Me

C

SIPRI

Stockholm International Peace Research Institute

SIPRI is an independent institute for research into problems of peace and conflict, with particular attention to disarmament and arms regulation. It was established in 1966 to commemorate Sweden's 150 years of unbroken peace.

The Institute is financed by the Swedish Parliament. The staff, the Governing Board and the Scientific Council are international. As a consultative body, the Scientific Council is not responsible for the views expressed in the publications of the Institute.

SIPRI

Stockholm International Peace Research Institute

Sveavägen 166, S-113 46 Stockholm, Sweden

Cable: Peaceresearch, Stockholm Telephone: 08-15 09 40

Medical Protection against Chemical-Warfare Agents

SIPRI

Stockholm International Peace Research Institute

Almqvist & Wiksell
International
Stockholm, Sweden

First published by
the Stockholm International Peace Research Institute

in collaboration with

Almqvist & Wiksell International
Gamla Brogatan 26, S-111 20 Stockholm, Sweden

ISBN 91-2200044-5

Printed in Sweden by
Almqvist & Wiksell, Uppsala 1976

PREFACE

Chemical weapons have the singular characteristic among weapons that, in principle, nearly perfect protection against their effects could be provided to individuals. Physical means of protection, such as protective masks and garments, already exist, and can provide a high degree of protection, but there are certain problems involved with their use. Hence, effective medical treatment of chemical-warfare casualties would be highly desirable.

A great deal of research is currently being undertaken on the problem of medical treatment of poisoning by organophosphorus compounds—the class of chemicals to which the chemical-warfare nerve agents belong. The drug-treatment methods available now, based on the use of atropine and certain oximes, are reasonably simple and can be used by laymen, even by the poisoned individuals themselves. However, they are by no means fully adequate, since they are not effective against all nerve agents and they cannot counter all of the toxic effects of exposure to nerve agents. The results of current research, however, indicate that much more effective treatment methods may become feasible in the not too distant future. It is argued in some quarters that were this to be achieved, chemical weapons, however sophisticated they might become, would be of no use or interest to an attacker. Hence, research into improved methods of protection may be seen as a possible way to assist and stimulate progress in the current international chemical disarmament negotiations. It may be noted that 100 per cent protection is not necessarily the objective: what is needed is a level of protection that is sufficiently high to render chemical-warfare attack uneconomical or otherwise unattractive.

In October 1974 a group of 31 scientists—toxicologists, pharmacologists and biochemists as well as disarmament experts—from 13 countries met in Herceg Novi in Yugoslavia at a symposium organized by the Yugoslav Toxicological Society in cooperation with SIPRI. The purpose of the symposium was to review the present state of knowledge of medical treatment of organophosphorus poisoning, to discuss the work that is currently under way in this field and to assess the possibilities for further progress in solving some of the problems that still remain. This book contains the scientific papers that were presented at that symposium, together with a summary of the discussions. It was edited by John Stares, a member of the SIPRI research staff, who was also involved with the organization of the symposium.

December 1975

Frank Barnaby
Director

CONTENTS

Introduction: defences against chemical warfare 1

I. Physical countermeasures 1
Respirators – Protective clothing – Protective skin ointments

II. Chemical countermeasures: decontamination 4

III. Medical treatment of nerve-agent poisoning 5

IV. Future possibilities for medical protection against nerve agents 7

List of participants 9

Abstracts of papers 12

Trivial names, chemical names and structural formulae of some of the 20
chemicals referred to in the text 20

Chapter 1. Clinical aspects of intoxication by cholinesterase inhibitors 22

I. Symptoms and diagnosis of organophosphate poisoning 22

II. Treatment of organophosphate poisoning 25

III. Experimental work on therapeutic compounds 26
Cholinolytic drugs – Oximes

Chapter 2. Acetylcholinesterase inhibitors: examples of their modes of action and their utility as scientific tools 36

I. Introduction 36

II. Effects of acetylcholinesterase inhibitors on neuromuscular transmission 36

III. Acetylcholinesterase inhibitors as scientific tools 37
Tetanic contractions – Permeability of biological barriers – Protection of acetylcholinesterase by the neuromuscular transmitter

Chapter 3. Success and failure of oxime therapy in acute poisoning by organophosphorus compounds 46

I. Introduction 46

II. Practical limitations of oxime therapy 47
Dose and time of administration of oximes – Specificity of oximes against various organophosphates – Oxime therapy and liver damage – Methods for monitoring enzyme activities during organophosphate intoxication

III. Other problems of oxime therapy 50

Chapter 4. The effects of antidotes in experimental animals intoxicated by carbamate and organophosphorus cholinesterase inhibitors 53

I. Effects of cholinesterase inhibition 53

Effects in the central nervous system – Effects in the autonomic nervous system – Effects in the voluntary nervous system – Effects of metabolic induction

II. Therapy of poisoning by cholinesterase inhibitors 56

Chapter 5. A comparative study of pralidoxime, obidoxime and trimedoxime in healthy men volunteers and in rats 65

I. Introduction 65

II. Comparative studies of oxime therapy 65

Chapter 6. Organophosphates and central cholinergic systems 74

I. Introduction 74

II. Time course of changes in brain acetylcholine level 74

III. Possible central actions of enzyme reactivators 75

IV. Effect of atropine on brain acetylcholine 79

Chapter 7. Reactivation of phosphorylated brain cholinesterase *in vivo* 82

I. Introduction 82

II. Summary of experimental studies 82

III. Discussion of results 84

Chapter 8. Kinetic studies on chemical reactions between acetylcholinesterase, toxic organophosphates and pyridinium oximes 88

I. Introduction 88

II. Reactivation and rephosphorylation 88

Inhibition by paraoxon in the absence of substrate – Inhibition by paraoxon in the presence of substrate – Inhibition by tabun

III. The direct reaction: inhibition by soman 95

Chapter 9. Comparative studies of the protective effects of pyridinium compounds against organophosphate poisoning 101

I. Introduction 101

II. Materials and methods 102

III. Results and discussion 104

Monopyridinium compounds – Bispyridinium compounds

IV. Conclusions 108

Chapter 10. Limitations of pharmacotherapy in organophosphate intoxications 109

I. Introduction 109

II. Pharmacotherapy 109

Cholinolytic compounds – Ganglia-blocking and enzyme-reactivating compounds – Treatment of central effects – Repetitive administration of drugs

III. Conclusions 114

Chapter 11. The possibility of complex therapy in acute dimethoate poisoning . 117
I. Introduction 117
II. Methodology 117
III. Discussion of results 118
IV. Conclusions 119

Chapter 12. The prophylactic value of oximes against organophosphate poisoning 120
I. Introduction 120
II. Experimental methods 122
Materials – Reactivation of phosphonylated acetylcholinesterase in vitro – *Biological half-life in rats and rabbits – Toxicity in mice – Prophylactic activity against sarin in mice – Activity in the central nervous system*
III. Results and discussion 125
Monopyridinium and bispyridinium oximes – Thiadiazole oximes – Aliphatic oximes – Central activity of the investigated oximes
IV. Conclusions 131

Chapter 13. An alternative therapy against organophosphate poisoning 134
I. Limitations of oxime therapy 134
II. An alternative approach: chemotherapy against respiratory paralysis . . 135
III. Conclusions 140

Chapter 14. Some toxicological consequences of the alkylating action of organophosphorus compounds 145
I. Introduction 145
II. Alkylating reactions of organophosphates 145

Chapter 15. Blood and brain cholinesterase activity in human death cases, in normal human subjects and in some laboratory and domestic animals 151
I. Introduction 151
II. Experimental methods 151
III. Results 154

Chapter 16. Medical protection against chemical-warfare agents 157
I. Introduction 157
II. Existing methods of treatment and their effectiveness 158
III. Current research on treatment of organophosphorus poisoning 161
IV. The need for further research 165

TABLES AND FIGURES AND PLATE

Chapter 1. Clinical aspects of intoxication by cholinesterase inhibitors

TABLES

1.1. Time required for heart-rate response in man to reach certain levels after intramuscular injection of 2 mg atropine sulphate in various volumes of solution 28
1.2. Reactivation of VX- and sarin-inhibited red cell cholinesterase by pyridine-2-aldoxime methochloride (2-PAM Cl) 30
1.3. Excretion rate of pralidoxime with and without treatment with thiamine 33
1.4. Effects of stress conditions on some kinetic parameters of pralidoxime chloride in man 34

FIGURES

1.1. Increase in heart rate due to intramuscular administration of 2 mg atropine sulphate by needle and syringe or by automatic injector 27
1.2. Number Facility (performance test) scores and cholinesterase activity in a patient treated with scopolamine or methscopolamine following accidental exposure to soman 29
1.3. Plasma oxime concentrations following intravenous infusion (over a period of 30 minutes) of one gram of oxime, either alone or in conjunction with 200 mg thiamine hydrochloride 32

Chapter 2. Acetylcholinesterase inhibitors: examples of their modes of action and their utility as scientific tools

TABLE

2.1. Cholinesterase activities in rat phrenic nerve diaphragm preparations exposed to cholinesterase inhibitors for one minute during motor nerve stimulation at two different frequencies 42

FIGURES

2.1. Correlation between acetylcholinesterase inhibition due to neostigmine bromide (0.5 μg/ml) and end-plate potential shape in isolated rat "cut" diaphragm preparations 38
2.2. Maternal and foetal erythrocyte acetylcholinesterase activities 16 hours after subcutaneous injection of the quaternary acetylcholinesterase inhibitor Tx-54 (0.325 mg/kg) in atropinized (5 mg atropine sulphate/kg) rats . 39
2.3. Maternal and foetal erythrocyte acetylcholinesterase activities 16 hours after subcutaneous administration of the tertiary acetylcholinesterase inhibitor Tx-60 (0.02 mg/kg) in atropinized (5 mg atropine sulphate/kg) rats 40

2.4. Acetylcholinesterase activities in various tissues 16 hours after subcutaneous administration of Tx-54 (0.325 mg/kg) in atropinized (5 mg atropine sulphate/kg) rats 41
2.5. Relationship between half decay time of end-plate potential (recorded by intracellular microelectrode) and stimulation frequency in rat phrenic nerve "cut" diaphragm preparations exposed to tensilon 43

Chapter 4. The effects of antidotes in experimental animals intoxicated by carbamate and organophosphorus cholinesterase inhibitors

TABLES

4.1. Signs and symptoms of acute intoxication by cholinesterase inhibitors . 54
4.2. Median protective doses of atropine sulphate and atropine methonitrate injected 60 minutes before the administration of a lethal dose of cholinesterase inhibitor in mice 57
4.3. Effects of therapeutic antidotes on the LD_{50} values of carbamate anticholinesterases in male rats 58
4.4. Effects of obidoxime and P2S on the anticholinesterase activity of carbamates in rat brain homogenates *in vitro* 59
4.5. Effects of therapeutic antidotes on the LD_{50} values of organophosphate anticholinesterases in female rats 61

FIGURES

4.1. Rate of survival of mice pretreated with atropine sulphate, by intraperitoneal injection, 60 minutes before subcutaneous injection of a lethal dose of a cholinesterase inhibitor 56
4.2. Effects of P2S and obidoxime on the toxicity of carbamate anticholinesterases: relationship between increase in pI_{50} values due to treatment with 10^{-3} M oxime and elevation of LD_{50} values due to administration of 250 μmol/kg oxime 60

Chapter 5. A comparative study of pralidoxime, obidoxime and trimedoxime in healthy men volunteers and in rats

TABLES

5.1. Nature and frequency of symptoms in healthy male subjects injected intramuscularly with pralidoxime, obidoxime or trimedoxime 66
5.2. Heart rate, blood pressure and respiration rate in healthy male subjects injected intramuscularly with pralidoxime, obidoxime or trimedoxime . . 67
5.3. Velocity constant, biological half-life and urinary excretion rate of pralidoxime, obidoxime and trimedoxime after intramuscular administration in man 68
5.4. Acute toxicity of trimedoxime and obidoxime in rats by different routes of administration 68
5.5. Concentrations of trimedoxime and obidoxime in the blood of rats after intramuscular administration (25 mg/kg) 69

5.6. Reactivation *in vivo* by trimedoxime and obidoxime of rat-blood acetylcholinesterase inhibited by sublethal doses of Gd-7 and Gd-42 compounds 69

FIGURES

5.1. Protective effects of oximes (25 mg/kg, *im*) in rats poisoned by 2 LD_{50} (0.72 mg/kg) of Gd-7 70

5.2. Protective effects of oximes (25 mg/kg, *im*) in rats poisoned by 2 LD_{50} (0.064 mg/kg) of Gd-42 71

Chapter 6. Organophosphates and central cholinergic systems

TABLE

6.1. Effect of obidoxime on acetylcholine content and cholinesterase activity in the pontomedullary region of rat brain after intoxication with armin . 78

FIGURES

6.1. Relationship between brain acetylcholine level, active avoidance (behavioural) performance and cholinesterase activity in rats poisoned with paraoxon 76

6.2. Total acetylcholine content and cholinesterase activity in brains of paraoxon-intoxicated rats treated with 2-PAM (20 mg/kg, *iv*) 10 minutes after intoxication 77

6.3. Effects of atropine (5 mg/kg, *ip*) on brain acetylcholine level of rats intoxicated with paraoxon (E 600) 79

Chapter 7. Reactivation of phosphorylated brain cholinesterase *in vivo*

TABLES

7.1. Rates of inhibition by organophosphates of rat blood and brain acetylcholinesterase 83

7.2. Inhibition of brain acetylcholinesterase and increase in blood pressure following intravenous injection of organophosphates in rats 83

7.3. Rates of reactivation by P2S of phosphorylated rat brain acetylcholinesterase *in vitro* 84

7.4. Effects of P2S and obidoxime on brain acetylcholinesterase inhibition in atropinized rats 85

Chapter 8. Kinetic studies on chemical reactions between acetylcholinesterase, toxic organophosphates and pyridinium oximes

TABLES

8.1. Kinetic data for the *in vitro* reactivation and rephosphorylation of paraoxon-inhibited acetylcholinesterase in the absence of substrate 91

8.2. Kinetic data for the *in vitro* reactivation and rephosphorylation of paraoxon-inhibited acetylcholinesterase in the presence of substrate 94

8.3. Kinetic data for the *in vitro* reactivation and rephosphorylation of tabun-inhibited acetylcholinesterase in the presence of substrate 95
8.4. Rate constants of formation of phosphorylated oximes formed in a "direct reaction" between the oxime (2×10^{-4} M) and soman (5.5×10^{-3} M) at 37°C and pH 7.6 99

FIGURES

8.1. Chemical reactions of acetylcholinesterase, organophosphates and pyridinium oximes 89
8.2. Rate of reactivation of paraoxon-inhibited acetylcholinesterase by Toxogonin and HS-6 90
8.3. Relationship between *in vivo* effectivity and *in vitro* reactivating potency of oximes with paraoxon-inhibited acetylcholinesterase 93
8.4. Relationship between *in vivo* effectivity and *in vitro* reactivating potency of oximes with tabun-inhibited acetylcholinesterase 96
8.5. Relationship between oxime concentration and degree of additional acetylcholinesterase inhibition due to the formation of toxic phosphonylated oximes in a "direct reaction" between oxime and soman 97
8.6. Possible chemical reactions arising from a "direct reaction" between an organophosphate and a pyridinium oxime 98

Chapter 9. Comparative studies of the protective effects of pyridinium compounds against organophosphate poisoning

TABLES

9.1. Chemical structures of monopyridinium compounds tested as antidotes against organophosphate intoxication 102
9.2. Chemical structures of bispyridinium compounds tested as antidotes against organophosphate intoxication 103
9.3. Monopyridinium compounds: antidotal effects against organophosphate intoxication in female NMRI mice 105
9.4. Bispyridinium compounds: antidotal effects against organophosphate intoxication in female NMRI mice 106

Chapter 10. Limitations of pharmacotherapy in organophosphate intoxications

TABLES

10.1. Effects of various cholinolytics (used in conjunction with P2S (30 mg/kg)) on the toxicity of sarin in the mouse 110
10.2. Effects of various oximes, given as adjuncts to atropine, on the toxicity of DFP in the rat 111
10.3. Effects of various drugs on the toxicity of DFP in the rat 113
10.4. Effects of combined therapy on the toxicity of DFP in the rat 114

Chapter 11. The possibility of complex therapy in acute dimethoate poisoning

TABLE

11.1. Effects of the prophylactic and therapeutic administration of some drugs on the LD_{50} of dimethoate (intraperitoneally) in mice 118

Chapter 12. The prophylactic value of oximes against organophosphate poisoning

TABLES

12.1. Pyridinium oximes: chemical structures, pK_a values, toxicities and reactivating potencies 124
12.2. Thiadiazole oximes: chemical structures, pK_a values, toxicities, reactivating potencies and biological half-lives 128
12.3. Aliphatic oximes: chemical structures, pK_a values, toxicities, reactivating potencies and biological half-lives 129

FIGURES

12.1. Rate of decrease of P2S and obidoxime concentration in the blood of rabbits after intravenous administration of the oximes 126
12.2. Effect of intraperitoneal injection of an aliphatic oxime on the hypothermia induced in rats by intravenous administration of soman and paraoxon 130

Chapter 13. An alternative therapy against organophosphate poisoning

TABLES

13.1. Variations in rapidity of ageing and sensitivity to oxime reactivation of cholinesterases inhibited by various organophosphorus compounds . . 136
13.2. The effects of U23223 on the respiratory paralysis caused by DFP, paraoxon or soman in anaesthetized, atropinized rats 139

FIGURES

13.1. Relationship between dose of several organophosphate anticholinesterases administered to rats and time during which artificial respiration was required before animals could breathe unaided for one hour 137
13.2. Events during normal respiration (left), after intoxication with a predominantly peripherally acting anticholinesterase (centre) and with a centrally acting anticholinesterase (right), and effects, in each case, of additional administration of ANCA on contractions of the diaphragm . 138
13.3. Effects of ANCA and EDTA on the ability of anaesthetized, atropinized rats to breathe spontaneously after intoxication with soman 141

PLATE

13.1. Bodies of rats injected with soman and ANCA (left) or killed in ether (right), five minutes after death 140

Chapter 14. Some toxicological consequences of the alkylating action of organophosphorus compounds

TABLES

14.1. Incidence of tumours in rats after treatment with trichlorphon 147
14.2. Incidence of tumours in rats after treatment with dimethoate 147
14.3. Location of tumours and histological diagnosis in rats after treatment with trichlorphon 148
14.4. Location of tumours and histological diagnosis in rats after treatment with dimethoate 149

FIGURE

14.1. Rate of alkylation of NBP by various organophosphates in 1.0 M methanol solution at 25°C 146

Chapter 15. Blood and brain cholinesterase activity in human death cases, in normal human subjects and in some laboratory and domestic animals

TABLES

15.1. Blood cholinesterase activities in humans and animals 152
15.2. Blood and brain cholinesterase activities in humans and animals 153
15.3. Blood and cerebellum cholinesterase activities in 17 fatal organophosphate-poisoning cases (suicides) 154
15.4. Blood and brain cholinesterase activities in rats and mice poisoned by parathion 155

Introduction: defences against chemical warfare

There are three basic lines of defence against attack by chemical-warfare agents. First, there are the possibilities for physical protection: if people can be shielded from the contaminated environment, they will not succumb to CW attack. The air they breathe can be filtered, their skin can be protected by special clothing or by skin protection ointments (barrier creams), or they can remain inside special air-conditioned shelters. Second, there are chemical countermeasures—decontamination methods—that can be used to destroy environmental contaminants before they do any harm. Finally, there are medical countermeasures, such as antidotes to counter the effects of poisons that have entered the body. Certainly, no one of these lines of defence will be perfect or foolproof, but together they can be expected to blunt most forms of CW attack, provided they are used with reasonable efficiency. In fact, 100 per cent protection is not necessarily the objective: what is needed is a level of protection that is sufficiently high to render CW attack uneconomical or otherwise unattractive to an attacker.

I. *Physical countermeasures*

Respirators

The respirator, or "gas mask", is the basic component of any CW defence. Most modern designs are refinements of pioneering developments, made in the 1920s and 1930s, of the trial-and-error expedients of World War I.

One of the first steps in improving respirator design after World War I was to increase the efficiency of existing particulate filters. One important advance was the development of resin-wool filters. The very high filtration efficiency, even for micron-sized particles, of mats of this material was due to electrostatic attraction between the particles and the fibres of the mat, for during carding of the resin-wool mixture the resin acquired a substantial negative charge. Resin-wool particulate filters were used in several World War II respirator designs, and remain in use today. Their principal deficiency was a tendency to become less retentive when they became damp, and approaches to overcoming this defect included the use of asbestos fibres and hydrophobic surfactants, and, more recently, micron-diameter glass and plastic fibres, in the preparation of the particulate filters. Adequate filtration of particulate aerosols is no longer a serious problem.

Current military specifications for respirators require that they be capable of removing 99.99 per cent of all possible contaminants from inhaled air. For contaminants in aerosol form, the particulate filters described above are capable of meeting this specification, even with particle sizes ranging down to 0.1 microns. For many gases and vapours, activated charcoal is easily capable of meeting the specification also: but much heavier challenges are possible with vapours than with particulate aerosols—a vapour cloud may have a very much higher agent concentration than any aerosol cloud—so that there is a danger of charcoal filters becoming saturated. Much of the post-World War I work on respirators was therefore concerned with improving the retentiveness of charcoal filters. One line of research was to look for more active charcoal, and satisfactory results have been obtained with wood, coal and lignite charcoals. Another approach was to seek charcoal impregnants that could catalyse the decomposition of chemical vapours to yield oxidation or other breakdown products that were either non-toxic or else were more easily adsorbed onto the charcoal than the agent itself. By the end of World War II, the charcoal in British, Canadian, German and US respirators, at least, contained various combinations of copper, silver, chromium and pyridine or picoline impregnants. The best of the World War II designs all proved adequate against the G-agent nerve gases, and, presumably, against the V-agents also.

In principle, therefore, adequate protection of the respiratory tract is possible. The main outstanding difficulty arises from the close fitting of the mask around the wearer's face. A respirator is much more likely to leak because the wearer has been careless in putting it on, or has not shaved properly, than because of inadequacies in filter or valve design. The face sealing method used must not delay the process of donning the respirator: today, soldiers are expected to do this within 10 seconds, although during exercises, at least twice this amount of time is common.

Once on, a respirator is an appreciable burden to its wearer, restricting his vision, limiting his ability to communicate and hampering his breathing. Respirators are of course designed to minimize these restrictions, and modern designs are a substantial improvement on those of World War II. In the current British service respirator, the S6, the wearer is allowed 75 per cent unimpeded vision and his voice carries over at least one-third of the normal range. The current US design, the M17A1, has a fitting that allows the wearer to drink safely from a canteen. It is said that, with sufficient training, combat soldiers can perform almost as efficiently when wearing respirators as without them.

Protective clothing

It is much more difficult to provide the same high level of protection to a man's skin as to his respiratory tract, or, at least, to do so without encumbering him to the point of military uselessness. Ordinary combat clothing can give some protection, but only for short periods: liquid nerve agent and mustard gas are remarkably penetrative substances, capable of soaking through most normal textiles, even through untreated shoe leather. Thus some special means of skin protection is necessary: ideally it should be clothing also suitable as regular combat uniform, but this is not yet technically feasible.

The oilcloth used to protect against vesicant agents in World War I was impermeable to mustard gas, but, as well as being heavy and uncomfortable, it was also impermeable to air and water vapour, so that the wearer quickly became overheated and exhausted. Since then, therefore, there has been an intensive search for clothing materials impermeable to CW agents but permeable to air and water vapour. There have been some promising approaches, but none has been more than partially successful: heat loss is always impaired to some extent and the effective lifetime of the clothing is never long.

A recent model of the British CB suit, a permeable protective overgarment that has been adopted by other NATO countries, is made from a nonwoven synthetic textile coated on the outside with a liquid repellent—one that is both hydrophobic and oleophobic—and having a layer of activated charcoal bonded to the inside. Several liquid repellents are available. For example, highly fluorinated hydrocarbons have been studied for nerve-agent repellency, and repellents made from Werner-type chrominuclear complexes, in which the acido-groups are long-chain perfluoroalkanoyl radicals, have proved satisfactory for certain synthetic textiles. This outer coating impedes penetration of liquid agents into the cloth, while the inner charcoal layer adsorbs any agent vapour that might still get through. The British suit looks heavy and cumbersome, but it is in fact remarkably light, and it is reported to have little effect on a man's efficiency, even in tropical climates. Its main defects seem to be its limited shelf-life and its poor tear-resistance.

Later versions of the CB suit may be made from a promising new material known as "carbon cloth", a woven activated-carbon-containing fabric that is strong and tear-resistant and might even be made into regular combat clothing. Nevertheless, it is considered in some quarters that the most satisfactory material will eventually emerge from a rather different approach—the use of clothing impregnants that destroy rather than merely adsorb invading chemicals. One of the earliest successes in this field was the US development in the late 1920s and early 1930s of a clothing-impregnating process based on a chloracetamide that chemically decomposes mustard gas. The impregnant, sym-bis-(chloro-2,4,6-trichlorophenyl) urea (code name CC-2), also reacts efficiently with the V-agent nerve gases, although not with the G-agents. The US CC-2 process was used throughout World War II and, in a modified form, is still used today: the current impregnant (code-named XXCC-3) is in micronized-powder form containing 10 per cent zinc oxide stabilizer.

The limitations of materials impregnated with CC-2 or other chloroimides are due mainly to the large amounts of impregnant that must be incorporated into the cloth. Thus there has been an active search for impregnants capable of catalysing the air-oxidation, autoxidation or hydrolysis of invading CW agents, since relatively small quantities of such catalysts may be effective. Protective clothing of this type would, however, probably be once-only garments: carbon cloth, on the other hand, could be reused after decontamination by suitable laundering processes.

A further possibility that is currently being explored is the use of air-conditioned, air-impermeable suits. Existing outfits of this type completely encapsulate the wearer, his head being inside a helmet that is integral with a one-piece suit of impermeable clothing that fastens closely round the wrists and ankles. The suit is fitted with air-inlet and -outlet valves through which the wearer's breathing and cooling requirements can be satisfied.

In the absence of adequate protective suits meeting the requirements of regular combat clothing, other means have to be used for skin protection of combat troops. The most widely used item today is the antigas cape, a lightweight impermeable overgarment that a soldier can wrap around himself and subsequently discard if it becomes contaminated. There are also lightweight impermeable hoods, leggings, gloves and overshoes. All these can be used in conjunction with existing types of impregnated battle dress or undergarments. The skin protection they afford is certainly not perfect: they offer no protection against vapours and in warm climates they cannot be worn for long periods. But they are believed capable of significantly reducing the number of percutaneous casualties that might otherwise occur.

Protective skin ointments

Protective skin ointments, or barrier creams, may represent an important extension of the protective-clothing concept of defence against exposure to chemical-warfare agents. Barrier creams are intended to cover those parts of the body that are not completely covered by a protective suit or where there may be weak points in the protection, such as at the wrists and ankles.

II. *Chemical countermeasures: decontamination*

In principle, decontamination of a man's skin or of matériel is a simple process, provided sufficient time is available. The main difficulty arises where the time available for decontamination is short or must be kept to a minimum, as on an active battlefield. The success of a CW attack may be measured not only in terms of the number of casualties secured, but also in terms of the time delay it forces on the enemy while he cleans himself.

During World War I, bleaching powder, and to a much lesser extent potassium permanganate, were used against mustard gas: both compounds destroyed the mustard gas by oxidizing it to its sulphoxide and sulphone. After the war, and especially after the discovery of the nerve agents, the main goal of decontamination research was to find faster and simpler methods of coping with contaminants on the battlefield, and a variety of other decontaminants were studied, chiefly compounds other than bleaching powder that contained active chlorine. By World War II, superchlorinated bleaching powder was the most common general-purpose decontaminant. It was cheap, and effective against all the standard involatile CW agents. In dust dispensers it remains standard antigas equipment for individual soldiers in many of today's armies. In many armies it is also s.andard equipment for terrain and matériel decontamination, although it has two important drawbacks: since it is a solid, it is not completely amenable to spraying, and although it can be made into a slurry, it tends to clog spray nozzles and in cold weather slurries may freeze; and its active chlorine content is both rather low and unstable.

Alternative agents resulting from pre-World War II work were trichlorocyanuric acid, N,N-dichloromethanesulphonamide and 1,3-dichloro-5,5-dimethylhydantoin. The first two, designated Entgiftungsstoff 40 and Waffenentgiftungsmittel (WEM), respectively, were adopted by the German Wehrmacht as special-purpose decontaminants alongside bleach. The third, as a 6.25 per cent solution in acetylene tetrachloride known as DANC solution, was adopted by the US Army, also for special purposes alongside bleach. DANC has disadvantages, notably the alarming toxicity of the solvent and the fact that it is ineffective against the G-agents (although it is effective against the V-agents), and it is now gradually being phased out of the US inventory.

The search for better liquid decontaminants was therefore accelerated, and moved away from active-chlorine decontaminants to explore the possibility of exploiting new types of CW-agent decomposition reactions, such as catalysed hydrolyses and various oxidations. One of the more recent decontaminants is the US Army formulation known as DS-2, the active ingredient of which is diethylenetriamine. It works by base-catalysed hydrolysis and is effective against all the standard CW agents. It is expensive, but it can be used effectively at temperatures as low as −25°C, and it is coming into increasing use in other armies.

III. *Medical treatment of nerve-agent poisoning*

The above discussion shows that although physical means of protection against chemical warfare, as well as chemical decontamination methods, have been developed to a high level of sophistication, a number of problems still remain. In many countries research and development work in this field is continuing and the level of protection provided for individual soldiers is being continuously improved, but in all armies the level of protection provided for ground troops is vulnerable to some form of CW attack, and no army yet has the capability for keeping its soldiers in a state of continuous physical protection while on combat duty. There is, however, a third line of defence against chemical warfare that may be used alongside these other methods, namely medical countermeasures.

At present, the possibilities for effective treatment of chemical-warfare casualties are limited: prophylaxis is possible only against certain protein agents such as some toxins, and very few specific antidotes are available for the multitude of different CW agents, so that, for the most part, medical treatment is merely supportive and palliative. But there is one important exception—the therapy of nerve-agent poisoning. This has now been refined to the stage where the simpler forms of treatment can be administered, with special autoinjectors, by a layman—even by the poisoned individual.

The principal mode of action of the nerve agents is to inactivate an enzyme in the body called acetylcholinesterase, which is essential for the normal functioning of the nervous system. Nerve impulses are transmitted between nerve fibres and between nerve endings and various organs and muscles by the compound acetylcholine. Once acetylcholine has performed its function, it is destroyed by acetylcholinesterase, thus leaving the nerve fibres or endings free to transmit further impulses. The action of the nerve agents is to inhibit acetylcholinesterase so that it is unable to break down the acetylcholine, with the result that acetylcholine accumulates and nerve function is blocked. Death from nerve-agent poisoning is most likely to be caused by acute oxygen deprivation following paralysis of the respiratory muscles or inhibition of the central respiratory centres, aggravated by severe cardiovascular failure.

Treatment of nerve-agent poisoning consists of the use of atropine, or related drugs, that block the effects of excess acetylcholine, and oxime-type drugs that are able to restore the activity of the acetylcholinesterase inhibited by some types of nerve agent. But these self-aid treatments are by no means completely adequate. Atropine cannot prevent paralysis of the respiratory muscles (although oximes may do so if the dose of nerve agent has not been too large), and so artificial respiration of the positive-pressure type may be essential, and the victim obviously cannot do this for himself. Oximes are not effective against all types of nerve agent, the most important example of this being their lack of effect against poisoning by soman. Nor is the treatment without risks of its own: the drugs must be administered very quickly after poisoning if they are to have any effect, but atropine is itself a powerful poison, so that ungassed individuals who inject themselves under the impression that they have been exposed to nerve agent may themselves become incapacitated. And as yet there is no effective prophylactic treatment against nerve-agent poisoning, although oximes and certain other compounds do offer a fair measure of promise for nerve-agent prophylaxis.

IV. *Future possibilities for medical protection against nerve agents*

Chemical weapons have the singular characteristic that in principle, if not yet in practice, nearly perfect protection against their effects can be provided to individuals. It is argued in some quarters that, were this ideal to be achieved, chemical weapons, however sophisticated they might become, would be of no use to an attacker. Hence research into better means of protection, physical or medical, may be seen as a possible way to assist progress in the current international chemical disarmament negotiations.

This book is concerned with just one aspect of defence against chemical warfare—the possibilities of medical protection against nerve agents. Chemical-warfare nerve agents, such as tabun, sarin, soman and VX, are organophosphorus compounds, a class of chemical that also includes many insecticides in widespread use in agriculture. These organophosphorus pesticides are less toxic than the nerve agents, but their mode of action in the human body is the same, and therefore there is much interest in studying the problems of poisoning by organophosphorus compounds in general, pesticides as well as nerve agents. In fact, active research programmes are in progress in many countries on the problems of medical treatment of organophosphorus poisoning, all of which are important in the present context since the results obtained from studies on these pesticides can, at least in principle, be extrapolated to the problems of protection against chemical-warfare nerve agents.

In October 1974 a group of 31 scientists—toxicologists, pharmacologists and biochemists as well as disarmament experts—from 13 countries met in Herceg Novi in Yugoslavia at a symposium organized by the Yugoslav Toxicological Society in cooperation with the Stockholm International Peace Research Institute (SIPRI). The purpose of the symposium was to review the present state of knowledge of medical treatment of organophosphorus poisoning, to discuss the work that is currently under way in this field, and to assess the possibilities for further progress in solving some of the problems that still remain, with special reference to the problems of protection against chemical-warfare agents.

This book contains the papers that were presented at the meeting. They describe the biochemical mode of action of organophosphorus compounds, current methods of protection and detailed studies of the modes of action of currently used drugs, the search for new compounds that might be more effective than the drugs currently available (for example, new oximes or drugs with other modes of action, such as anticonvulsant agents), some attempts at solving the problem of intoxications that are not responsive to oxime therapy, the possibilities for prophylactic use of oximes and a promising approach to overcoming the problem of respiratory failure by the use of muscle stimulants. There are also discussions of some of the delayed effects and side-effects of organophosphorus compounds, and of methods for determining acetylcholinesterase activities in biological tissues. Finally, there is a summary based on the papers and on the discussions that took place at the symposium.

LIST OF PARTICIPANTS

Dr Hussein A. Ads
NRC Biochemical Unit
3 Ebn El Wardy Street
El Nozzha
Cairo
Egypt

Dr Johannes A. B. Barstad
Department of Environmental Toxicology
National Institute of Public Health
Geitmyrsveien 75
Oslo
Norway

Professor Zlatko Binenfeld
Kraševa 14
Zagreb
Yugoslavia

Dr Bogdan Bošković
Institute of Technical and Medical Protection
Department of Pharmacology and Toxicology
Vojvode Stepe 445
POB 1011
11001 Belgrade
Yugoslavia

Dr Adel A. El Mehy
NRC Organic Technology Unit
4 Mohamed Wagieh Khalil Street
Sante Fatima
Heliopolis
Cairo
Egypt

Professor Wolf Dieter Erdmann
Institute of Pharmacology and Toxicology
University of Göttingen
Geiststrasse 9
D-34 Göttingen
FR Germany

Dr Wolfgang Gibel
Institute of Cancer Research
Academy of Sciences of the GDR
1115 Berlin
GDR

Dr Henri Kienhuis
Chemical Laboratory TNO
137 Lange Kleiweg
POB 45
Rijswijk (Z.H.)
The Netherlands

Professor Tadeusz Kisieliński
Department of Toxicology
Military Institute of Hygiene and Epidemiology
Kozielska 4
POB 45
01-163 Warsaw 42
Poland

Professor Karlheinz Lohs
Forschungsstelle für Chemische Toxikologie
Academy of Sciences of the GDR
Johannisalle 20
701 Leipzig
GDR

Dr Johan Lundin
National Defence Research Institute FOA
Fack
S-104 50 Stockholm
Sweden

Dr Bela Matkovics
Jate–Termeszettudomanyi kar
Tancsics Mihaly U. 2
POB 539
6701 Szeged
Hungary

Dr Tore Mellstrand
Försvarets Sjukvårdsstyrelse
Fack
S-104 40 Stockholm 14
Sweden

Professor Jorma K. Miettinen
Department of Radiochemistry
University of Helsinki
Unioninkatu 35
00170 Helsinki
Finland

Professor Milenko P. Milošević
Department of Pharmacology
Medical Faculty
POB 662
11000 Belgrade
Yugoslavia

Dr Ian L. Natoff
Department of Pharmacology
Roche Products Ltd
Broadwater Road
Welwyn Garden City
Hertfordshire
England

Dr Hubert Oldiges
Fraunhofer-Gesellschaft
Institut für Aerobiologie
D-5948 Schmallenberg-Grafschaft
FR Germany

Mr Bernard Reiff
Shell Research Ltd
Tunstall Laboratory
Broad Oak Road
Sittingbourne
Kent
England

Dr Else Reiner
Institute for Medical Research and Occupational Health
Yugoslav Academy of Sciences and Arts
Moše Pijade 158
POB 291
41000 Zagreb
Yugoslavia

Mr Julian Perry Robinson
Science Policy Research Unit
University of Sussex
Brighton BN1 9RF
Sussex
England

Dr Nedeljko Rosić
Institute of Technical and Medical Protection
Department of Pharmacology and Toxicology
Vojvode Stepe 445
POB 1011
11001 Belgrade
Yugoslavia

Dr Vesa Riihimäki
Institute of Occupational Health
Haartmaninkatu 1
00290 Helsinki
Finland

Dr Slawomir Rump
Department of Toxicology
Military Institute of Hygiene and Epidemiology
Kozielska 4
POB 45
01-163 Warsaw 42
Poland

Dr Maher M. Sary El Din
NRC Agricultural Unit
173 Higaz Square
Heliopolis
Cairo
Egypt

Dr Klaus Schoene
Fraunhofer-Gesellschaft
Institut für Aerobiologie
D-5948 Schmallenberg-Grafschaft
FR Germany

Dr Frederick R. Sidell
Clinical Research Branch
Biomedical Laboratory
Edgewood Arsenal, Md. 21010
USA

Mr John Stares
Stockholm International Peace Research Institute (SIPRI)
Wenner-Gren Center
Sveavägen 166
S-113 46 Stockholm
Sweden

Dr Milutin Vandekar
Vector Biology and Control Unit
WHO
Geneva
Switzerland

Professor Vladimir Vojvodić
Institute of Technical and Medical Protection
Department of Pharmacology and Toxicology
Vojvode Stepe 445
POB 1011
11001 Belgrade
Yugoslavia

Dr Otto L. Wolthuis
Medical Biological Laboratory TNO
139 Lange Kleiweg
POB 45
2100 Rijswijk (Z.H.)
The Netherlands

Dr Hassan Z. Youssef
El Nasr Chemical Company
Department of Research and Development
5 Ahmed Amin Street
Doki
Cairo
Egypt

Chapter 1. Clinical aspects of intoxication by cholinesterase inhibitors

F. R. SIDELL
Clinical Research Branch, Biomedical Laboratory, Edgewood Arsenal, Md. 21010, USA

The signs and symptoms of intoxication by compounds that inhibit cholinesterase depend on the particular compound involved, the route of exposure and the size of the dose: the classic picture of miosis, rhinorrhea and bronchoconstriction may not be seen if the exposure is by the oral or percutaneous route. The most important aspect of therapy is to keep the poisoned patient adequately oxygenated. In addition, cholinolytic compounds, atropine being the one most commonly used, are important in blocking the effects of excess acetylcholine, and oximes will reactivate the inhibited enzyme following intoxication by some (but not all) cholinesterase inhibitors. Some recent research on different pharmaceutical preparations of atropine and oximes is presented.

Chapter 2. Acetylcholinesterase inhibitors: examples of their modes of action and their utility as scientific tools

J. A. B. BARSTAD
Department of Environmental Toxicology, National Institute of Public Health, Geitmyrsveien 75, Oslo, Norway

Various aspects of acetylcholinesterase inhibitors are discussed. The post-synaptic, as well as the possible presynaptic, effects of acetylcholinesterase inhibitors on neuromuscular transmission are dealt with on the basis of experiments with normal as well as "cut" rat phrenic-nerve-diaphragm preparations. Some examples of the use of acetylcholinesterase inhibitors, sometimes together with reactivators of the inhibited enzyme, as tools for studying certain physiological phenomena are also presented. For instance, special acetylcholinesterase inhibitors (tertiary and quaternary nitrogen compounds) have been used to study the permeability of biological barriers, such as the placenta and the blood-brain barrier. And it was possible to estimate the transmitter concentration at the neuromuscular junction, found to be 10^{-3} M, which is considerably higher than was generally supposed.

Chapter 3. Success and failure of oxime therapy in acute poisoning by organophosphorus compounds

W. D. ERDMANN
Institute of Pharmacology and Toxicology, University of Göttingen, Geiststrasse 9, D-34 Göttingen, FR Germany

Therapy of organophosphate intoxication is based on the use of atropine and reactivating oximes. However, there are some doubts and misunderstandings about this treatment among clinical physicians. In order to help clarify this situation, various aspects of oxime therapy are discussed: (*a*) the time of application of oximes after poisoning, the dosage that should be used and the specificity of oximes against various organophosphates; (*b*) the question of whether liver damage results from oxime treatment or from the intoxication itself; (*c*) the value of analytical procedures for monitoring enzyme activities as means of assessing the progress of the intoxication and the oxime treatment; (*d*) the possibility of reactivating phosphorylated acetylcholinesterases after ageing; (*e*) the problem of diffusion of oximes across the blood-brain barrier; and (*f*) the possibilities of oral administration of oximes, especially in a mass-casualty situation.

Chapter 4. The effects of antidotes in experimental animals intoxicated by carbamate and organophosphorus cholinesterase inhibitors

I. L. NATOFF
Department of Pharmacology, Roche Products Ltd, Broadwater Road, Welwyn Garden City, Hertfordshire, England

The effects of intoxication by cholinesterase inhibitors in the central nervous system, the autonomic nervous system and the voluntary nervous system are reviewed. Laboratory methods of measuring, in qualitative and quantitative terms, the efficiency of antidotes to intoxication are considered. The acute toxicity of carbamate pesticides is influenced by oximes in parallel with their effect on the anticholinesterase activity of these carbamates *in vitro,* while marked potentiation of the antidotal effect of atropine by oximes in the presence of organophosphorus intoxication is quantitatively demonstrated.

Chapter 5. A comparative study of pralidoxime, obidoxime and trimedoxime in healthy men volunteers and in rats

V. VOJVODIĆ and B. BOŠKOVIĆ

Institute of Technical and Medical Protection, Department of Pharmacology and Toxicology, Vojvode Stepe 445, POB 1011, 11001 Belgrade, Yugoslavia

Experimental observations on healthy male volunteers have shown that there are no differences in the nature or frequency of symptoms following intramuscular administration of pralidoxime, obidoxime or trimedoxime, and that the side-effects produced by these compounds do not differ in frequency, intensity or duration from those reported for other oximes administered in therapeutic doses. The effects of all three oximes on heart rate, blood pressure and respiration were found to be negligible. Comparison of the biological half-lives has shown that trimedoxime is the most persistent of the three oximes tested.

Experiments in rats on the acute toxicities, blood concentrations, reactivating potencies and protective efficacies of obidoxime and trimedoxime in poisoning by the organophosphate anticholinesterases Gd-7 and Gd-42 have shown that trimedoxime, in spite of its greater toxicity, is more effective as an antidote than obidoxime.

The results obtained from studies on men and rats suggest that the toxicity of a particular oxime should not be the sole factor used in determining the superiority of one oxime over another in cases of poisoning by different organophosphorus compounds.

Chapter 6. Organophosphates and central cholinergic systems

M. P. MILOŠEVIĆ

Department of Pharmacology, Medical Faculty, POB 662, 11000 Belgrade, Yugoslavia

In the early phase of paraoxon intoxication in rats, neurological symptoms and behavioural depression are well correlated with the decrease in brain cholinesterase activity and the increase in brain acetylcholine content. During the later phase of intoxication, brain acetylcholine level returns to normal within a few hours, while brain cholinesterase activity remains at a low level. The disappearance of behavioural depression seems to correlate fairly well with the normalization of brain acetylcholine content, but shows little relationship to brain cholinesterase activity. Some actions of cholinolytic drugs (atropine) and reactivators of phosphorylated cholinesterase (quaternary oximes) on the brain acetylcholine level of paraoxon-intoxicated rats are also discussed.

Chapter 7. Reactivation of phosphorylated brain cholinesterase *in vivo*

B. REIFF
Shell Research Ltd, Tunstall Laboratory, Broad Oak Road,
Sittingbourne, Kent, England

The therapeutic role of oximes in anticholinesterase intoxication with regard to reactivation of phosphorylated cholinesterase in the brain has not yet been fully elucidated. This paper describes work on the measurement of the bimolecular rate constants between brain enzyme and a number of organophosphates, the reactivation rates of phosphorylated enzyme in the presence of oximes, the velocity of penetration of the inhibitors into the central structures and the actual amounts of oximes which enter the brain. The conclusion drawn from these studies is that parenteral administration of oximes may help to reactivate brain cholinesterase inhibited by diethoxyphosphates but that oximes are unlikely to be of benefit after intoxication with dimethoxy- or diisopropoxyphosphates.

Chapter 8. Kinetic studies on chemical reactions between acetylcholinesterase, toxic organophosphates and pyridinium oximes

K. SCHOENE
Fraunhofer-Gesellschaft, Institut für Aerobiologie,
D-5948 Schmallenberg-Grafschaft, FR Germany

Paraoxon-inhibited acetylcholinesterase was reactivated with pyridinium oximes in the absence of substrate. By kinetic analysis of the reactivation-rephosphorylation equilibrium, the rate constants of reactivation and rephosphorylation (by the corresponding phosphorylated oxime), as well as the decomposition rate constants of the phosphorylated oximes, could be calculated. Reactivation in the presence of substrate was used to characterize the pyridinium oximes in terms of their affinity and reactivity towards the phosphorylated acetylcholinesterase.

The results of the latter experiments correlate well with the antidotal efficacy of the pyridinium compounds observed *in vivo*. In the case of tabun-inhibited acetylcholinesterase, however, no such correlation could be found. This might be explained by the formation of an additional inhibitor in a reaction between the oxime and the less toxic stereoisomers of tabun. In experiments with soman it could in fact be shown that the less toxic stereoisomers of this compound react with oximes to form phosphorylated oximes with high anticholinesterase activity.

Chapter 9. Comparative studies of the protective effects of pyridinium compounds against organophosphate poisoning

H. OLDIGES
Fraunhofer-Gesellschaft, Institut für Aerobiologie,
D-5948 Schmallenberg-Grafschaft, FR Germany

Female mice were intoxicated with paraoxon (2 LD_{50}), tabun (3 LD_{50}), sarin (2 LD_{50}) or soman (1.2 LD_{50}), administered subcutaneously. The antidotal efficacy of a large number of pyridinium salts was determined by evaluating the ED_{50} of the compound injected intramuscularly either one minute after intoxication (therapeutic treatment) or five minutes before intoxication (prophylactic treatment). The results show that the protective potency of a pyridinium salt depends on the chemical structure both of the antidote and of the intoxicating organophosphorus compound. The paper discusses these structure-activity relationships in detail, with special emphasis on protection against soman poisoning.

Chapter 10. Limitations of pharmacotherapy in organophosphate intoxications

S. RUMP and J. FAFF
Department of Toxicology, Military Institute of Hygiene and Epidemiology,
Kozielska 4, POB 45, 01-163 Warsaw 42, Poland

Experimental methods of therapy against acute organophosphate intoxications are described. Special attention is paid to the dependence of the effectiveness of therapy on such factors as the type and dose of the drugs used and the time of administration. In animal experiments it was found that the most effective therapy consisted of the use of a combination of a cholinolytic drug, an acetylcholinesterase reactivator, an acetylcholinesterase protector, an anticonvulsant drug and a veratrine-like agent. However, even this treatment could not save the lives of animals intoxicated with more than 90 LD_{50} of an organophosphate. This value, therefore, probably represents the limit of the efficacy of experimental pharmacotherapy of organophosphate intoxication at the present time.

Chapter 11. The possibility of complex therapy in acute dimethoate poisoning

T. KISIELIŃSKI, D. GAJEWSKI, H. OWCZARCZYK and J. SOŃTA
Department of Toxicology, Military Institute of Hygiene and Epidemiology, Kozielska 4, POB 45, 01-163 Warsaw 42, Poland

The resistance of dimethoate intoxication to oxime therapy cannot be explained, as can the similar resistance of soman poisoning, on the basis of rapid ageing of the inhibited acetylcholinesterase. Experiments on mice show that atropine sulphate is an effective therapeutic agent against dimethoate poisoning, and that its therapeutic effect is enhanced by the use of Toxogonin, HS-6 or SAD-128. In contrast to results of other workers, it was found that HS-6 and SAD-128 have little value as prophylactic agents, that the use of two cholinolytics together does not give additional therapeutic effect, and that the use of Valium in conjunction with atropine and an oxime has little additional value.

Chapter 12. The prophylactic value of oximes against organophosphate poisoning

H. P. BENSCHOP, L. A. P. de JONG, J. A. J. VINK and H. KIENHUIS
Chemical Laboratory TNO, 137 Lange Kleiweg, POB 45, Rijswijk (Z.H.), The Netherlands

and

F. BERENDS, D. M. W. ELSKAMP, L. A. KEPNER, E. MEETER and R. P. L. S. VISSER
Medical Biological Laboratory TNO, 137 Lange Kleiweg, POB 45, Rijswijk (Z.H.), The Netherlands

Several new oximes with greater liposolubility than P2S were synthesized. It was hoped that these oximes would be eliminated slowly from the body, thus rendering them suitable for prophylactic use against organophosphorus poisoning. The increased liposolubility of the oximes, relative to P2S, was obtained by: (*a*) substitution of the methyl group in P2S by larger aryl or alkyl groups; or (*b*) synthesis of oximes that lack a quaternary group, for example, thiadiazole-5-carboxaldoximes and derivatives of oximinoacetic acid. The oximes were tested with regard to their *in vitro* reactivating capacity, LD_{50} values in mice (intraperitoneally), biological half-lives after intravenous administration in rats and rabbits, and prophylactic activities against sarin after intraperitoneal administration in mice.

Chapter 13. An alternative therapy against organophosphate poisoning

O. L. WOLTHUIS
Medical Biological Laboratory TNO, 139 Lange Kleiweg, POB 45, Rijswijk (Z. H.), The Netherlands

Since the standard therapy against organophosphate poisoning—the use of atropine and oximes—is only partially successful, alternative means of therapy are investigated. One of the alternatives is based on the observation that atropinized rats poisoned with large doses of organophosphates resume spontaneous breathing after several hours, provided they are kept alive with artificial respiration during the period of respiratory paralysis. This paper discusses the question of whether it is possible, by means of muscle stimulants with veratrinic properties, to maintain respiration until spontaneous respiration is restored. The results so far have been partially successful. Although good therapeutic results have been obtained against poisoning with sarin, DFP and paraoxon, only a delay of the onset of respiratory failure has been obtained after poisoning by soman. The main problem is the side-effects that occur after repeated injections of the muscle stimulants.

Chapter 14. Some toxicological consequences of the alkylating action of organophosphorus compounds

KH. LOHS, W. GIBEL and G. W. FISCHER
Academy of Sciences of the GDR, 108 Berlin, GDR

The problem of the delayed effects of exposure to organophosphorus compounds has so far received little attention, the reason being that these effects are mainly the results of the little-known alkylating properties and side-reactions, rather than of the well-understood phosphorylating actions, of organophosphates. The work described in this paper is based on studies carried out in 1966–67 on some phosphoric- and phosphonic-ester preparations, and on some new studies of the alkylating actions of these compounds *in vivo*. It was found that two organophosphorus compounds—trichlorphon and dimethoate—show distinct carcinogenic activity, in addition to their haematotoxic and hepatotoxic effects. The possibility of sub-acute damage, and consequently the risk of carcinogenic and other delayed effects in man resulting from exposure to organophosphorus compounds, must be accepted. It is also possible that biochemical alkylation reactions are responsible for the psychopathological and neurological side-effects that have been observed following exposure to organophosphorus compounds.

Chapter 15. Blood and brain cholinesterase activity in human death cases, in normal human subjects and in some laboratory and domestic animals

A. R. ALHA, A. RUOHONEN and M. TELARANTA

Department of Forensic Medicine, Division of Forensic Chemistry, University of Helsinki, Helsinki, Finland

Acetylcholinesterase and butyrylcholinesterase activities in blood and in brain homogenates were estimated using a kinetic spectrophotometric DTNB method. The average blood acetylcholinesterase activity of human subjects fatally poisoned with organophosphates was found to be about 25 per cent of the normal value. The average acetylcholinesterase activity in the cerebellum of human organophosphate-poisoning cases was about 15 per cent of the value found in normal death cases. Acetylcholinesterase and butyrylcholinesterase activities in normal animal blood were considerably lower than in normal human blood: there were no large differences in acetylcholinesterase activities among the species investigated, but butyrylcholinesterase activities varied considerably. The acetylcholinesterase activities in the brains of normal rats and mice were higher than in the human cerebellum. After poisoning with parathion, decreased acetylcholinesterase activities were found in whole brains of rats and mice and in the blood of mice, and decreased butyrylcholinesterase activities were found in the blood of mice.

TRIVIAL NAMES, CHEMICAL NAMES AND STRUCTURAL FORMULAE OF SOME OF THE CHEMICALS REFERRED TO IN THE TEXT

Trivial name	Chemical name	Structural formula
Organophosphates		
DFP	O,O-diisopropyl phosphorofluoridate	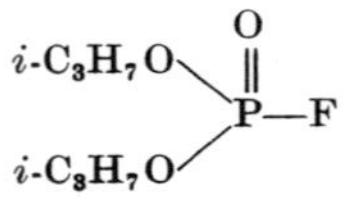
Dimethoate	O,O-dimethyl S-(N-methylcarbamoyl) methyl phosphorodithioate	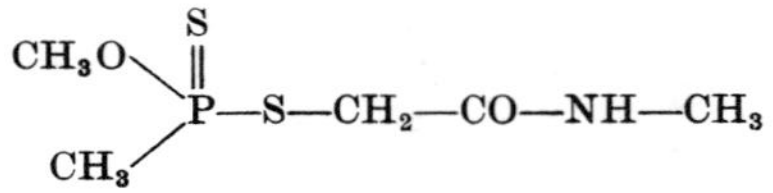
Paraoxon, E 600	O,O-diethyl O-4-nitrophenyl phosphate	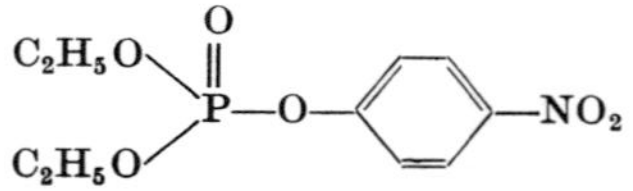
Parathion, E 605	O,O-diethyl O-4-nitrophenyl phosphorothioate	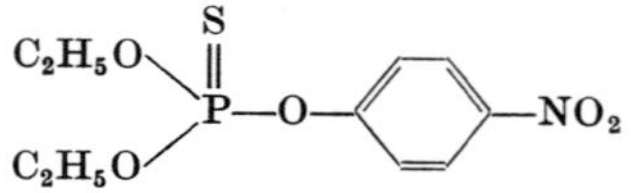
Sarin, GB	O-isopropyl methylphosphonofluoridate	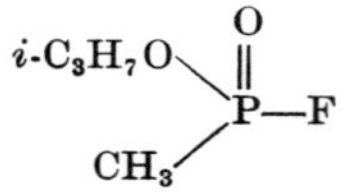
Soman, GD	O-1,2,2-trimethylpropyl methylphosphonofluoridate	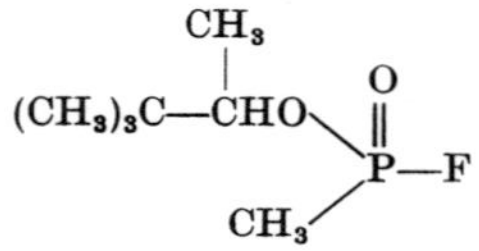
Tabun, GA	O-ethyl N,N-dimethyl phosphoramidocyanidate	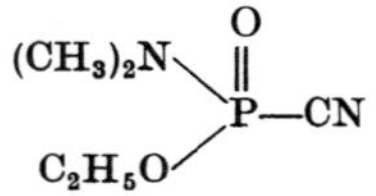

VX	O-ethyl S-2-diisopropylaminoethyl methylphosphonothioate	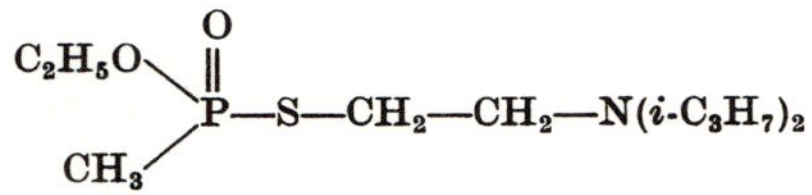
Cholinolytics		
Atropine		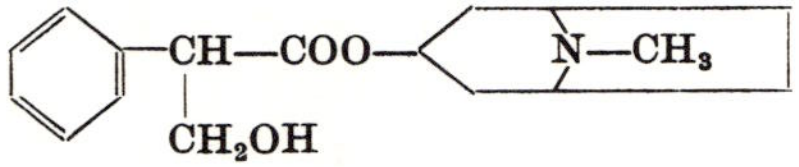
PMCG	N-ethyl-2-pyrrolidylmethyl cyclopentylphenyl glycollate	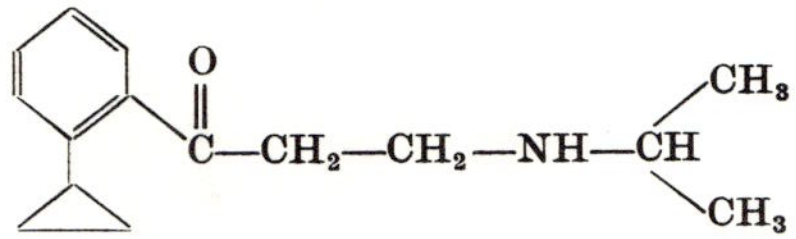
Oximes		
Obidoxime, Toxogonin, LüH6	Bis-[(4-hydroxyimino-methyl)-pyridine-1-methyl]-ether dichloride	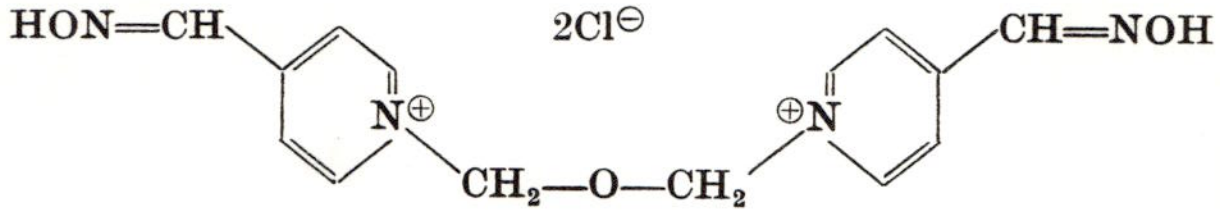
Pralidoxime 2-PAM	(2-hydroxyimino-methyl)-pyridine-1-methyl chloride (or iodide)	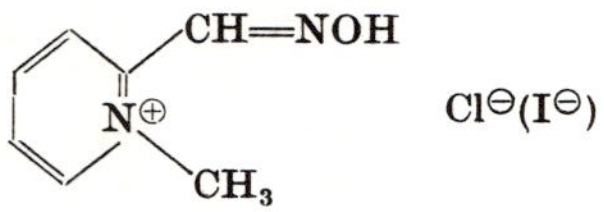
P2S	(2-hydroxyimino-methyl)-pyridine-1-methyl methanesulphonate	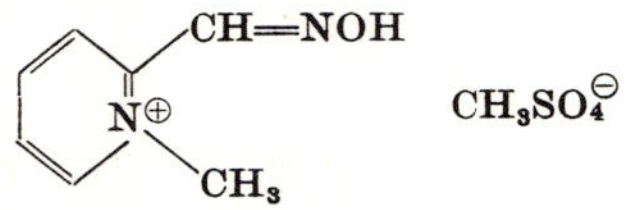
Trimedoxime, TMB-4	1,3-bis-[(4-hydroxyimino-methyl)-pyridine-1]-propane dichloride (or dibromide)	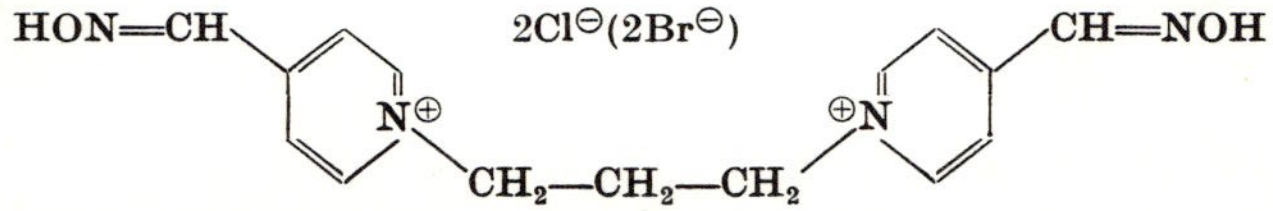

1. Clinical aspects of intoxication by cholinesterase inhibitors

F. R. SIDELL

Square-bracketed numbers, thus [1], *refer to the list of references on page 35.*

I. *Symptoms and diagnosis of organophosphate poisoning*

Many of the clinical consequences of cholinesterase inhibition are predictable, at least insofar as the peripheral neural systems are concerned. At muscarinic sites, the accumulation of acetylcholine stimulates the secretory and contractile activity of glands and smooth muscle fibres. In the sympathetic ganglia, including the adrenal medulla, rising levels of acetylcholine cause sympathetic stimulation followed by depression. As the concentration of acetylcholine increases, the neuromuscular junction displays a progression of nicotinic effects, beginning with heightened irritability and fasciculations and proceeding to paralysis.

In the central nervous system, the situation is more complicated. Although there is considerable evidence for the existence of cholinergic systems within brain structures, our limited knowledge of the details of nervous organization do not always allow the prediction of the end-result of cholinergic excess in these systems. Clinically, dizziness, anxiety and nausea might be considered early signs of mild intoxication; these might proceed to convulsions, which may be a manifestation of hyperexcitability of one part, or depression of another part, of the brain. The end-result is a generalized depression of the central nervous system, including the respiratory centre. Central-nervous-system symptoms, such as nightmares, disturbances of concentration and memory and depression of mood are typical behavioural manifestations of cholinesterase inhibition and may be most prevalent during the period of recovery from the more life-threatening effects of the inhibition.

The clinical manifestations of anticholinesterase intoxication depend on the particular inhibitor involved, the route of exposure and the size of the dose. If the exposure is by the vapour or aerosol route, the first signs and symptoms may be localized in the sensitive areas around the face: miosis, with eye pain and dim vision, may be the first sign noted and, if the dose is quite low, may be the only sign. Usually, but not always, rhinorrhea accompanies miosis. As the dose increases and the individual finds it difficult to breathe, symptoms and signs relating to the lungs begin to appear. These, of course, are due to bronchoconstriction and increased secretions of the bronchial tree. If the exposure is only moderate, these may be the only signs and symptoms, but if the dose is overwhelming, the progression continues with gastrointestinal signs, muscular weakness, possibly convulsions and unconsciousness, and ultimately general depression and death.

Exposure by a droplet on the skin may cause a different sequence of events. Usually there is increased sweating and localized muscular fasciculations at the exposure site, but these may be overlooked if the exposure is unexpected. More commonly, the first symptoms are of gastrointestinal origin, such as nausea, vomiting and diarrhea, followed by bronchoconstriction, generalized muscular weakness and paralysis, convulsions and death. In small amounts, rather potent and quite lipid-soluble materials, such as sarin, present low hazards by this means of exposure, because their volatility causes them to disseminate into the air before they can penetrate the skin. However, large amounts of such compounds can be extremely toxic by this route.

Oral ingestion is probably the most common route of exposure and is usually seen in cases of suicide or attempted suicide, or in accidents involving children. The first signs and symptoms are those relating to the gastrointestinal tract, with nausea and vomiting. Such symptoms are usually attributed to the local action of the agent on the gut wall. However, in a small group of subjects who received VX orally in an experimental study [1], there were fewer subjects with gastrointestinal symptoms than in another group who received the compound intravenously—even though the former group showed slightly greater cholinesterase depression—which suggests that at least part of the gastrointestinal symptomology may be of central-nervous-system origin.

The time course of symptom progression varies, and again depends on exposure route, size of dose and compound. A very large vapour exposure may cause unconsciousness within minutes, as may some smaller doses by other routes. An example is the case of a chemist who had accidentally taken a very small amount of soman into his mouth. He immediately washed it out and was able to walk to the emergency room without difficulty. Immediately afterwards, however, he collapsed, and within minutes was comatose and almost totally apneic [2]. On the other hand, small, but lethal, amounts of organophosphates on the skin may not produce any symptoms for hours, and it may be longer before the first symptoms progress in severity.

When organophosphorus compounds are administered to animals intravenously in large doses, they cause bradycardia or heart block, but it is unusual to see these signs clinically. In fact, in almost all reported cases tachycardia is the universal finding and this probably reflects the stimulation of the autonomic ganglion or is a manifestation of a generalized stress reaction. Miosis, which is often considered a diagnostic sign, may also not necessarily be present unless the exposure directly involves the eyes.

The diagnosis of a typical case of anticholinesterase intoxication is not difficult, particularly if a good history is available. The patient may be a farmer who has used organophosphate insecticides, a worker in an insecticide plant, a laboratory worker, a child who has accidentally swallowed such compounds, or someone intent on suicide. Fortunately, some of the material, or an empty container, is usually available as an aid to diagnosis.

A more difficult case may be, for example, that of a person who works with or around such materials and, without being aware of it, has been repeatedly exposed to small amounts of the compound. He may have no acute symptoms, but may complain of feeling tired, and may exhibit some mental changes, such as intellectual dullness, depression, memory impairment or troubled sleep. The estimation of cholinesterase activity in the blood may be a useful diagnostic procedure in such cases: many insecticides, such as parathion, preferentially cause a depression in the serum cholinesterase (or pseudocholinesterase), whereas the more potent materials, such as sarin and VX, preferentially inhibit the cholinesterase found in red blood cells, so that when the enzyme activity in either plasma or red blood cells is negligible, the diagnosis is rather straightforward. However, there are instances when the enzyme activity is only slightly depressed, and in such cases the question arises whether the individual has been exposed or whether his cholinesterase activity is in the low part of the normal range: how much variability in cholinesterase activity can one expect to see?

Two recent studies provide some information on this point. In one study, the cholinesterase activity of 22 subjects was estimated every other week for a year. These subjects were healthy, ranged in age from 25 to 69 years, and were either male or female. Although there were large differences in enzyme activity among the subjects, the activity of each individual subject varied very little throughout the year. In general, the range of red-blood-cell activity for each individual was within 10 per cent of the mean, and for each person the standard deviation from the mean was about 5 per cent. Therefore, for any given individual, a change in activity greater than 10 per cent of the mean should be regarded with suspicion. The range of plasma cholinesterase activity was slightly greater—about 10–20 per cent—and the standard deviation was about 8 per cent.

In the second study, the cholinesterase activities of about 450 men and 200 women were measured, and it was found that the average activity varies with sex and age, and under the influence of certain medications. The average plasma cholinesterase activity was about 15–20 per cent lower in females than in males of the same age, until the age of 50 years; thereafter the activities of males and females were about the same. Women taking birth-control pills had, on average, an even lower activity—about 15 per cent lower than women of the same age who did not take oral contraceptives. Red-blood-cell cholinesterase activity varied with age in both sexes.

It was lower in those under 30 and highest in those in their 50s. The activity of women taking birth-control pills was again different, but in this case it was significantly higher than in other women in the same age groups.

II. *Treatment of organophosphate poisoning*

The treatment of a severe case of poisoning by a cholinesterase inhibitor is a medical emergency and requires constant care from a team of medical personnel. Although rather straightforward in theory, therapy may well be difficult in practice, particularly if there are multiple casualties or if adequate medical facilities are not available. There are four principal factors in treatment: termination of the exposure; blockade of the excess acetylcholine; oxygenation; and reversal of the cholinesterase inhibition, if possible. The order of priority depends on the condition of the patient.

The most desirable first step is termination of the exposure, either by removing the casualty from the contaminated environment or by removing the compound from the casualty, for example, if it is on his skin or in his gastrointestinal tract. This is one of the more important—and one of the most often overlooked—aspects of therapy, since both the skin and the gut can act as a reservoir from which the compound may be continuously absorbed for hours or days.

Blockade of the excess acetylcholine is achieved by the administration of a cholinolytic compound. Atropine is used almost universally for this, although other cholinolytics might possibly be used for certain purposes (see page 27). To be most effective, the drug should be given as soon as possible after the exposure, should be given by a means which promotes rapid absorption into the circulation (intravenous administration is obviously the best), and should be given in adequate doses. Two milligrams seems to be a recommended starting dose, but if the casualty is severe, the dose should be several times larger. Although there are no set rules regarding the total amount of atropine that should be given, or the length of time for which it should be continued, one general rule might be to give an adequate amount often enough and over a long enough period of time to keep secretions dry. Several doses may be adequate, but there are cases where several hundred milligrams have been administered over a 24-hour period. The most important single factor in therapy is to keep the patient breathing, or to maintain artificial respiration until he recovers sufficiently to breathe for himself. One's first instinct on confronting a cyanotic non-breathing patient is to give air, but the intense bronchoconstriction might make this extremely difficult. Atropine, apart from its antidotal activity, is also important in this context, since it promotes oxygenation by drying secretions and relieving bronchoconstriction, but quite large pressures by a pressure respirator might still be necessary, at least for the first few breaths.

In addition to bronchoconstriction, the respiratory muscles may be weakened or paralyzed and the central respiratory centre severely depressed.

Since the poisoning effects of anticholinesterase compounds are caused by the binding of a foreign compound to the enzyme, the most logical way of reversing this process is to break this bond and remove the foreign material. The oximes do just that, but, unfortunately, although they might reactivate the enzyme, we know that, clinically at least, the oximes are not nearly as effective as atropine in reversing the muscarinic effects of the poison. We also know that, depending on the time between poisoning and administration of the antidote, the oximes are relatively ineffective against certain organophosphate compounds because of the "ageing" process, by which the inhibited enzyme becomes resistant to reactivation. Furthermore, it is questionable whether oximes enter the central nervous system in significant amounts to reverse the process in these vital areas.

Nonetheless, these compounds are useful and when administered in combination with a cholinolytic such as atropine, they are reasonably effective in reducing the lethality of many organophosphates.

Since the oximes are rapidly excreted by the kidneys, and so only have a relatively short half-life of about 1–1½ hours, a second or third dose may be needed at appropriate intervals to maintain adequate blood concentrations.

The oximes in common use are pralidoxime chloride (PAM), pralidoxime methanesulphonate (P2S) and obidoxime (Toxogonin). The differences between them are for the most part small. On a weight basis, Toxogonin is more potent, but it is also more toxic. The major hazard from acute administration of pralidoximes is hypertension, but this may sometimes be an advantage in a patient with a failing circulation. If the hypertension becomes too severe it can be quickly reversed with phentolamine, a rapid acting alpha-adrenergic blocking compound.

III. *Experimental work on therapeutic compounds*

Cholinolytic drugs

Although the necessary rapid administration of atropine is easily and effectively carried out in a hospital or other medical facility, a person poisoned in the field must adopt other procedures. The autoinjector is a pressure-sensitive, spring-operated device designed for such circumstances: all the user need do is remove the safety cap and press the other end against his muscle, and as the needle comes out and enters the muscle the solution is expelled, creating a spray effect into the muscle. This spray effect creates a larger area or volume for drug absorption and, as a result, the drug takes effect faster than with the usual intramuscular injection (see figure 1.1) [3].

Even faster drug absorption can be obtained by using a smaller volume of

Figure 1.1. Increase in heart rate due to intramuscular administration of 2 mg atropine sulphate by needle and syringe or by automatic injector

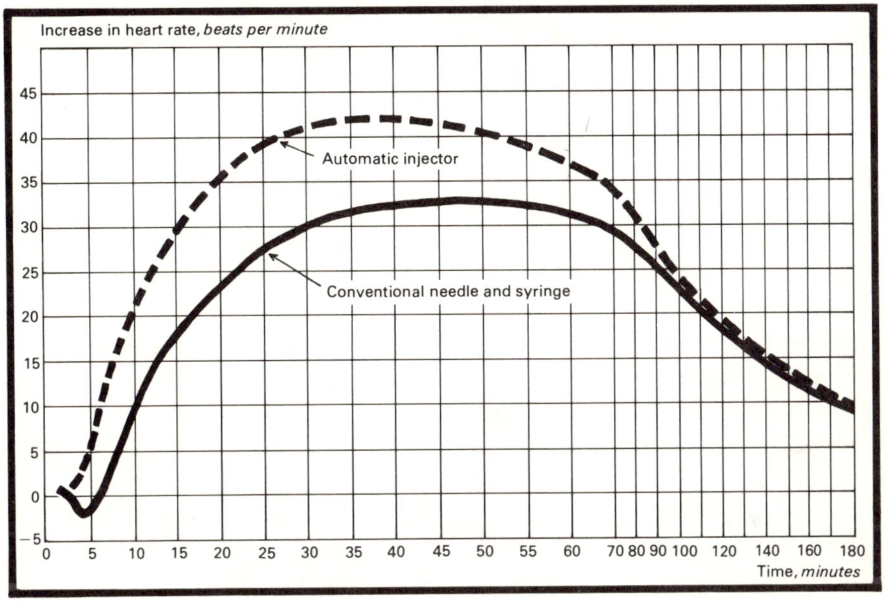

solution. A comparison of the effects of 2 mg of atropine given in 2.0 ml, 0.1 ml and 0.7 ml of solution—the last volume being the volume contained in the autoinjector—shows that the effects from the smallest volume are most rapid in onset (table 1.1). It seems that the way to achieve rapid onset of effects is to use a very small amount of a highly concentrated solution in a mini-injector.

The possible use of cholinolytic compounds other than atropine has been mentioned above. Several synthetic compounds have been shown to be better than atropine as therapy for anticholinesterase intoxication and it is felt that these are more effective because they have a higher central-nervous-system activity. However, this very property is also a major drawback to the routine use of these compounds. If an individual thinks he has been exposed and thus gives himself a large dose, when in fact he has had only a very mild exposure or none at all, these compounds may well produce undesirable central-nervous-system effects, such as confusion and disorientation. There may, however, be a use for such compounds under carefully controlled conditions.

The effectiveness of one of these alternative cholinolytic compounds has been investigated in the case of an individual who was severely ill from soman intoxication [2]. After the acute effects had been successfully treated, he began to have mental disturbances, such as inability to con-

Table 1.1. Time required for heart-rate response in man to reach certain levels after intramuscular injection of 2 mg atropine sulphate in various volumes of solution

	Time taken for heart-rate level to be reached *min*			
Volume of solution, *ml*	Lowest heart rate	10 beats/min above normal	More than 80 beats/min	Maximal heart rate
0.1	3.25	7.8	12.8	29.0
0.7 (autoinjector)	2.8	8.0	16.3	34.4
0.7	4.2	14.7	22.8	40.7
2.0	7.75	19.3	26.3	47.0

centrate, depression, poor sleep and so on. Each day for the next week he was given either scopolamine or methscopolamine: scopolamine has prominent central effects and, in the dose given, might have been expected to produce mild confusion and difficulty in concentration; methscopolamine was given as a placebo, as it causes the peripheral but not the central effects of scopolamine. Each day that the patient received scopolamine he felt better, he was less depressed, and he could concentrate and think better. His scores on an arithmetic test were also better on the days he received scopolamine (see figure 1.2).

Fortunately, we have not seen another patient under these circumstances on whom to try this therapy again and it would be interesting to know of other experiences with it. The psychiatric sequelae following severe anticholinesterase intoxication, although minor in terms of being life-threatening, may be a cause of severe disability and perhaps more attention should be given to reducing this morbidity.

Oximes

The patient described in the above section was given pralidoxime chloride, which seemingly had no effect on his red-cell cholinesterase. Despite this, he physically improved over the first few days, which may indicate that the circulating-cholinesterase activity does not reflect that in the tissues, or that the tissues can adapt to a lack of cholinesterase, or both. Whether or not this is true, this case does provide a good clinical example of an inhibitor/enzyme bond that is refractory to oxime reactivation: ageing was probably complete within minutes, as the patient was given oxime within 10–15 minutes of exposure. For other compounds, the ageing process is not so rapid. When an oxime is given as long as 48 hours after exposure to VX there is still significant reactivation of the enzyme, at least of circulating enzyme [1]. Table 1.2 shows that at all times studied, from 0.5 to 48 hours after exposure to VX, and at all doses of pralidoxime, from 2.5 mg/kg to 29 mg/kg, there was a small amount of enzyme that was not reactivated, but

Figure 1.2. Number Facility (performance test) scores[a] and cholinesterase activity in a patient treated with scopolamine or methscopolamine following accidental exposure to soman

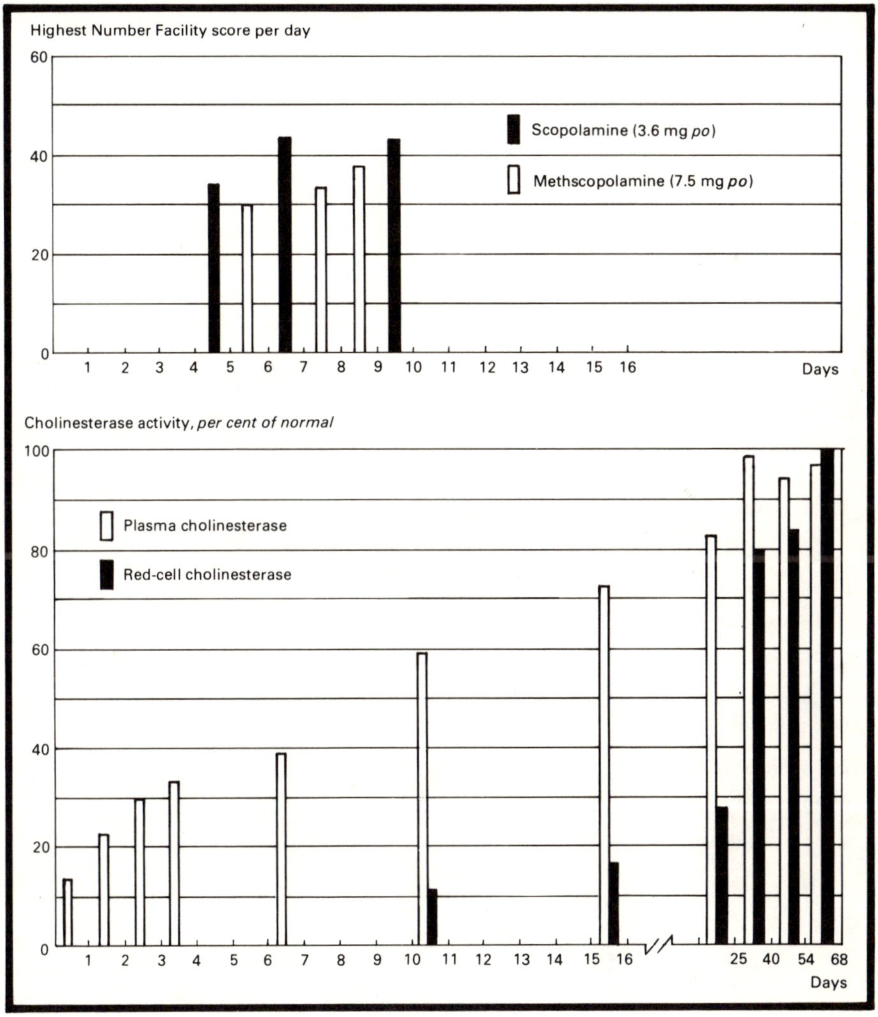

[a] The Number Facility test is a three-minute addition task, and the score is the number of problems solved correctly during that time.

this did not change as time increased or as the dose of oxime changed. In a more limited study with sarin, also shown in table 1.2, the findings were somewhat different [1]: one hour after exposure to sarin, a small dose of oxime—10 mg/kg—did not cause as much reactivation as a larger dose—25 mg/kg—and the larger dose did not work as well after five hours as it did after three hours.

These examples probably indicate the extremes of ageing times: soman is

Table 1.2. Reactivation of VX- and sarin-inhibited red cell cholinesterase by pyridine-2-aldoxime methochloride (2-PAM Cl)

Dose of 2-PAM Cl *mg/kg*	Time of adminis-tration, after VX or sarin *hours*	Number of sub-jects	Cholinesterase activities (per cent of control (mean±SD)): Lowest activity reached after intoxication	Activity just prior to oxime administra-tion[a]	Activity after oxime adminis-tration	Total per cent re-activation
After VX intravenously						
15	0.5	2	17±17	18±18	79± 6	75± 2
15	1.0	1	23	28	80	72
2.5	3	3	39± 3	41± 4	79± 1	65± 2
15	3	3	32± 7	34± 7	71±10	51±12
25	3	2	15± 8	24±21	83± 4	78± 1
2.5	6	4	22± 6	33±15	75± 5	62± 9
15	6	3	32± 8	35± 8	80± 8	69±11
25	6	1	14	39	89	82
2.5	24	3	32± 2	53± 5	83± 1	62± 2
5	24	4	22± 4	50± 9	78±14	59±23
15	24	2	22± 6	48± 7	83± 1	68± 2
25	24	2	15± 4	51± 2	85± 1	70± 2
After VX orally						
5	5	7	23±11	34± 9	85± 7	77±11
10	5	7	29±13	39± 9	89±10	82±13
20	24	1	24	56	90	77
25	24	2	24± 1	54± 7	83±10	61±28
30	24	2	23± 2	59± 7	90± 6	74±18
24[b]	27[d]	5	27±14	55± 3	88±10	74±24
29[c]	27[e]	3	21± 9	56±14	101±20	85±25
15	48	1	33	70	87	57
20	48	1	42	63	87	62
After sarin intravenously						
10	1	3	54± 1	56± 2	68± 6	28±11
15	1	2	54±13	58±11	83± 1	58±12
20	1	2	52± 7	53± 6	81± 1	58± 7
25	1	2	48± 3	51± 2	83± 3	66± 8
2.5	3	2	37± 2	41± 2	40± 2	0
5	3	2	37± 5	41± 4	47± 4	10±13
10	3	2	39±11	50± 1	76± 6	53±12
15	3	2	41± 3	48± 6	76± 8	53±21
20	3	2	28± 4	35± 4	65±10	46±19
25	3	2	59± 5	62± 6	85± 3	64± 2
25	5	2	35± 4	38± 4	64±13	43±16

[a] The difference between this value and the value in the previous column (for the lowest cholinesterase activity reached) represents spontaneous reactivation during the interval before oxime administration.
[b] Average (range=20–25 mg/kg).
[c] Average (range=26.2–31.6 mg/kg).
[d] Average (range=25–30 hours).
[e] Average (range=26–28 hours).

almost completely aged within minutes, while there is very little ageing of VX, even after 48 hours.

Several routes of administration of several oximes have been studied in man. The indications for giving oximes orally are few. Oral administration might be used for prophylaxis. It might also be used when the aim is to maintain a certain blood concentration of oxime over a long period of time without repeated injections. Such might be the case if the cholinesterase inhibitor is being released from a depot, such as the gut, from where it cannot be removed, or if the inhibitor requires metabolic conversion, for example, the conversion of parathion to paraoxon, and hence time to act. Of course, oximes should not be given orally to a vomiting patient.

Toxogonin is poorly absorbed from the gastrointestinal tract, and only 2–3 per cent of the dose is found in the urine. Because it has a much smaller volume of distribution than the pralidoximes, however, blood concentrations after a given dose of Toxogonin are only slightly lower than those after a similar dose of pralidoxime.

We studied four different preparations of pralidoxime—one of pralidoxime chloride and three of the methanesulphonate salt [4–5]. The maximal plasma concentrations varied by as much as 100 per cent between the different preparations.

We looked at the absorption of pralidoxime chloride given orally while men were exercising. The subjects took five grams of pralidoxime and either rested in bed for the test period or walked about 11 miles during the next four hours. There was no difference in absorption, or at least in the plasma concentration, of oxime, or in the urinary excretion of the drug.

Pralidoxime methanesulphonate was given to subjects who had fasted for 12 hours and to subjects who had just eaten a large breakfast [5]. The plasma concentration of oxime was about 20 per cent higher in the subjects who had eaten, suggesting that food promotes absorption of the drug.

We also examined the blood concentrations of oxime following the administration of 600 mg of oxime with an autoinjector [3], and found that in the early minutes the concentration of oxime given by autoinjector was 82 per cent higher than with the same dose of oxime given by needle and syringe. Moreover, a concentration of 4 μg/ml is reached much sooner with autoinjector administration.

The use of the value 4 μg/ml is somewhat arbitrary, because the concentration of oxime needed to reverse cholinesterase inhibition is not well defined: it varies according to the inhibitor, the time after poisoning that the oxime is given, and probably other factors. Perhaps these factors should be better defined. Another interesting question is how long the oxime need be present to be effective. Is a concentration of 5 μg/ml for five minutes as effective as the same concentration for two hours?

After autoinjector administration, the concentration is above 5 μg/ml for about 30 minutes; would the effectiveness be increased by a higher concentration for a longer period? It would be helpful to know the answers to some of these questions when trying to evaluate pharmaceutical preparations of oximes, as well as when comparing oximes.

If atropine is good therapy, and if an oxime is good therapy, and if

Figure 1.3. Plasma oxime concentrations following intravenous infusion (over a period of 30 minutes) of one gram of oxime, either alone or in conjunction with 200 mg thiamine hydrochloride

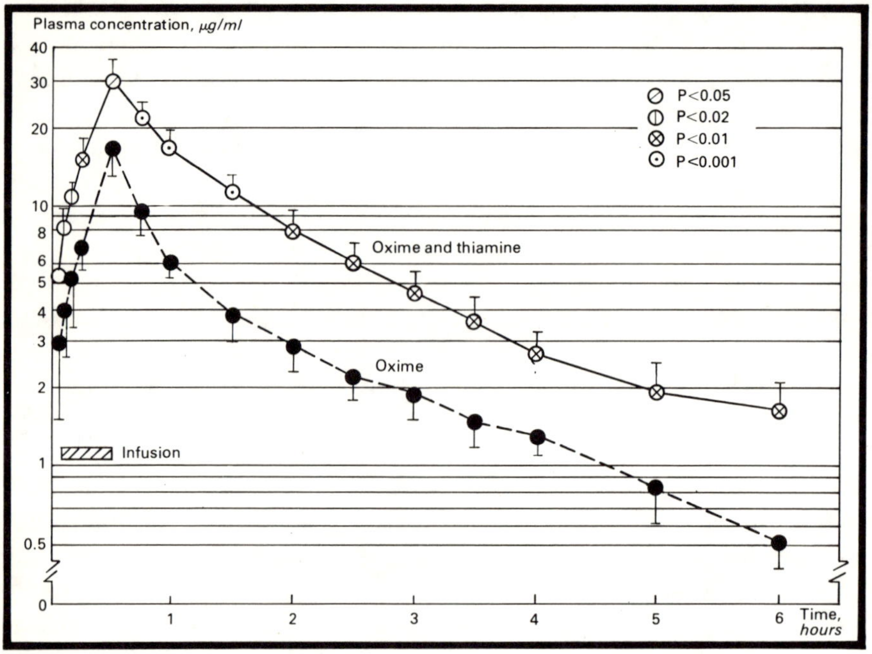

Note: Each point represents the mean ± SD.

administration by an autoinjector can hasten absorption, why not put both drugs into an autoinjector? Several years ago, we conducted a series of trials in which atropine was given intramuscularly and then was given in the same 2-ml solution with 600 mg of pralidoxime chloride [6]. We found that the effects of atropine on the heart rate were significantly delayed when the mixture was administered. Holland and White, using 600 mg/2 ml of P2S instead of pralidoxime chloride, found no delay in the effects of atropine [7]. Since pralidoxime methanesulphonate has a larger molecular weight than pralidoxime chloride, the osmolarity of the P2S solution, at the same dose, is lower, and so we repeated our study, using a concentration of pralidoxime chloride with the same osmolarity as the solution of P2S used by Holland and White. At this osmolarity, the time course of atropine effects was not significantly altered [8], and we concluded that the delay was a function of the concentration of oxime or osmolarity of the solution, and was not caused by the oxime itself.

A distinct difference between Toxogonin and the pralidoximes is their mode of excretion. The renal clearance rate of pralidoxime is almost the same as that of para-amino hippuric acid, indicating that pralidoxime is

Table 1.3. Excretion rate of pralidoxime with and without treatment with thiamine

Compounds administered	Per cent of oxime dose excreted				
	In 0–1½ hours	In 1½–3 hours	In 3–6 hours	In 6–24 hours	**Total**
Pralidoxime	61.7	12.8	8.3	2.8	**85.6**
Pralidoxime + thiamine	33.9[a]	13.0[b]	19.5[c]	20.8[c]	**87.2**

[a] $p = < 0.01$, compared with pralidoxime alone.
[b] $p = < 0.8$, compared with pralidoxime alone.
[c] $p = < 0.001$, compared with pralidoxime alone.

actively secreted by the renal tubule cells. The renal clearance of Toxogonin, on the other hand, is about the same as that of creatinine, suggesting that it is filtered at the glomerulus but not secreted by the tubule cells [9]. One possible way of prolonging the plasma half-life of pralidoxime might be to block its secretion by the tubule cell. One substance which does this effectively is thiamine, vitamin B_1 [10]. Figure 1.3 shows the plasma concentrations of oxime after an intravenous infusion of one gram of pralidoxime alone and pralidoxime combined with 200 mg of thiamine: the plasma concentrations are more than doubled when thiamine is added. Table 1.3 shows the excretion pattern, and it is clear that in the first few hours, while thiamine is in the body, much less oxime is excreted. However, since Toxogonin is probably not excreted by the tubule cells of the kidney, it is doubtful whether thiamine would be effective in increasing the plasma concentration of this compound.

Men were given intravenous pralidoxime and underwent various conditions of stress [11]—walking at three miles per hour, staying in a hot environment (40°C) for three hours, or a combination of these conditions. Some subjects also went without fluids for 12 hours before the study (table 1.4). Exercise alone prolonged the half-life and reduced the renal excretion, but had no effect on plasma concentration. Heat did not change the half-life, but caused a slight decrease in plasma concentration. Heat and exercise together caused a more marked decrease in renal clearance, a prolongation of the half-life by 21 per cent, and a 20 per cent increase in plasma concentration. Dehydration also caused a decrease in renal clearance, and a 25 per cent increase in plasma concentration. Such factors as stress should be considered when drugs are administered, as they can influence the plasma concentration and half-lives of drugs.

Acknowledgements

The author wishes to thank Dr R. D. Swartz and Dr J. Josselson for allowing him to use some of their data, published and unpublished.

Table 1.4. Effects of stress conditions on some kinetic parameters of pralidoxime chloride in man

Per cent change

Stress conditions	Kinetic parameters for pralidoxime chloride						Renal clearance of creatinine	Renal clearance of para-amino hippuric acid
		Per cent of dose excreted in urine						
	Renal clearance	In 0–3 hours	In 3–24 hours	Biological half-life	Plasma clearance	Plasma con-centration		
Control	645 ml/min	84	10	71 min	686 ml/min	–	130 ml/min	770 ml/min
Exercise	*–11*	*–10*	*0*	*+24*	*0*	*0*	*–8*	*–10*
Exposure to heat	+5	*–10*	*0*	*0*	*+19*	*–15*	*–8*	*+10*
Exercise and exposure to heat	*–16*	*–10*	*0*	*+21*	*–7*	*+20*	*–15*	*–15*
Fluid deprivation	*–15*	*0*	*0*	*0*	*–22*	*+25*	–	*–15*

References

1. Sidell, F. R. and Groff, W. A., "The reactivatibility of cholinesterase inhibited by VX and sarin in man", *Toxicol. Appl. Pharmacol.,* **27,** 241–52 (1974).
2. Sidell, F. R., "Soman and sarin; clinical manifestation and treatment of accidental poisoning by organophosphates", *Clin. Toxicol.,* **7** (1), 1–17 (1974).
3. Sidell, F. R., Markis, J. E., Groff, W. A. and Kaminskis, A., "Enhancement of drug absorption after administration by an automatic injector", *J. Pharmacok. Biopharmaceu.,* **2**, 197–210 (1974).
4. Sidell, F. R., Groff, W. A. and Ellin, R. I., "Blood levels of oxime and symptoms in humans after single and multiple oral doses of 2-pyridine aldoxime methochloride", *J. Pharm. Sci.,* **58** (9), 1093–98 (1969).
5. Sidell, F. R., Groff, W. A. and Kaminskis, A., "Pralidoxime methanesulfonate: plasma levels and pharmacokinetics after oral administration to man", *J. Pharm. Sci.,* **61** (7), 1136–40 (1972).
6. Sidell, F. R., Magness, J. S. and Bollen, T. E., "Modification of atropine on human heart rate by pralidoxime", *Clin. Pharmacol Ther.,* **11** (1), 68–76 (1970).
7. Holland, P. and White, R. G., "Atropine sulfate absorption in humans after intramuscular injection of a mixture of the oxime-P2S and atropine", *Brit. J. Pharmacol.,* **42,** 645P–646P (1971).
8. Sidell, F. R., "Modification by diluents of effects of intramuscular atropine on heart rate in man", *Clin. Pharmacol. Ther.,* **16** (4), 711–15 (1974).
9. Sidell, F. R., Groff, W. A. and Kaminskis, A., "Toxogonin and pralidoxime: kinetic comparison after intravenous administration to man", *J. Pharm. Sci.,* **61** (11), 1765–69 (1972).
10. Swartz, R. D. and Sidell, F. R., "Renal tubular secretion of pralidoxime in man, *Proc. Soc. Exp. Biol. Med.,* **146,** 419–24 (1974).
11. Swartz, R. D. and Sidell, F. R., "Effects of heat and exercise on the elimination of pralidoxime in man", *Clin. Pharmacol. Ther.,* **14** (1), 83–89 (1973).

2. Acetylcholinesterase inhibitors: examples of their modes of action and their utility as scientific tools

J. A. B. BARSTAD

Square-bracketed numbers, thus [1], *refer to the list of references on page 44.*

I. *Introduction*

The effect of acetylcholinesterase inhibitors on the functioning of the neuromuscular junction or synapse has been understood, at least to some extent, for a long time: the treatment of myasthenia gravis with physostigmine and neostigmine, for example, was first practised more than 40 years ago [1–2]. At that time, biochemistry was a rather immature discipline, but since World War II, the mechanisms of action of acetylcholinesterase inhibitors have been elucidated in more detail. Much of this research has been motivated by the discovery and development of the organophosphorus compounds, which are extremely important not only as pesticides and scientific tools, but also as potential chemical-warfare agents.

II. *Effects of acetylcholinesterase inhibitors on neuromuscular transmission*

The alkyl phosphates are acid-transferring compounds that donate their acyl group—a substituted phosphoryl group—to the acetylcholinesterase, which is then said to be phosphorylated (in the same way as the enzyme is carbamylated by the carbamates and acetylated by acetylcholine). The stability of the enzyme/inhibitor complex produced by the various acylating inhibitors varies considerably, the phosphorylated acetylcholinesterases being, with few exceptions, the most stable (hence the term "irreversible inhibitors"). This property of the organophosphates accounts for their toxic effects, including those at the neuromuscular junction. For example, the prolongation of the end-plate potential, which gives rise to repetitive firing in the muscle and thus increased contraction height, is typical of all acetylcholinesterase inhibitors, but is more persistent in the case of the organophosphates than, for example, the carbamates. The same is true of the effects on the synaptic potentials at all cholinergic synapses.

But acetylcholinesterase inhibitors may perhaps also act presynaptically. Masland and Wigton have demonstrated the so-called antidromic activity in motor nerves under the influence of acetylcholinesterase inhibitors [3]. When the motor nerve was stimulated, the orthodromic nerve impulse was followed by an echo-like antidromic impulse, or train of impulses, which usually followed the same nerve fibres as did the orthodromic impulse. This was shown by longitudinal division of the nerve. Sometimes, however, the antidromic pulses were conducted by fibres which were not primarily stimulated. The antidromic activity was counteracted by curare.

The antidromic activity could be due either to intramuscular nerve fibres being stimulated electrically from the muscle fibres (ephaptic transmission) during muscle activity, particularly during the repetitive firing in the muscle, or to a presynaptic effect of the transmitter. The effect of curare could be compatible with both explanations.

In "cut" diaphragm preparations from rat [4], where the muscle fibres, due to demarcation, are unable to set up action potentials, I have recorded antidromic firing in the phrenic nerve after treatment with acetylcholinesterase inhibitors. The antidromic activity was elicited by neostigmine more easily than by diisopropyl phosphorofluoridate (DFP). The antidromic activity was enhanced by acetylcholine in low concentrations (0.6 μg/ml) whereas it was blocked by acetylcholine in higher concentrations (15 μg/ml) as well as by *d*-tubocurarine at a concentration known to induce neuromuscular block (2.5 μg/ml).

This seems to indicate that the neuromuscular transmitter under the influence of acetylcholinesterase inhibitors, even at the presynaptic nerve endings, generates a graded local response, which outlasts the refractory period of the adjacent "all or nothing" responding nerve membrane, and sets up antidromic activity in the nerve. The fibrillation and fasciculation seen in organophosphate poisoning may perhaps be partly due to antidromic impulses conducted by axon reflexes orthodromically to nerve terminals in the vicinity of where the impulse started.

III. *Acetylcholinesterase inhibitors as scientific tools*

The irreversibility of their inhibitory effect on acetylcholinesterase makes the alkyl phosphates unique scientific tools for certain purposes.

Tetanic contractions

We have used DFP to study the correlation between acetylcholinesterase inhibition and the pattern of indirectly induced tetanic contractions in phrenic-nerve-diaphragm preparations. High-frequency inhibition, or

Figure 2.1. Correlation between acetylcholinesterase inhibition due to neostigmine bromide (0.5 μg/ml) and end-plate potential shape in isolated rat "cut" diaphragm preparations

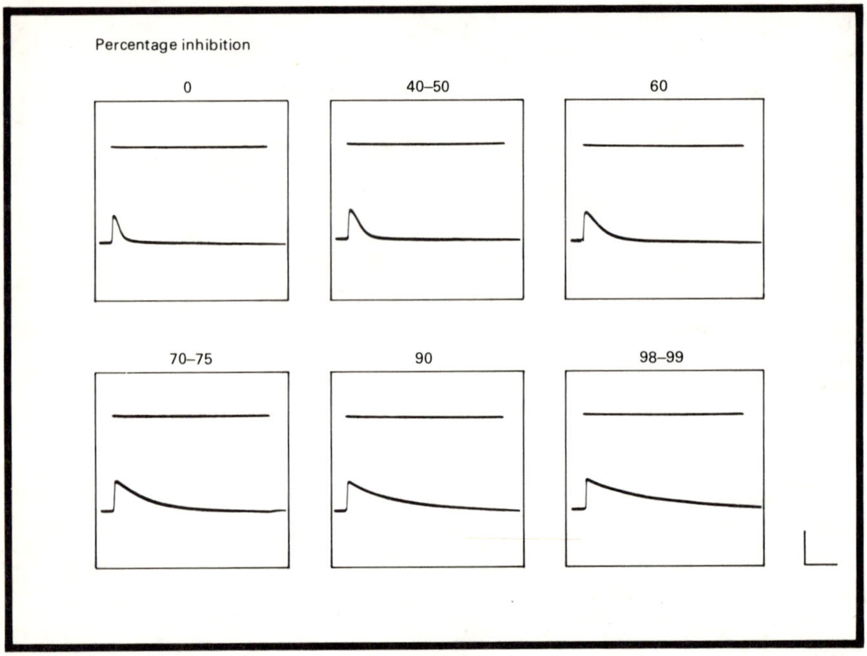

Notes: Stimulation frequency=12 stimuli/minute at 37°C. Percentage acetylcholinesterase inhibition was calculated from second-order rate constants. A calibration scale is shown at right: vertical line (voltage calibration) corresponds to 10 mV; horizontal line (time calibration) corresponds to 4 msec.

Wedensky inhibition, resulting from the addition of DFP to an isolated phrenic-nerve-diaphragm preparation, was seen to persist for hours after washing out the DFP from the bath. The diaphragm preparations were homogenized and the acetylcholinesterase activity measured [5]. It was found that indirectly evoked "five-second" tetanic contractions were well sustained at a frequency of 60 stimuli per second if the acetylcholinesterase activity was above a level between 10 and 15 per cent of the normal. The acetylcholinesterase level necessary for normal sustenance of tetani at a frequency of 120 stimuli per second was between 15 and 20 per cent.

The directly determined acetylcholinesterase activity corresponding to a given tetanic contraction pattern was rather close to the value calculated from the rate constants of inhibition or reactivation of acetylcholinesterase [5–6]. A similar quantitative correlation between the half-decay-time of end-plate potential and the degree of acetylcholinesterase inhibition has been demonstrated in our laboratories partly directly and partly by calculations based on rate constants as mentioned above (see figure 2.1).

Figure 2.2. Maternal and foetal erythrocyte acetylcholinesterase activities 16 hours after subcutaneous injection of the quaternary acetylcholinesterase inhibitor Tx-54[a] (0.325 mg/kg) in atropinized (5 mg atropine sulphate/kg) rats

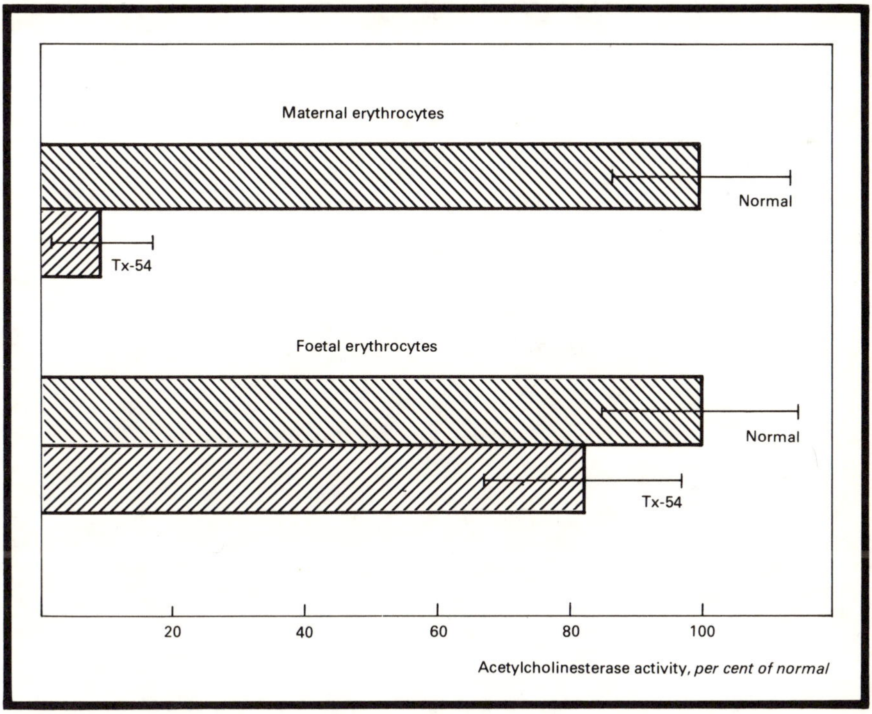

Note: Each column represents the mean of results from six animals (P=0.05).

[a] Tx-54=

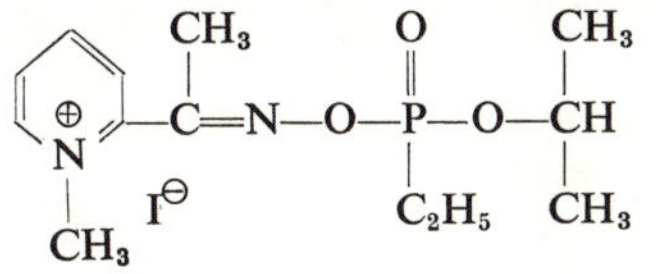

Permeability of biological barriers

Irreversible inhibition of acetylcholinesterase by diethyl paranitrophenylphosphate (paraoxon), and its subsequent reactivation by means of oximes such as pralidoxime methanesulphonate (P2S) or bis-(4-hydroxyiminomethyl)-pyridine-1-methyl)-ether dichloride (Toxogonin), has been used to study the permeability of biological barriers such as the blood-brain barrier, the blood-retina barrier and the placenta barrier [7–10].

For the same purpose we employed tertiary and quaternary nitrogen compounds that were also irreversible acetylcholinesterase inhibitors. In all these experiments the degree of acetylcholinesterase inhibition on both sides of the barrier concerned was determined and the results used as an indicator of barrier penetration. In the experiments on the placenta barrier,

Figure 2.3. Maternal and foetal erythrocyte acetylcholinesterase activities 16 hours after subcutaneous administration of the tertiary acetylcholinesterase inhibitor Tx-60[a] (0.02 mg/kg) in atropinized (5 mg atropine sulphate/kg) rats

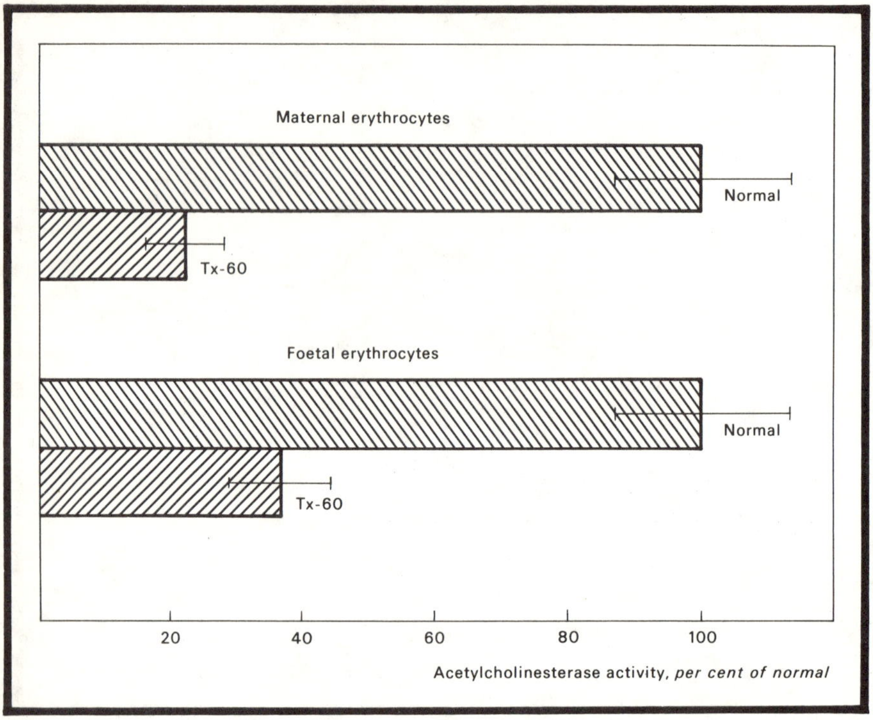

Note: Each column represents the mean of results from six animals (P=0.05).
[a] Tx-60=

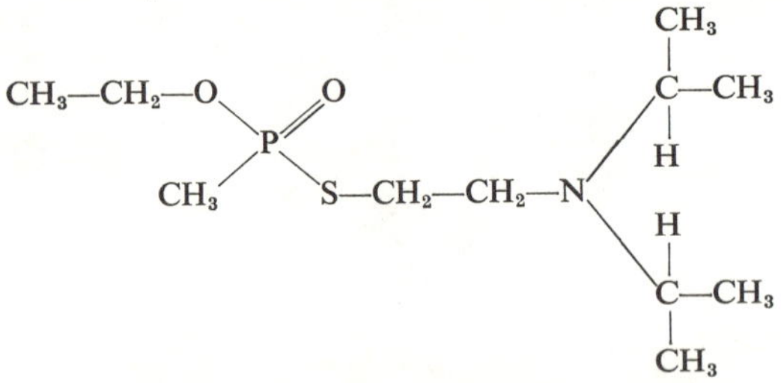

acetylcholinesterase activities were measured in maternal and foetal erythrocytes, while in those on the blood-brain barrier and the blood-retina barrier, brain and retina enzyme activities were compared with that of erythrocytes.

All the three above-mentioned barriers were found to be fairly easily permeable to tertiary compounds, whereas the quaternary ones penetrated at a far lower rate (see figures 2.2 to 2.4). This bears on both inhibitors and reactivators, and is in accordance with the results of other authors [11–14]. With regard to penetration, we found no significant difference between mono- and bisquaternary compounds.

Figure 2.4. Acetylcholinesterase activities in various tissues 16 hours after subcutaneous administration of Tx-54[a] (0.325 mg/kg) in atropinized (5 mg atropine sulphate/kg) rats

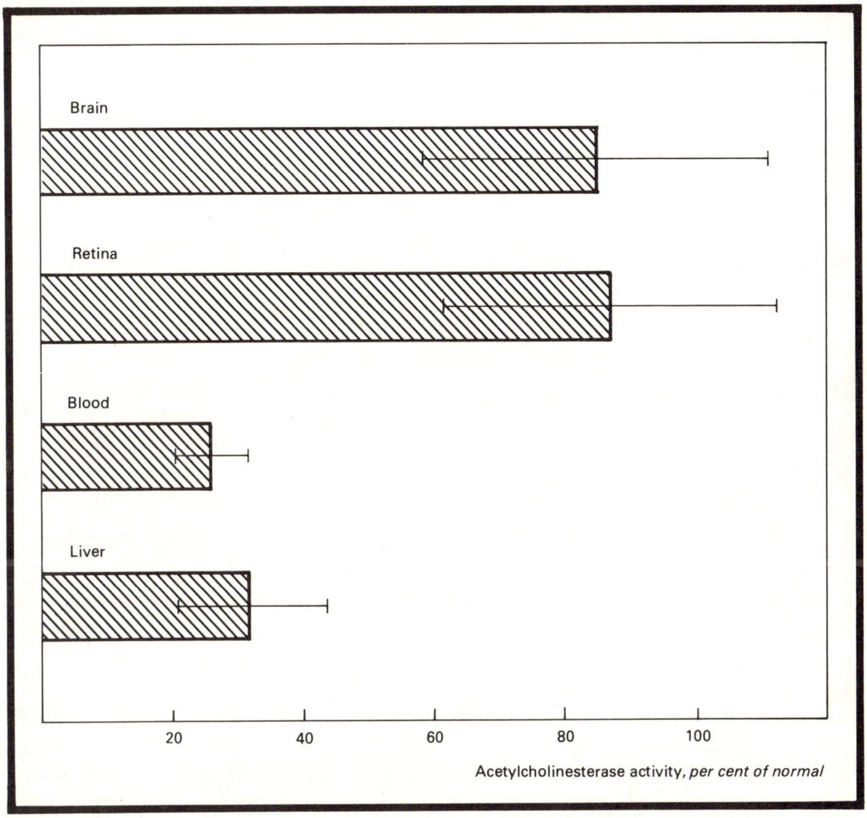

Note: Each column represents the mean of results from six animals ($P=0.05$).
[a] The chemical structure of Tx-54 is shown in footnote *a* to figure 2.2.

Protection of acetylcholinesterase by the neuromuscular transmitter

It is well known that acetylcholinesterase can be protected *in vitro* by its substrate, acetylcholine, against inhibition by various inhibitors. Acetylcholine being the cholinergic transmitter, it is reasonable to anticipate that such a protection might even occur *in vivo,* for example, at the neuromuscular junction, if transmitter concentration at the surface of the junctional acetylcholinesterase is high enough and is maintained for a sufficiently long period.

This was the idea behind a series of experiments made on isolated rat phrenic-nerve-diaphragm preparations with various acetylcholinesterase inhibitors. Stimulation of the phrenic nerve at a frequency of 120 stimuli per second during exposure to DFP or tetraethyl pyrophosphate (TEPP) was shown to retard the progressive acetylcholinesterase inhibition as compared

Table 2.1. Cholinesterase activities in rat phrenic nerve diaphragm preparations exposed to cholinesterase inhibitors for one minute during motor nerve stimulation at two different frequencies

Cholinesterase inhibitor	Concentration *M*	Motor nerve stimulation frequency *stimuli/sec*	Percentage of normal cholinesterase activity[a]
TEPP	3.3×10^{-6}	120	38±8.2 (12.7)
TEPP	3.3×10^{-6}	0.2	18±6.2 (9.6)
DFP	4.3×10^{-5}	120	26±6.3 (9.8)
DFP	4.3×10^{-5}	0.2	12±6.0 (9.3)

[a] Each value is the mean of six preparations, P=0.05. Figures in parentheses show scatter at P=0.01.

with preparations stimulated at a low rate (0.2 stimuli per second) during similar exposure (see table 2.1). This was shown by enzyme determination, supplemented by certain physiological criteria dependent on acetylcholinesterase activity (high-frequency inhibition, neuromuscular block caused by added acetylcholine, increase in single contraction height resulting from a second addition of acetylcholinesterase inhibitor, and histochemical demonstration of the enzyme activity). Control experiments with direct stimulation—the acetylcholine output being reduced by drugs (procaine, nupercaine, mytilotoxin and *d*-tubocurarine)—did not show any protection against acetylcholinesterase inhibition under otherwise comparable conditions.

If the observed protective effect is in fact a substrate protection exerted by the transmitter, this would seem to indicate a higher transmitter concentration than is generally supposed to exist.

In electrophysiological experiments on the "cut" diaphragm preparation [4], the falling phase of the end-plate potential, elongated by the rapidly reversible inhibitor tensilon (10 μg/ml), became shortened and more curved (convexity downwards) when the frequency of phrenic-nerve stimulation was increased from 0.5 to 50 stimuli per second (see figure 2.5). Return to the lowest frequency was accompanied by recurrence of the elongated end-plate-potential shape.

This phenomenon is assumed to be due to competition between the transmitter and the rapidly reversible inhibitor, the competitive power of the transmitter being higher at the higher stimulation frequencies, thus giving rise to some reactivation of acetylcholinesterase, which in turn results in the shortening of the end-plate potential. This "elbowing effect" could not be demonstrated in acid-transferring inhibitors such as the carbamates and alkyl phosphates. This is in accordance with the much slower reversibility of these inhibitors.

The shape of the end-plate potential as a function of acetylcholinesterase

Figure 2.5. Relationship between half decay time of end-plate potential (recorded by intracellular microelectrode) and stimulation frequency in rat phrenic nerve "cut" diaphragm preparation exposed to tensilon

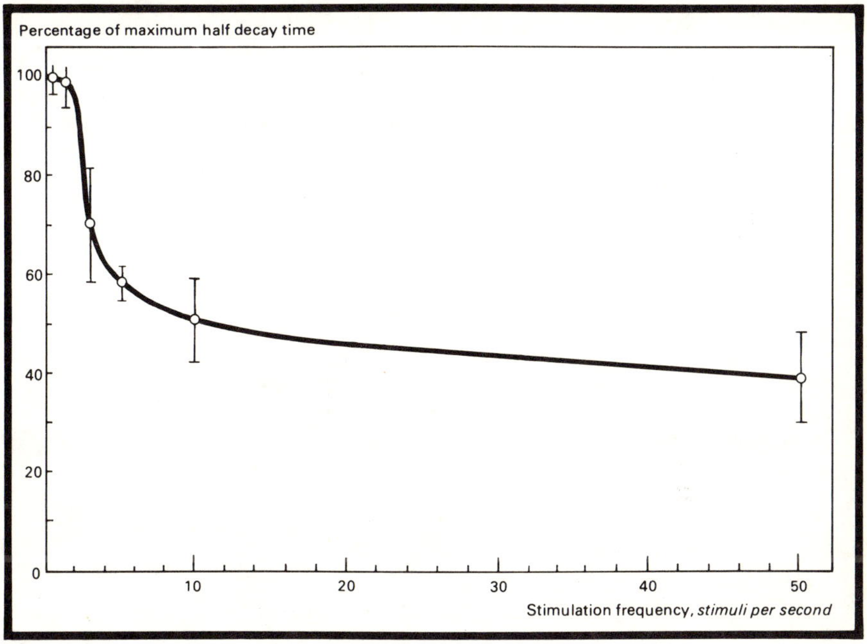

Note: Bars denote scatter of the mean at $P=0.05$.

inhibition was "calibrated" by means of acid-transferring inhibitors whose inhibition and spontaneous reactivation rate constants are known (see figure 2.1). The end-plate potentials recorded in the experiments with tensilon at varying stimulation frequencies were compared with the "calibrated" ones. If it is presupposed that end-plate potentials with similar shapes correspond to similar degrees of acetylcholinesterase inhibition, and that approximately the same equilibrium between transmitter, tensilon and acetylcholinesterase exists *in vivo* as *in vitro,* some conclusions about the order of magnitude of transmitter concentration seem to be justified.

The degree of acetylcholinesterase inhibition at the tensilon concentration employed in these experiments, and without acetylcholine present, was calculated to be just above 98 per cent. The "elbowing effect" may represent approximately 10–15 per cent reactivation of the enzyme. This is what would be achieved by an acetylcholine concentration in the order of 10^{-3} M. Although the most widely held view seems to be that the transmitter concentration in the synaptic cleft is markedly lower (by three or four orders of magnitude) [15], the concentration in presynaptic vesicles has been estimated as 0.11 M [16] and 0.16 M [17]. These are of course very rough estimates. If the amount of transmitter estimated to be contained in one presynaptic vesicle is inserted into the general diffusion equation for an isotropic medium, then the maximum concentration of acetylcholine at a receptor site, say 500 Å away from the point source (site of release of an acetylcholine quantum) is calculated to be approximately 10^{-2} M. Although most receptor sites may be further away from the point of release and therefore acted upon by far lower transmitter concentrations, the estimate presented here (10^{-3} M) seems to be supported by such calculations as well as by similar ones based on electrophoretic point application of acetylcholine [18].

References

1. Remen, L., "Zur Pathogenese und Therapie der Myasthenia gravis pseudoparalytica", *Deut. Z. Nervenheilk.*, **128,** 66–78 (1932).
2. Walker, M., "Treatment of myasthenia gravis with physostigmine", *Lancet,* **1,** 1200–201 (1934).
3. Masland, R. L. and Wigton, R. S., "Nerve activity accompanying fasciculation produced by prostigmine", *J. Neurophysiol.,* **3,** 269–75 (1940).
4. Barstad, J. A. B., "Presynaptic effect of the neuro-muscular transmitter", *Experientia,* **18,** 579 (separatum 1962).
5. Barstad, J. A. B., "Cholinesterase inhibition and the effect of anticholinesterases on indirectly evoked single and tetanic contractions in the phrenic-nerve-diaphragm preparation from the rat", *Arch. Int. Pharmacodyn.,* **128,** 143–68 (1960).
6. Barstad, J. A. B., "An investigation into neuro-muscular transmission in rat diaphragm" (Kjeller (Norway), Norwegian Defence Research Establishment, 1968) NDRE Report No. 55.
7. Aarseth, P. and Barstad, J. A. B., "Blood-brain-barrier permeability in various parts of the central nervous system", *Arch. Int. Pharmacodyn.,* **176,** 434–42 (1968).
8. Andersen, R. A., Barstad, J. A. B. and Laake, K., "Permeability of the blood-retina barrier to quaternary nitrogen compounds", *Acta Pharmacol. Toxicol.,* **28,** suppl. 1 (1970).
9. Andersen, R. A., Barstad, J. A. B. and Laake, K., "Access of quaternary drugs to the central nervous system", *Progr. Brain Res.,* **36,** 189–95 (1972).
10. Andersen, R. A. and Barstad, J. A. B., "Passage of tertiary and quaternary nitrogen compounds through the rat placenta", *Arch. Int. Pharmacodyn.,* **210,** 232–40 (1974).
11. Thesleff, S., "Succinylcholine iodide. Studies on its pharmacological properties and clinical use", *Acta Physiol. Scand. Suppl.,* **99,** 1–36 (1952).
12. Hansson, E. and Smiterlöw, C. G., "A comparison of the distribution, excretion and metabolism of a tertiary (promethazine) and a quaternary (aprobit®) phenothiazine compound labelled with S^{35}", *Arch. Int. Pharmacodyn.,* **131,** 309–24 (1961).
13. Schanker, L. S., "Passage of drugs across body membranes", *Pharmacol. Rev.,* **14,** 501–30 (1967).
14. Sjöqvist, F., "Transplacentär passage av läkarmedel", *Nord. Med.,* **78,** 1354–58 (1967).

15. Ehrenpreis, S., "Molecular aspects of cholinergic mechanisms", in Berger, A., ed., *Drugs affecting the peripheral nervous system* (New York, Marcel Dekker Inc., 1967) Volume 1, pp. 1–76.
16. MacIntosh, F. C., "Formation, storage and release of acetylcholine at nerve endings", *Can. J. Biochem. Physiol.*, **37,** 343–56 (1959).
17. Whittaker, V. P. and Sheridan, M. N., "The morphology and acetylcholine content of isolated cerebral cortical synaptic vesicles", *J. Neurochem.,* **12,** 363–72 (1965).
18. Krnjević, K. and Miledi, R., "Acetylcholine in mammalian neuro-muscular transmission", *Nature,* **182,** 805–806 (1958).

3. Success and failure of oxime therapy in acute poisoning by organophosphorus compounds

W. D. ERDMANN

Square-bracketed numbers, thus [1], *refer to the list of references on page 51.*

I. *Introduction*

The high toxicity of a large number of organophosphorus compounds depends on the almost irreversible inhibition of acetylcholinesterase by phosphorylation. The inhibited enzyme is unable to hydrolyse acetylcholine—the transmitting substance involved in axonal excitation—and the resulting accumulation of acetylcholine in all organs causes an endogenous acetylcholine intoxication with severe and dangerous muscarinic and nicotinic symptoms.

It is logical that the most important therapeutic measure against organophosphate poisoning is the injection of atropine as a pharmacodynamic antagonist of acetylcholine. Although atropine has only a symptomatic antidotal effect—it does not influence the root of the intoxication, the inhibition of the enzyme—it is fast and reliable in action, and is effective in combatting cramp and spasm of the bronchi [1] and of the glottis [2]. It is thus a valuable means of gaining the time necessary for applying additional therapeutic measures such as artificial respiration and the injection of reactivating antidotes.

The reactivating potency of pyridinium oximes was reported in 1955 by Wilson and Ginsburg [3]. The antidotal action of pralidoxime (2-PAM), trimedoxime (TMB-4) and obidoxime (Toxogonin) is based on the dephosphorylation of the inhibited acetylcholinesterase, a reaction which restores the enzyme activity. But the difficulties of research on reactivating antidotes is well illustrated by the fact that 2-PAM was introduced in 1955 and obidoxime in 1964 [4], and that since then, although hundreds of oxime derivatives have been tested, no new highly effective ones have been found.

Furthermore, there are still many misunderstandings and doubts about therapy with atropine and reactivating oximes: there are hospitals in the Federal Republic of Germany, for example, where it is the practice *not* to use reactivators in the therapeutic treatment of organophosphate poisoning. Certainly it is possible to save the life of an organophosphate-poisoned patient without using reactivators, but this requires the enormous equipment of an intensive care unit and the application of atropine and artificial respiration over a period of weeks. Moreover, if this type of treatment becomes widely accepted, there is a danger that the incentive to develop new antidotal therapy might be lost, and that physicians will remain inexperienced in the application of antidotes. And in cases of mass poisoning by organophosphorus compounds, for example, as a result of the use of nerve gases in wartime, or of accidents during the manufacture or transport of insecticides, the limitations of such treatment would be extremely serious: the number of lives that could be saved would depend on the number of respiratory machines available, and would only be a fraction of the number that could be saved by the large-scale use of reactivating antidotes.

II. *Practical limitations of oxime therapy*

The hesitation of some medical practitioners to use reactivating oximes is probably the result of misunderstandings and lack of experience on the following four questions: (*a*) What dose of the pyridinium oxime should be used and when should it be given? (*b*) Should pyridinium oximes be used as antidotes against all types of organophosphate intoxication? (*c*) Are pyridinium oximes responsible for the liver damage that is often observed in poisoned patients? and (*d*) Is the determination of acetylcholinesterase activity in a patient's blood an adequate indicator of the success of oxime therapy? These problems will be discussed in the following sections.

Dose and time of administration of oximes

In contrast to atropine, which must be given in high doses very rapidly after organophosphate intoxication, and then at regular intervals for many days or even weeks, pyridinium oximes must be administered in limited doses and only over a limited period of time (for example, two or three injections over a period of no more than 48 hours). These limits are necessary because the phosphorylated enzymes become "aged" (the rapidity of the ageing process depending on the particular organophosphate involved) and hence resistant to any further reactivation. Moreover, the oxime can react with the phosphorylated enzyme, or with organophosphate bound to the tissue, to form a phosphorylated oxime which may itself be toxic, and this reaction becomes significant at high oxime concentrations—concentrations which might result from repeated administration. The phosphorylated derivatives of the pyridinium-4-oximes in particular are known to be extremely toxic, sometimes even more toxic than the original organophosphates.

There is good experimental evidence that an overdose of 4-PAM, trimedoxime or obidoxime is more dangerous than an overdose of 2-PAM or HS-6. The structural features of oximes that determine the toxicity of the phosphorylated derivatives have been elucidated from an investigation of 27 pyridinium aldoximes [5]. In this study, it was found that none of the pyridinium compounds with only a methyl group on the nitrogen atom, irrespective of whether the aldoxime group is in position 2, 3 or 4, had a stronger inhibitory effect on acetylcholinesterase after phosphonylation by soman than did soman itself. Of the pyridinium compounds with an aldoxime group at position 4, all those connected by a bridge of the type $-CH_2-CH_2-CH_2-$ or $-CH_2-O-CH_2-$ to a phenyl group, a quaternary nitrogen atom or another pyridinium group, formed phosphonylated derivatives with a stronger inhibitory effect than soman. And an additional aldoxime group in position 4 of the second pyridinium group further intensified the inhibitory effect: the velocity constants for the inhibition of acetylcholinesterase by the phosphonylation products of obidoxime and trimedoxime, for example, were more than 10 times higher than the velocity constant for soman. A bridge of the type $-CH_2-CO-NH-CO-CH_2-$, on the other hand, did not intensify the inhibitory effect. Moreover, phosphonylated derivatives of pyridinium compounds with the above-mentioned bridges, but with the aldoxime group in position 2, did not have a stronger inhibitory effect than soman. The same was true for phosphorylated imidazolium derivatives, although the imidazolium compounds themselves did have a strong, direct inhibitory effect on acetylcholinesterase.

Specificity of oximes against various organophosphates

Provided oximes are administered only in limited doses and over limited periods of time, they will present no additional danger to an organophosphate-poisoned patient. Unfortunately, however, this does not mean that oxime therapy is always successful, and with some cases of organophosphate poisoning, oximes will have very little, if any, effect.

Oxime therapy frequently fails in cases of intoxications caused by extremely high doses of organophosphate compounds, when reabsorption of the organophosphate compound from the intestine, body fat or other tissue leads to a continuous rephosphorylation of the oxime-reactivated acetylcholinesterase [7]. This situation is often seen in cases of suicidal poisoning, and in one case of a severe intoxication, we were able to detect parathion in the patient's stomach eight days after the ingestion [6].

In a study by Boelcke *et al* [6] of the change in acetylcholinesterase and cholinesterase activity during treatment of an extremely severe parathion poisoning with obidoxime, it was found that the effect of repeated oxime injections is small. The repeated inhibition of acetylcholinesterase by excess parathion, absorbed from the intestine and reabsorbed from other tissues, was demonstrated in a fascinating way in this study by the decrease of acetylcholinesterase activity in blood after exchange transfusion. This technique can be repeated until the depots of parathion are exhausted, and recovery can finally take place. It is unfortunate that no analogous technique is available to replace inhibited acetylcholinesterase in nerve tissue.

Thus the effect of antidotal treatment with oximes may vary considerably according to the severity of the organophosphate intoxication. But variations in antidotal efficacy can also be explained by different structural features of the organophosphates. For example, in the Federal Republic of Germany, the normal preparation of the insecticide parathion has the name E 605. But in fact, two different esters of thiophosphoric acid are sold under this same name: one is the highly toxic diethyl ester with the name "E 605 forte", while the other, the dimethyl ester preparation with the name "E 605 Pulver", is about 100 times less toxic. A layman taking E 605 in an attempt at suicide does not know this difference, with the result that most of the suicide attempts are made with the more readily available, but less toxic dimethyl thiophosphate. However, our experience of treating these intoxications shows that this compound's lower toxicity does not, as might be expected, lead to a more favourable prognosis.

Pyridinium oximes are not effective against the dimethyl thiophosphate intoxications, and a very high dose is undoubtedly noxious in such cases. In fact, difficulties arise in the treatment of many intoxications caused by relatively less toxic dimethyl esters: frequently three or more weeks of treatment are required for such intoxications, and even then they are often fatal. A possible explanation for these difficulties comes from the work of Nenner [8], whose recent *in vitro* investigations on undiluted bovine blood have shown that dimethyl-phosphorylated acetylcholinesterase undergoes a rapid decrease in reactivatibility. This also seems to be true for dimethyl phosphates and dimethyl thiophosphates in general. If these results can be reproduced *in vivo,* this might be a good argument for the commerical use of diethyl derivatives rather than the dimethyl ones, even though they have a higher toxicity.

Oxime therapy and liver damage

Liver damage is often cited as a side-effect of the therapeutic use of oximes against organophosphate poisoning. Statistical data certainly show an increase in the incidence of liver damage since the advent of oxime therapy, but we believe that liver damage is caused by the organophosphate itself, and not by the oxime therapy, and that this increase simply represents a greater survival rate among severely poisoned patients. We could detect no influence of obidoxime on liver-enzyme activity in volunteer subjects [9], while we were able to induce liver damage by organophosphate intoxication in animal experiments, especially when therapy was insufficient or was started too late. It seems that if hypoxemia can be prevented by therapeutic measures such as artificial respiration or treatment with atropine and obidoxime, no liver damage will occur [10–11].

Methods for monitoring enzyme activities during organophosphate intoxication

The method generally used in West German hospitals to follow the course of an organophosphate intoxication is the photometric determination of cholinesterase activity in plasma. However, there seems to be only a poor correlation between this activity and the activity of acetylcholinesterase in erythrocytes and in nerve tissue, and this could lead to false assessments of the treatment. In an investigation of the course of an experimental poisoning with dimethoate (a "less toxic" dimethyl phosphate), it was discovered that the early injection of obidoxime causes an additional inhibition of cholinesterase activity in plasma [12], and on the basis of such observations, doctors have warned against the use of obidoxime in such cases of intoxication. Such a warning, however, seems to be unjustified, since the obidoxime can be shown to have a positive effect on the activity of erythrocyte-bound acetylcholinesterase. This would suggest that the acetylcholinesterase of nerve tissue, whose function is well known, should be compared with the acetylcholinesterase of the erythrocytes, and not with the great variety of cholinesterases in plasma.

What is needed, therefore, is a suitable laboratory method for the determination of the activity of erythrocyte-bound acetylcholinesterase. In 1961, Ellman and co-workers [13] demonstrated that their photometric method, which uses acetylthiocholine as the substrate, was suitable for blood and for tissue homogenates, but although many modifications of this method have been described since then, none has so far been introduced for general use in the clinical laboratory. Our own (unpublished) experience indicates that the major difficulties with such measurements result from the sedimentation of the cells and from haemoglobin absorption.

The extent to which the activity of erythrocyte-bound acetylcholinesterase correlates with the acetylcholinesterase activity of other tissues is under investigation. In cooperation with Okonek, we determined the acetylcholinesterase activity of muscle tissue from poisoned patients. In all cases, the activity in muscle was inhibited to a smaller extent than that in the erythrocytes, but as only 15 samples have so far been tested, these results should not be regarded as reliable.

III. *Other problems of oxime therapy*

Apart from the practical limitations of antidotal oxime therapy discussed above, there are also a number of other problems with oxime therapy which must be solved in the future.

Perhaps the most difficult problem in the field of antidote research is the restoration of the functional activity of acetylcholinesterase after ageing. Using soman, which produces a phosphonylated acetylcholinesterase with a half-time of ageing of about three minutes, we have tested a few hundred oximes, mainly pyridinium oximes, synthesized by the working groups of Hagedorn at Freiburg and of Engelhard at Göttingen. HS-3, an isomer of obidoxime, is able to restore an inhibited function *in vitro* and also shows some promising effects *in vivo*. Other compounds also seem to have an effect on the aged enzyme [14], but probably by a mechanism other than reactivation of phosphonylated acetylcholinesterase. Possibly the effect depends on a regeneration process based on axonal flow, as has been suggested by Filbert, Fleisher and Lochner [15]. Our experiments are in accordance with data from Weger [16], who intoxicated beagle dogs with 8 LD_{50} of soman and achieved a survival rate of two from five.

Another serious problem with oxime therapy is the slow penetration of pyridinium oximes across the blood-brain barrier into the central nervous system. Undoubtedly the recovery of vital functions after organophosphate poisoning depends on the reactivation of acetylcholinesterase in the central nervous system. Data from animal experiments show that the achievement of an effective oxime level in the central nervous system requires a blood concentration 10 times higher than that recommended for therapeutic use [17]. But, as mentioned above, such high concentrations pose considerable dangers for the patient, because of the formation of more toxic reaction products from oxime and organophosphate. Michelssen [18] has shown that it is possible to obtain a therapeutically sufficient concentration in the cerebrospinal fluid of dogs either by giving a single, very high dose intravenously or by giving a smaller dose followed by a long-lasting intravenous infusion. Namba, in Japan, has applied this technique with pralidoxime in severe cases of organophosphate intoxication [19] and it seems to show some promise.

Finally, in a mass-casualty situation, the application of antidotes by injection will pose serious problems. In such a situation, it would be desirable to administer antidotes orally. A great deal of experimental work has been done on this approach, but unfortunately, all the pyridinium oximes that are effective as antidotes show poor absorption behaviour when taken by the mouth, which means that enormous amounts have to be taken in order to achieve an effective concentration in the blood. Not only is it unrealistic to assume that 10 to 20 tablets of the corresponding antidote will be available for every person involved in a mass intoxication, but all efforts to improve absorption by the use of substances such as Na-EDTA or by changing the molecular structure of the pyridinium derivatives have been unsuccessful [20].

References

1. Holmstedt, B., "Synthesis and pharmacology of dimethylamido-ethoxyphosphoryl cyanide (tabun) together with a description of some allied anti-

cholinesterase compounds containing the N-P bond", *Acta Physiol. Scand. Suppl. 90.*, **25,** 11–120 (1951).
2. Kuga, T. and Erdmann, W. D., "Versuche zur Wirkung von Paraoxon auf Atem- und Vaguszentren und der Einfluss verschiedener Antidote", *Naunyn-Schmiedebergs Arch. Pharmakol. Exp. Pathol.*, **251,** 445–64 (1965).
3. Wilson, I. B. and Ginsburg, S., "A powerful reactivator of alkylphosphate-inhibited acetylcholinesterase", *Biochim. Biophys. Acta,* **18,** 168–70 (1955).
4. Erdmann, W. D. and Engelhard, H., "Pharmakologisch-toxikologische Untersuchungen mit dem Dichlorid des Bis (4-hydroxyiminomethyl-pyridinium-(1)-methyl) äthers, einem neuen Esterase-Reaktivator", *Arzneimittel-Forsch.*, **14,** 5–11 (1964).
5. Nenner, M., "Phosphonylierte Aldoxime. Hemmwirkung auf Acetylcholinesterase und hydrolytischer Abbau", *Biochem. Pharmacol.*, **23**, 1255–62 (1974).
6. Boelcke, G., Butigan, N., Lavar, H., Erdmann, W. D., Gaaz, J. W. and Nenner, M., "Neue Erfahrungen bei der toxikologisch kontrollierten Therapie einer ungewöhnlich schweren Vergiftung mit Nitrostigmin (E 605 forte)", *Deut. Med. Wochschr.*, **95,** 2516–21 (1970).
7. Erdmann, W. D., Sakai, F. and Scheler, F., "Erfahrungen bei der spezifischen Behandlung einer E 605-Vergiftung mit Atropin und dem Esterasereaktivator PAM", *Deut. Med. Wochschr.*, **83,** 1359–62 (1958).
8. Nenner, M., unpublished.
9. Boelcke, G., Creutzfeldt, W., Erdmann, W. D., Gaaz, J. W. and Jacob, G., "Untersuchungen zur Frage der Lebertoxizität von Obidoxim (Toxogonin) am Menschen", *Deut. Med. Wochschr.*, **95,** 1175–78 (1970).
10. Okonek, S. and Boelcke, G., "Hyperventilation zur Vermeidung von Störungen der exkretorischen Leberfunktion im Initialstadium der Nitrostigmin (E 605 forte) Vergiftung an Ratten", *Arch. Toxicol.*, **28,** 24–38 (1971).
11. Gaaz, J. W., Poser, W. and Erdmann, W. D. "Untersuchungen zur Lebertoxizität von Nitrostigmin (Parathion, E 605) and der perfundierten Rattenleber", *Arch. Toxicol.*, **33,** 31–40 (1974).
12. Erdmann, W. D., "Antidotbehandlung bei Alkylphosphatvergiftungen", *Arch. Toxicol.*, **24,** 30–40 (1968).
13. Ellmann, G. E., Courtney, J. D., Andres, V., Jr. and Featherstone, R. M., "A new and rapid colorimetric determination of acetylcholinesterase activity", *Biochem. Pharmacol.*, **7,** 88–95 (1961).
14. Erdmann, W. D., "Ein neues Antidotprinzip zur Behandlung von Alkylphosphat-vergiftungen", *Naunyn-Schmiedebergs Arch. Pharmakol. Exp. Pathol.*, **263,** 61–72 (1969).
15. Filbert, M. G., Fleisher, J. H. and Lochner, M. A., "Failure of Toxogonin to reactivate soman-inhibited brain acetylcholinesterase in monkeys and regeneration of the enzyme", *Biochim. Biophys. Acta,* **284,** 164–74 (1972).
16. Weger, N., unpublished.
17. Falb, A. and Erdmann, W. D., "Über die Permeation von ^{14}C-Obidoxim durch die sog. Blut-Hirnschranke von Mäusen und Ratten", *Arch. Toxicol.*, **24,** 123–32 (1969).
18. Michelssen, A., unpublished.
19. Namba, T., "Cholinesterase inhibition by organophosphorus compounds and its clinical effects", *Bull. World Health Organ.*, **44,** 289–307 (1971).
20. Erdmann, W. D. and Okonek, S., "Über die gastroenterale Resorption des Esterasereaktivators Obidoxim und die Möglichkeiten einer Resorptionsförderung", *Arch. Toxicol.*, **24,** 91–101 (1969).

4. The effects of antidotes in experimental animals intoxicated by carbamate and organophosphorus cholinesterase inhibitors

I. L. NATOFF

Square-bracketed numbers, thus [1], *refer to the list of references on page 62.*

I. *Effects of cholinesterase inhibition*

The inhibition of cholinesterases by carbamates or organophosphates leads to an accumulation of endogenous acetylcholine at postsynaptic receptor sites, and a potentiation of the effects of the neurohormone [1]. The resulting increased activity at nicotinic, muscarinic and central-nervous synapses results in the signs and symptoms of intoxication.

Table 4.1 lists the principal signs evident on acute intoxication with cholinesterase inhibitors [2]. They are all peripheral in location, except for hypothermia [3] and respiratory arrest [4] which result from an action of the inhibitor in the central nervous system. Death is usually due to respiratory arrest, caused by depression of the central-nervous medullary centres together with paralysis of the diaphragm [4].

Effects in the central nervous system

The manifestations of poisoning by cholinesterase inhibitors depend not so much on the degree of inhibition of the enzyme as on the rate of onset of this inhibition [1]. When brain cholinesterase is inhibited, the concentration of free acetylcholine rises. Peripheral signs of intoxication (for example, fasciculations) become apparent only when the free acetylcholine level rises to 60 per cent above normal, and this occurs when the brain enzyme is 75 per cent inhibited [5]. The observation that receptors can adapt to continuous cholinergic stimulation [6–9] suggests an explanation of this phenomenon: those organophosphorus inhibitors which have a slow rate of onset of inhibition *in vivo* allow the gradual accumulation of acetylcholine, to which adaptation, or tolerance, may develop, while those inhibitors which produce a rapid onset of effect cause the sudden appearance of relatively large amounts of the neurohormone at the receptor before adaptation may develop [1]. In our laboratory we found that rats intoxicated with a lethal dose of the slow-acting organophosphate chlorfenvinphos had 80 per cent inhibition of their brain cholinesterase at death, the animals dying in a mean time of 30 hours. In rats intoxicated with a lethal dose of the

Table 4.1. Signs and symptoms of acute intoxication by cholinesterase inhibitors

Miosis
Hypotension Vasodilation Bradycardia
Salivation
Intestinal spasm
Bronchoconstriction Bronchosecretion
Voluntary nerve muscle junction fasciculation and blockade
Respiratory arrest
Hypothermia

more rapidly acting dicrotophos, brain cholinesterase was 50 per cent inhibited at death, and the animals died in a mean time of 19 minutes.

Inhibitors of cholinesterase may not only cross the blood-brain barrier, but may also increase the permeability of this structure to other compounds, such as anaesthetics [10] and sulphanilamide [11]. For example, Schradan (OMPA), which does not cross the blood-brain barrier, and therefore does not inhibit brain cholinesterase following systemic administration, nevertheless facilitates penetration of the blood-brain barrier by systemically administered sulphanilamide [11]. It is therefore not improbable that some cholinesterase inhibitors may, to a greater or lesser extent, facilitate penetration of the blood-brain barrier to themselves [1] and to oximes. The nucleophilic oximes which can reactivate phosphorylated cholinesterase before it has "aged" [12–13] are thought to be unable to cross the blood-brain barrier in sufficiently high concentrations to exert an effect, because of their quaternary ammonium structure. Firemark, Barlow and Roth [14] nevertheless demonstrated that isotopically labelled pyridine-2-aldoxime methiodide (^{14}C-2-PAM) is able to enter the brains of rats, the highest concentration appearing in the cerebellar cortex and lesser amounts being found in other areas. These amounts were increased by prior exposure of the rats to dipterex, but not to eserine or neostigmine. Mayer and Michalek [15] reported that the rise in free acetylcholine in the brain of rats intoxicated with DFP is prevented by later administration of obidoxime, whereas the inhibition of brain cholinesterase by DFP was not affected. Falb and Erdmann [16] found that ^{14}C-obidoxime enters the brains of mice and rats; this penetration was not affected by prior intoxication with paraoxon. Nevertheless, the administration of 2-PAM (pralidoxime) or TMB-4 after paraoxon exposure has been reported to reactivate the cholinesterase in the cerebellum [17] and cortex [18] of rats and rabbits [19]. Similarly, obidoxime has been reported to reduce the inhibition of cholinesterase in the pontomedullary region of the mouse brain following intoxication with isopropyl methylphosphonofluoridate [20]. Thus there is evidence of a central effect of quaternary oximes following systemic administration to experimental animals treated with anticholinesterase agents.

Effects in the autonomic nervous system

By far the most obvious signs of acute intoxication by cholinesterase inhibitors are those in the peripheral areas of the body. These may be attributed to hyperactivity at cholinergic sites in the autonomic nervous system, and are predominately at the post-ganglionic parasympathetic nerve endings (muscarinic sites). When the muscarinic receptors of the dog are blocked with atropine, nicotinic stimulation by acetylcholine is not enhanced by eserine. When the nicotinic ganglia are blocked with mecamylamine, however, muscarinic stimulation by acetylcholine is noticeably potentiated by eserine [21].

Effects in the voluntary nervous system

Cholinesterase inhibitors have been reported to produce structural and functional derangements in the voluntary nervous system. Jager, Roberts and Wilson [22] reported an impairment of the electromyograms of workers engaged in the manufacture of organophosphates, and a reversible necrosis has been reported to occur at the motor end-plate of voluntary muscle in rats poisoned with DFP, paraoxon or tabun [23].

A number of organophosphorus cholinesterase inhibitors (for example, TOCP, DFP and mipafox) produce a motor paralysis in many species of animals, and in man. This is associated with a demyelination of the voluntary nerve fibres [24]. The most sensitive experimental species for demonstrating this effect is the fowl [25]. In both man and fowl the signs of this neurotoxicity do not occur until eight days after exposure [26] and take the form of a slowly developing ataxia with flaccid paralysis of the hind limbs. This phenomenon has been the subject of many hypotheses and studies in the past, but the recent work of Johnson [27] has suggested a biochemical system on which this effect may depend. A small fraction of esterase activity present in homogenates of hen brain will hydrolyse the phenyl ester of phenylacetic acid [28]. This activity is inhibited by organophosphates which produce a delayed neurotoxicity *in vivo,* but is unaffected by organophosphates not causing delayed neurotoxic effects (such as paraoxon) [28]. It is possible to protect fowl against the neurotoxic action of an organophosphate by pretreating them with a reversible carbamate anticholinesterase, such as phenylbenzylcarbamate. During the time that the carbamate is producing signs of cholinesterase inhibition, that is, while it is occupying the esteratic site of cholinesterase [29–30], the neurotoxic organophosphate is unable to gain access to the enzyme, or that fraction of it concerned with the production of the delayed neurotoxicity.

Figure 4.1. Rate of survival of mice pretreated with atropine sulphate, by intraperitoneal injection, 60 minutes before subcutaneous injection of a lethal dose of a cholinesterase inhibitor

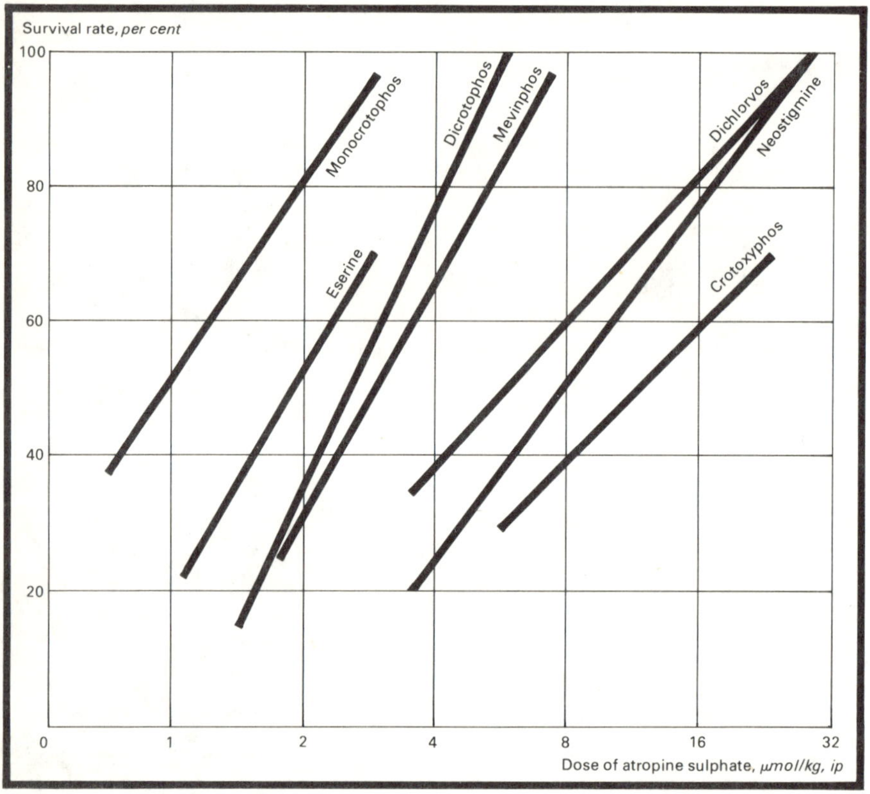

Effects of metabolic induction

The inactivation and elimination of many cholinesterase inhibitors *in vivo* proceed via hepatic microsomal enzymes. Thus, stimulation of these enzyme systems by exposure of rats to chlorinated hydrocarbons or to phenobarbitone reduces the toxicity of parathion, EPN, disulfoton, dioxathion and others [31–32]. This effect may be prevented by ethionine, which competes with the essential amino acid, methionine, for incorporation into new enzyme protein synthesized under the influence of these inducing agents [31, 33].

II. *Therapy of poisoning by cholinesterase inhibitors*

The various experimental methods outlined above for altering the toxicity of cholinesterase inhibitors are *prophylactic* in that they involve pretreatment of the animals with reversible carbamates or enzyme inducers. Of greater

Table 4.2. Median protective doses of atropine sulphate and atropine methonitrate injected 60 minutes before the administration of a lethal dose of cholinesterase inhibitor in mice

Cholinesterase inhibitor	Lethal dose (LD_{99}), *sc* *μmol/kg*	Median protective doses (PD_{50})	
		Atropine sulphate, *ip* *μmol base/kg*	Atropine methonitrate, *icv* *nmol base/mouse*
Monocrotophos	58	1.9	6.7
Dicrotophos	59	5.5	1.8
Crotoxyphos	55	23.0	3.7
Dichlorvos	145	12.5	55.0
Mevinphos	7	5.1	2.0
Neostigmine	4	1.9	–
Eserine	4	3.9	0.4

relevance to the human experience, however, is the *therapeutic* application of antidotes to intoxication. Apart from the danger of the use of organophosphate compounds as chemical-warfare agents, the use of organophosphorus and carbamate anticholinesterase compounds as pesticides in agriculture is widespread, and the accidental exposure of humans to these compounds may lead to toxic effects. The scientific community is obliged to anticipate and understand these effects, and to seek measures to counteract them. At the present state of our knowledge, this may only be done with any meaning by experiments with laboratory animals.

In treating poisoning by cholinesterase inhibitors, one must remember that the treatment is essentially symptomatic, since the intoxicating factor is not so much the inhibitor, but the rapid accumulation of endogenous acetylcholine that it causes at vital receptor sites. Because of the predominance of muscarinic signs of intoxication, the use of atropine sulphate for blocking those hyperstimulated receptors at the muscarinic nerve endings and at the synapses in the central nervous system is generally recommended. Gastric lavage and artificial respiration should also be available, and used if the need arises.

Figure 4.1 shows the effect of atropine sulphate pretreatment in increasing the rate of survival of mice exposed to normally lethal doses of some cholinesterase inhibitors. Atropine methonitrate, the quaternary salt of the alkaloid, afforded no such protection, in spite of its ability to block peripheral muscarinic receptors. When methylatropine was given intracerebroventricularly, however, protection was achieved. Table 4.2 shows the median protective doses of intraperitoneal atropine sulphate and intracerebral methylatropine against some cholinesterase inhibitors. The toxicity of subcutaneously injected neostigmine, which does not cross the blood-brain barrier to enter the brain, was not reduced by intracerebrally injected methylatropine, which does not cross this barrier to leave the brain.

Atropine sulphate may be used prophylactically or therapeutically. On the other hand, nucleophilic substances such as oximes, which can reacti-

Table 4.3. Effects of therapeutic antidotes on the LD_{50} values of carbamate anticholinesterases in male rats

Therapy		LD_{50} values[a] *μmol/kg, sc*			
Antidote	Dose *μmol/kg*	Carbaryl	Temik	Neostigmine	Eserine
Control	–	397	3.5	1.0	5.3
Obidoxime	250	**101**	**8.2**	**20.8**	17.9[b]
P2S	250	**173**	**5.4**	**2.2**	**15.9**
Atropine sulphate	50	2 572[b]	18.0[b]	**5.9**	**49.3**
Atropine sulphate + obidoxime	50 250	717	>24[b]	**34.9**	>100[b]
Atropine sulphate + P2S	50 250	2 412[b]	22.4[b]	**6.5**	92.6[b]

[a] Bold figures indicate values significantly different from control values ($P < 0.05$).
[b] For these figures it was not possible to assess whether or not they were statistically significantly different from control values (at $P<0.05$), since experimental data did not allow estimation of confidence limits.

Source: Natoff, I. L. and Reiff, B., "Effect of oximes on the acute toxicity of anticholinesterase carbamates", *Toxicol. Appl. Pharmacol.*, **25**, 569–75 (1973).

vate organophosphate-inhibited cholinesterase before ageing has occurred, may only be used effectively as a therapeutic measure after exposure to cholinesterase inhibitors. Oximes, while often not as effective as atropine sulphate as antidotes against acute organophosphate intoxication, may nevertheless markedly potentiate its therapeutic effect [34–36].

Carbamate intoxication also responds well to atropine therapy, but is little or not affected by oximes [37]. Indeed it has been widely held for some time that oximes are positively contra-indicated in the therapy of carbamate intoxication because of an early report that the toxicity of the insecticide carbaryl was increased by N-methyl-pyridine-2-aldoxime (pralidoxime) [38]. Nevertheless, the literature shows that the toxicity of some other carbamates is either reduced or unaffected by oximes. Pralidoxime did not affect the acute toxicity of eserine or neostigmine in mice [39–40] or guinea-pigs [41], of Isolan in mice [42], or of carbaryl in rats [38, 43]. However, this oxime reduced the toxicity of pyridostigmine in mice [44], of dimetilan in rats [43] and mice [45], and of Isolan in rats [43]. The bis-quaternary dioxime TMB-4 (N,N′-trimethylene-bis-(pyridine-4-aldoxime)) similarly does not affect the toxicity of bisneostigmine in mice [40], but lowers the toxicity of neostigmine and bispyridostigmine [40, 46], and of pyridostigmine [44], in this species.

We studied a series of carbamates, and the influence of oximes on their toxicity in rats [37], and found that N-methyl-pyridine-2-aldoxime methanesulphonate (P2S) and obidoxime influenced their toxicity proportionally to their effect on the cholinesterase inhibitory activity of the carbamates *in vitro*. Table 4.3 shows the LD_{50} values for carbamates administered subcutaneously in rats and the influence of atropine sulphate,

Table 4.4. Effects of obidoxime and P2S on the anticholinesterase activity of carbamates in rat brain homogenates *in vitro*

Oxime concentration *M*	pI_{50} values Carbaryl	Temik	Neostigmine	Eserine
Obidoxime				
0	4.6	5.4	8.2	7.5
10^{-6}	4.5	5.4	7.2	7.4
10^{-5}	5.0	5.5	7.4	7.4
10^{-4}	5.0	5.4	6.7	6.8
10^{-3}	5.7	5.2	6.2	6.3
P2S				
0	4.2	5.4	8.5	7.4
10^{-6}	4.3	5.5	9.1	7.1
10^{-5}	4.1	5.5	8.6	7.4
10^{-4}	4.6	5.5	7.9	7.4
10^{-3}	4.8	5.2	7.3	6.4

Source: Natoff, I. L. and Reiff, B., ''Effect of oximes on the acute toxicity of anticholinesterase carbamates'', *Toxicol. Appl. Pharmacol.*, **25**, 569–75 (1973).

obidoxime and P2S and of atropine sulphate in combination with these oximes, on these values. Two groups of results are apparent: the toxicity of Temik, neostigmine and eserine was reduced by the oximes, while the toxicity of carbaryl was increased by the oximes. Both oximes potentiated the therapeutic effect of atropine sulphate, with one notable exception, where obidoxime significantly reduced the protection afforded by atropine against carbaryl toxicity.

The pI_{50} values (negative logarithm (base 10) of the molar concentration of carbamate required for 50 per cent inhibition of rat brain homogenate cholinesterase activity compared with controls) were determined in the presence of increasing concentrations of the oximes, and table 4.4 shows three groups of results to be apparent: (*a*) those in which the oximes did not affect carbamate inhibitory potency (Temik); (*b*) those in which the oximes decreased carbamate inhibitory potency (neostigmine and eserine); and (*c*) those in which the oximes increased carbamate inhibitory potency (carbaryl). Plotting the changes in the pI_{50} values due to 10^{-3} M oxime against the logarithm of the LD_{50} values due to the therapeutic administration of 250 μmol/kg oxime (see figure 4.2) gave a linear relationship, with correlation coefficients of 0.74 for obidoxime and 0.73 for P2S. These results indicate that oximes influence the acute toxicities and the anticholinesterase activities of the carbamates in parallel. Therefore, intoxication by carbamate anticholinesterases is a function of their cholinesterase inhibitory activity, and may best be treated with atropine sulphate. The additional use of oximes may be synergistic, and only in the case of carbaryl intoxication is therapy with oximes contra-indicated.

The synergistic effect of oximes with atropine sulphate in treating or-

Figure 4.2. Effects of P2S and obidoxime on the toxicity of carbamate anticholinesterases: relationship between increase in pI_{50} values due to treatment with 10^{-3} M oxime and elevation of LD_{50} values due to administration of 250 μmol/kg oxime

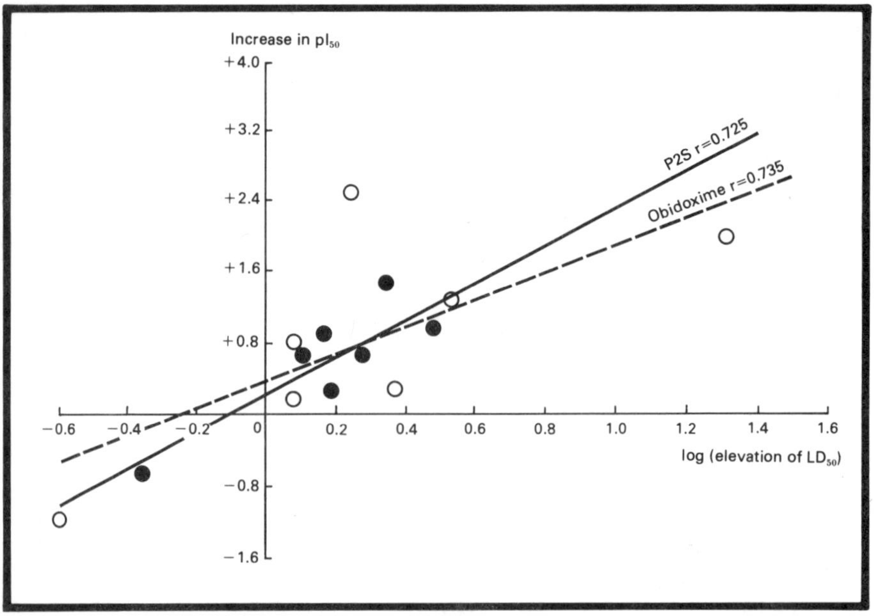

Key: ○=obidoxime; ●=P2S.
Note: r=correlation coefficient.

ganophosphorus intoxication of experimental animals, and man, is well documented [36]. Nucleophilic attack of the phosphorylated cholinesterase in the early stages of intoxication before ageing occurs [12–13] results in the reactivation of the cholinesterase and treats the cause, rather than the effect, of intoxication. Table 4.5 shows the effect of therapeutically administered atropine sulphate, atropine methonitrate, obidoxime and P2S, as well as combinations of the oximes with atropine sulphate, in reducing the toxicity of some organophosphates. In all instances, the toxicity was reduced by these regimens and, except in the case of crotoxyphos, there was marked potentiation of the therapeutic effect of atropine sulphate by the oximes [47]. The elevation of the LD_{50} of paraoxon with atropine sulphate and obidoxime was most dramatic.

An interesting feature of this experiment is the therapeutic superiority of an equimolar dose of atropine base as the sulphate over that of atropine base as the methonitrate. Methylatropine salts may penetrate to the central nervous system, but not in concentrations sufficient for therapeutic activity at this site [54]. Its major locus of activity is, therefore, restricted to the peripheral areas of the body. Atropine sulphate, however, acts both centrally and peripherally. With those organophosphates studied, the thera-

Table 4.5. Effects of therapeutic antidotes on the LD_{50} values of organophosphate anticholinesterases in female rats

Therapy		LD_{50} values[a] *μmol/kg, sc*						
Antidote	Dose *μmol/kg*	Mono-croto-phos	Dicroto-phos	Chlor-fen-vinphos	Crotoxy-phos	Dichlor-vos	Mevin-phos	Para-oxon[b]
Control	–	31	34	43	149	52	5	1
Methylatropine	50	**95**	79[c]	62	**223**	64	6	1[c]
Atropine sulphate	50	**365**	**251**	**104**	**298**	**177**	**8**	3[c]
P2S	250	**82**	**94**	54	**239**	**259**	**9**	3[c]
Obidoxime	250	**146**	**142**	**87**	207	**360**	**11**	9[c]
Atropine sulphate with P2S	50 } 250 }	**890**	**250**	**216**	**279**	**940**	**10**	6[c]
Atropine sulphate with obidoxime	50 } 250 }	**730**	**346**	**800**	**257**	**1 212**	**24**	261[c]

[a] Bold figures indicate values significantly different from control values ($P<0.05$).
[b] Previously unpublished results.
[c] For these figures it was not possible to assess whether or not they were statistically significantly different from control values (at $P<0.05$), since experimental data did not allow estimation of confidence limits.

Source: Natoff, I. L. and Reiff, B., "Quantitative studies of the effects of antagonists on the acute toxicity of organophosphates in rats", *Brit. J. Pharmacol.*, **40**, 124–34 (1970).

peutic superiority of atropine sulphate would suggest that their anticholinesterase activity predominates in the central nervous system.

Obidoxime and P2S are quaternary-nitrogen-containing compounds and, therefore, are thought to be unable to enter the central nervous system following systemic administration. Their action in reactivating "non-aged" phosphorylated cholinesterase is in the periphery, and they may act not only at muscarinic sites, but also at nicotinic sites in the autonomic ganglia and at voluntary motor synapses. In offering protection against all the organophosphates (table 4.5), they were as effective as methylatropine. Generally, obidoxime was superior to P2S as a therapeutic agent. The action of these oximes is presumably related to their action at the voluntary motor synapses of the respiratory muscles (diaphragm, intercostals) and this would account for the marked mutual potentiation seen in the therapeutic effects of these compounds with atropine sulphate.

Although there is no evidence that oximes decarbamylate cholinesterase inhibited by carbamates (as they dephosphorylate cholinesterase that has been inhibited by organophosphates [48]) they may owe part of their therapeutic effects in cases of poisoning by both types of inhibitors to "cholinesterase-stimulating" properties [49], parasympathetic-receptor-blocking properties [50], neuromuscular blocking action [51], or a direct effect on the "receptivity" of nicotinic receptors in sympathetic ganglia [52–53]. Except in cases of intoxication by carbaryl, there would appear to be no reason for the contra-indication of oxime therapy in cases of carbamate intoxication [37].

References

1. Natoff, I. L., "Organophosphorus pesticides: pharmacology", *Progr. Med. Chem.*, **8,** 1–37 (1971).
2. Holmstedt, B., "Pharmacology of organophosphorus cholinesterase inhibitors", *Pharmacol. Rev.* **11,** 567–688 (1959).
3. Meeter, E. and Wolthuis, O. L., "The effects of cholinesterase inhibitors on the body temperature of the rat", *Eur. J. Pharmacol.*, **4,** 18–24 (1968).
4. De Candole, C. A., Douglas, W. W., Evans, C. L., Holmes, R., Spencer, K. E. V., Torrance, R. W. and Wilson, K. M., "The failure of respiration in death by anticholinesterase poisoning", *Brit. J. Pharmacol. Chemother.*, **8,** 466–75 (1953).
5. Holmstedt, B., Härkönen, M., Lundgren, G. and Sundwall, A., "Relationship between acetylcholine and cholinesterase activity in the brain following an organophosphorus cholinesterase inhibitor", *Biochem. Pharmacol.*, **16,** 404–406 (1967).
6. Krivoy, W. A. and Wills, J. H., "Adaptation to constant concentrations of acetylcholine", *J. Pharmacol. Exp. Ther.*, **116,** 220–26 (1956).
7. Gissen, A. J. and Nastuk, W. L., "The mechanism underlying neuromuscular block following prolonged exposure to depolarizing agents", *Ann. N.Y. Acad. Sci.*, **135,** 184–94 (1966).
8. Kim, K. C. and Karczmar, A. G., "Adaptation of the neuromuscular junction to constant concentrations of acetylcholine", *Int. J. Neuropharmacol.*, **6,** 51–61 (1967).
9. Brodeur, J. and DuBois, K. P., "Studies on the mechanism of acquired tolerance by rats to O,O-diethyl S-2-(ethylthio) ethyl phosphorodithioate (Di Syston)", *Arch. Int. Pharmacodyn. Ther.*, **149,** 560–70 (1964).
10. Greig, M. E. and Mayberry, T. C., "The relationship between cholinesterase activity and brain permeability", *J. Pharmacol. Exp. Ther.*, **102,** 1–4 (1951).
11. Paulet, G., Marsol, H. and Coq, H., "Cholinésterase et perméabilité de la barrière hématoencéphalique", *J. Physiol. (Paris),* **49,** 342–45 (1957).
12. Hobbiger, F., "Effect of nicotinhydroxamic acid methiodide on human plasma cholinesterase inhibited by organophosphates containing a dialkylphosphato group", *Brit. J. Pharmacol. Chemother.*, **10,** 356–62 (1955).
13. Hobbiger, F., "Chemical reactivation of phosphorylated human and bovine true cholinesterases", *Brit. J. Pharmacol. Chemother.*, **11,** 295–303 (1956).
14. Firemark, H., Barlow, C. F. and Roth, L. J., "The penetration of 2-PAM-C^{14} into brain and the effect of cholinesterase inhibitors on its transport", *J. Pharmacol. Exp. Ther.*, **145,** 252–65 (1964).
15. Mayer, O. and Michalek, H., "Effects of DFP and obidoxime on brain acetylcholine levels and on brain and peripheral cholinesterases", *Biochem. Pharmacol.*, **20,** 3029–37 (1971).
16. Falb, A. and Erdmann, W. D., "Über die Permeation von ^{14}C-Obidoxim durch die sog. Blut-Hirnschranke von Mäusen und Ratten", *Arch. Toxikol.*, **24,** 123–32 (1969).
17. Hobbiger, F. and Vojvodić, V., "The reactivation by pyridinium aldoximes of phosphorylated acetylcholinesterase in the central nervous system", *Biochem. Pharmacol.*, **16,** 455–62 (1967).
18. Milošević, M. P. and Andjelković, D., "Reactivation of paraoxon-inactivated cholinesterase in the rat cerebral cortex by pralidoxime chloride", *Nature,* **210,** 206–207 (1966).
19. Rosenberg, P., "*In vivo* reactivation by PAM of brain cholinesterase inhibited by paraoxon", *Biochem. Pharmacol.*, **3,** 212–19 (1960).

20. Bajgar, J., Jakl, A. and Hrdina, V., "The influence of obidoxime on acetylcholinesterase activity in different parts of the mouse brain following isopropylmethyl phosphonofluoridate intoxication", *Eur. J. Pharmacol.,* **19,** 199–202 (1972).
21. Gillis, R. A., Flacke, W., Garfield, J. M. and Alper, M. H., "Actions of anticholinesterase agents upon ganglionic transmission in the dog", *J. Pharmacol. Exp. Ther.,* **163,** 277–86 (1968).
22. Jager, K. W., Roberts, D. V. and Wilson, A., "Neuromuscular function in pesticide workers", *Brit. J. Ind. Med.,* **27,** 273–78 (1970).
23. Ariens, A. Th., Meeter, E., Wolthuis, O. L. and van Bentham, R. M. J., "Reversible necrosis at the end plate region in striated muscles of the rat poisoned with cholinesterase inhibitors", *Experientia,* **25,** 57–59 (1969).
24. Barnes, J. M. and Denz, F. A., "Experimental demyelination with organophosphorus compounds", *J. Pathol. Bacteriol.,* **65,** 596–605 (1953).
25. Davies, D. R., "Neurotoxicity of organophosphorus compounds", in Koelle, G. B., ed., *Cholinesterases and anticholinesterase agents,* Volume XV of *Handbuch der experimentellen Pharmakologie* (Berlin, Göttingen and Heidelberg, Springer-Verlag, 1963) pp. 865–69.
26. Aldridge, W. N. and Barnes, J. M., "Further observations on the neurotoxicity of organophosphorus compounds", *Biochem. Pharmacol.,* **15,** 541–48 (1966).
27. Johnson, M. K., "Delayed neurotoxic action of some organophosphorus compounds", *Brit. Med. Bull.,* **25,** 231–35 (1969).
28. Johnson, M. K., "An enzyme in hen brain hydrolyzing phenyl phenylacetate: possible connection with the delayed neurotoxic effect of some organophosphorus compounds", *Biochem. J.,* **110,** 13P (1968).
29. Johnson, M. K. and Lauwerys, R., "Protection by some carbamates against the delayed neurotoxic effects of di-isopropyl phosphorofluoridate", *Nature,* **222,** 1066–67 (1969).
30. Johnson, M. K., "Organophosphorus and other inhibitors of brain 'neurotoxic esterase' and the development of delayed neurotoxicity in hens", *Biochem, J.,* **120,** 523–31 (1970).
31. Triolo, A. J. and Coon, J. M., "The protective effect of aldrin against the toxicity of organophosphate anticholinesterases", *J. Pharmacol. Exp. Ther.,* **154,** 613–23 (1966).
32. DuBois, K. P. and Kinoshita, F., "Stimulation of detoxification of O-ethyl O-(4-nitrophenyl) phenyl phosphonothioate (EPN) by nikethamide and phenobarbital", *Proc. Soc. Exp. Biol. Med.,* **121,** 59–62 (1966).
33. Triolo, A. J. and Coon, J. M., "Toxicological interactions of chlorinated hydrocarbon and organophosphate insecticides", *J. Agr. Food Chem.,* **14,** 549–55 (1966).
34. Kewitz, H. and Wilson, I. B., "A specific antidote against lethal alkylphosphate intoxication", *Arch. Biochem.,* **60,** 261–63 (1956).
35. Davies, D. R. and Green, A. L., "The chemotherapy of poisoning by organophosphate anticholinesterases", *Brit. J. Ind. Med.,* **16,** 128–34 (1959).
36. Hobbiger, F., "Reactivation of phosphorylated acetylcholinesterase. II. Enhancement of the antidotal action of atropine", in Koelle, G. B., ed., *Cholinesterases and anticholinesterase agents,* Volume XV of *Handbuch der experimentellen Pharmakologie* (Berlin, Göttingen and Heidelberg, Springer-Verlag, 1963) pp. 950–52.
37. Natoff, I. L. and Reiff, B., "Effect of oximes on the acute toxicity of anticholinesterase carbamates", *Toxicol. Appl. Pharmacol.,* **25,** 569–75 (1973).
38. Carpenter, G. P., Weil, C. S., Palm, P. E., Woodside, M. W., Nair, J. H. III and

Smyth, H. F. Jr., "Mammalian toxicity of 1-naphthyl-*N*-methylcarbamate (Sevin insecticide)", *J. Agr. Food Chem.*, **9,** 30–39 (1961).

39. Kewitz, H., Wilson, I. B. and Nachmansohn, D., "A specific antidote against lethal alkylphosphate intoxication. II. Antidotal properties", *Arch. Biochem. Biophys.*, **64,** 456–65 (1956).
40. Hobbiger, F. and Sadler, P. W., "Protection against lethal organophosphate poisoning by quaternary pyridine aldoximes", *Brit. J. Pharmacol. Chemother.*, **14,** 192–201 (1959).
41. Bethe, K., Erdmann, W. D., Lendle, L. and Schmidt, G., "Spezifische Antidotbehandlung bei protahierter Vergiftung mit Alkylphosphater (Paraoxon, Parathion, D.F.P.) und Eserine an Meerschweinen", *Arch. Exp. Pathol. Pharmakol.*, **231,** 3–22 (1957).
42. Stenger, E. G., "Zum Wirkungsmechanismus des Pyridin-2-aldoxim-*N*-methyljodids", *Arzneimittel-Forsch.*, **12,** 617–18 (1962).
43. Sanderson, D. M., "Treatment of poisoning by anticholinesterase insecticides in the rat", *J. Pharm. Pharmacol.*, **13,** 435–42 (1961).
44. Lehman, R. A., Fitch, H. M., Block, L. P., Jewell, H. A. and Nicholls, M. E., "Antidotes and potentiating agents for phospholine iodide", *J. Pharmacol. Exp. Ther.*, **128,** 307–17 (1960).
45. Stenger, E. G., "Beitrag zur Antidotwirkung des Pyridin-2-aldoxim-*N*-methyljodids (PAM)", *Med. Exp.*, **3,** 143–49 (1960).
46. Milošević, M. P., Vojvodić, V. and Milošević, V., "The action of *N, N'*,-trimethylenebis (4-hydroxyimino methyl-pyridinium bromide) (TMB-4) on acute lethal anticholinesterase poisoning in mice", *Arhiv Hig. Rada,* **10,** 213–16 (1959).
47. Natoff, I. L. and Reiff, B., "Quantitative studies of the effect of antagonists on the acute toxicity of organophosphates in rats", *Brit. J. Pharmacol.*, **40,** 124–34 (1970).
48. Wilson, I. B. and Ginsburg, S., "Reactivation of acetylcholinesterase inhibited by alkylphosphates", *Arch. Biochem. Biophys.*, **54,** 569–71 (1955).
49. Kühnen, H., "Activation and inhibition of acetylcholinesterase by Toxogonin", *Eur. J. Pharmacol.*, **9,** 41–45 (1970).
50. Kühnen-Clausen, D., "Investigations on the parasympatholytic effect of toxogonin on the guinea-pig isolated ileum", *Eur. J. Pharmacol.*, **9,** 85–92 (1970).
51. Erdmann, W. D. and Englehard, H., "Pharmakologisch-toxikologische Untersuchungen mit dem Dichlorid des Bis-(4-hydroxyiminomethyl-pyridinium-(1)-methyl) äthers, einem neuen Esterase-Reaktivator", *Arzneimittel-Forsch.*, **14,** 5–11 (1964).
52. Zarro, V. J. and di Palma, J. R., "The sympathomimetic effects of 2-pyridine aldoxime methylchloride (2-PAM C1)", *J. Pharmacol. Exp. Ther.*, **147,** 153–60 (1965).
53. Milošević, M. P., Terzić, M. and Simić, D., "Ganglionare Wirkungen einiger Oxime", *Naturwissenschaften,* **55,** 134–35 (1968).
54. Albanus, L., Sundwall, A. and Vangbo, B., "On the metabolic disposition of methylatropine in animals and man", *Acta Pharmacol. Toxicol.*, **27,** 97–111 (1969).

5. A comparative study of pralidoxime, obidoxime and trimedoxime in healthy men volunteers and in rats

V. VOJVODIĆ and B. BOŠKOVIĆ

Square-bracketed numbers, thus [1], *refer to the list of references on page 72.*

I. *Introduction*

It is well known that certain oximes, when used in combination with atropine, can provide an effective therapy in humans and animals exposed to lethal doses of organophosphorus cholinesterase inhibitors. Of the many hundreds of oximes that have been synthesized, however, only three—pralidoxime (2-PAM), trimedoxime (TMB-4) and obidoxime (LüH6)—have so far found a place in medical practice. And for various reasons, there is no agreement from country to country on which of these compounds is the "best". In the United States, for example, pralidoxime chloride is the only oxime commercially available; in some European countries, obidoxime (Toxogonin) and trimedoxime are the preferred compounds; while in Britain, France and Canada, the methanesulphonate salt of pralidoxime (P2S) is the most commonly used [1].

Obidoxime and trimedoxime are sometimes used in preference to pralidoxime in treating human organophosphorus poisoning [5–8]. The explanation lies in the fact that obidoxime and trimedoxime are in many respects superior to pralidoxime as antidotes in animal poisoning with organophosphorus compounds (for example, they induce stronger and more rapid reactivation of the inhibited cholinesterase). It is interesting, however, to note that obidoxime and trimedoxime have not yet replaced pralidoxime as the basic antidote, probably because, on a weight basis in animals, both of these compounds, but particularly trimedoxime, show a higher toxicity than pralidoxime. This paper presents an evaluation of these three oximes, based on studies on healthy men volunteers and experimental animals.

II. *Comparative studies of oxime therapy*

Our results in healthy men have shown that there are no differences in the nature or frequency of symptoms after the application of pralidoxime, obidoxime or trimedoxime (see table 5.1), and that the side-effects pro-

Table 5.1. Nature and frequency of symptoms in healthy male subjects injected intramuscularly with pralidoxime, obidoxime or trimedoxime

Symptom	Number of subjects having symptoms[a]		
	Pralidoxime (2-PAM Cl) (dose= 1.0 g/person)	Obidoxime (LüH6 Cl_2) (dose= 0.25 g/person)	Trimedoxime (TMB-4 Cl_2) (dose= 0.25 g/person)
Total number of subjects	**14**	**12**	**14**
Sensation of pain at site of injection	14	12	14
Sensation of warmth, a "hot feeling", especially in face	14	12	14
Sensation of cold (similar to that caused by menthol) in nasopharynx	14	12	14
Dizziness	5	6	7
Blurred vision	4	4	4
Sensation of "pins and needles" in arms and fingers	1	3	4
Impaired concentration	2	3	3
Headache	2	3	4
Diplopia	–	2	2
Impaired accommodation	1	2	2
Sensation of "numbness" in lips	1	3	2
Nausea	–	–	1

[a] No symptoms were observed in control subjects injected with saline.

duced in man by these compounds do not differ in frequency, intensity or duration from those reported in the literature for other oximes in doses that are likely to be effective as antidotes [5, 9–16]. The oximes invariably produced pain, described as "burning" or discomfort at the site of injection. Some subjects also complained of sciatica in the leg at the injection site, which lasted for several hours, although no local reactions were noticed at the site of injection. Five to 10 minutes after the injection of the oximes, all subjects had a feeling of weakness in the facial muscles. In addition, a sensation of cold, similar to that caused by menthol, was noticed in the nasopharynx during inspiration. A frequent complaint was dizziness, beginning five to 10 minutes after the injection and lasting for up to one hour. Blurring of vision was noticed by a few persons in each group, but this persisted on average for only 10 minutes. A few subjects in each group complained of a diffuse headache, most pronounced in the orbital region.

The effects of all three oximes on heart rate, blood pressure and respiration rate were small (table 5.2). Routine haematological and urinary analyses failed to show any abnormalities following administration of the oximes.

Comparison of the biological half-lives of the three oximes shows (table 5.3) that TMB-4 is the most persistent compound. Moreover, the urinary excretion rate of trimedoxime is significantly lower than that of pralidoxime or obidoxime (table 5.3). Therefore, since the side-effects in man of

Table 5.2. Heart rate, blood pressure and respiration rate in healthy male subjects injected intramuscularly with pralidoxime, obidoxime or trimedoxime

Time after injection of oxime *min*	Heart rate *beats/min (mean±SE)*	Blood pressure *mm Hg (mean±SE)*		Respiration rate *cycles/min (mean±SE)*
		Systolic	Diastolic	
Pralidoxime (2-PAM Cl) (dose=1.0 g/person)				
0	78.4±3.0	124.6±3.4	78.0±2.4	15.0±1.2
10	78.2±3.2	124.4±3.4	78.0±2.4	15.4±1.2
20	82.0±3.4	125.5±2.8	80.0±2.2	16.2±1.0
30	84.4±3.2	120.5±3.0	76.4±1.8	17.6±1.4
45	82.4±3.0	120.0±2.0	78.0±2.0	17.6±1.2
60	82.6±2.8	122.0±2.4	76.8±2.4	17.0±1.6
90	82.0±2.4	124.0±3.2	78.0±2.0	16.4±1.4
120	78.0±3.2	124.5±3.2	78.2±2.2	16.2±1.2
240	78.2±2.8	124.0±3.0	78.0±2.0	16.0±1.4
Obidoxime (LüH6 Cl_2) (dose=0.25 g/person)				
0	76.2±4.2	125.2±3.6	80.0±2.0	14.8±1.4
10	80.0±3.2	125.0±3.2	80.0±2.0	15.6±1.2
20	85.2±3.4	126.5±3.8	80.5±2.4	16.0±1.0
30	86.0±2.8	126.0±3.2	80.2±2.2	16.4±1.2
45	86.2±2.8	122.0±3.0	78.0±2.4	16.8±1.0
60	86.0±2.6	118.0±3.6	75.2±2.1	17.2±1.4
90	85.0±2.8	118.2±3.0	76.0±2.2	16.6±1.2
120	80.0±3.4	122.5±3.0	80.0±2.2	16.6±1.2
240	76.6±3.4	124.8±3.2	80.2±2.4	15.0±1.0
Trimedoxime (TMB-4 Cl_2) (dose=0.25 g/person)				
0	80.3±2.4	125.0±3.2	79.3±2.0	15.7±1.2
10	84.8±3.2	125.4±3.8	80.0±1.8	16.0±1.0
20	86.0±3.6	128.5±3.2	80.5±2.2	16.0±1.0
30	86.8±3.0	128.3±3.8	77.5±2.4	17.4±1.4
45	87.2±3.2	123.3±3.6	75.0±1.6	17.1±1.1
60	87.0±2.8	118.0±3.0	75.8±1.8	18.0±1.2
90	86.8±2.8	117.5±4.0	75.0±2.1	16.8±1.2
120	82.4±3.6	120.0±3.8	77.5±2.3	16.3±1.0
240	80.8±3.4	123.8±3.2	80.2±2.2	16.0±1.2

pralidoxime, obidoxime and trimedoxime are essentially similar, the fact that trimedoxime is the most persistent would suggest that this is the most promising of the three oximes investigated. However, experimental evidence indicates that the two bispyridinium oximes—TMB-4 and LüH6—are stronger reactivators of organophosphate-inhibited cholinesterase than the monopyridinium oxime, pralidoxime. Furthermore, when used in antidotal therapy, alone or in combination with atropine, against experimental poisoning by organophosphorus compounds, they are more effective than other oximes [2, 17]. It has been found from studies on laboratory animals that LüH6 is less toxic than TMB-4 [5], which is the main reason why some authors recommend the use of LüH6 in human organophosphorus poisoning [6, 18]. But some pharmacological results have shown that TMB-4 is at least equal, or superior, to LüH6 [19–21].

In order to contribute to the further evaluation of the efficacy of TMB-4

Table 5.3. Velocity constant, biological half-life and urinary excretion rate of pralidoxime, obidoxime and trimedoxime after intramuscular administration in man

Oxime	Dose *mg/kg*	Velocity constant (k)[a] *min*$^{-1}$	Biological half-life (t/2) *min*	Per cent of oxime dose excreted (*mean*[b]*±SE*) In 2 hours	In 4 hours	In 8 hours
Pralidoxime (2-PAM Cl)	10.0–14.08	1.120×10^{-2}	61.8	*54.2±6.5*	*69.5±10.8*	*88.6± 6.6*
Obidoxime (LüH6 Cl_2)	2.5– 3.52	6.380×10^{-3}	108.62	*50.0±8.4*	*64.5± 8.2*	*84.0±10.0*
Trimedoxime (TMB-4 Cl_2)	2.5– 3.52	5.484×10^{-3}	126.36	*28.0±6.2*	*46.0± 4.3*	*80.0±10.2*

[a] The velocity constant, k, is a measure of the drug-elimination rate from the bloodstream to urine.
[b] For the excretion-rate studies, pralidoxime was received by 14 subjects, obidoxime by 12 subjects and trimedoxime by 14 subjects.

and LüH6, we compared them in relation to their acute toxicity, their blood concentrations and their protective and reactivating potencies, in poisoning by tertiary (Gd-7) and quaternary (Gd-42) organophosphorus anticholinesterases in rats. Jakovljev *et al* [22] have found that Gd-7 and Gd-42 are strong cholinesterase inhibitors, and according to our results, the LD_{50} values of these compounds in rats (by subcutaneous administration) are 0.36 (0.31–0.4) mg/kg for Gd-7 and 0.032 (0.03–0.035) mg/kg for Gd-42. The signs and symptoms of poisoning by these compounds in rats were basically similar to those seen in poisoning by other organophosphorus compounds, but the onset of symptoms and the time of death were similar to those seen with organophosphorus compounds of a thiocholine type described by Aquilonius *et al* [23].

The results of studies on the acute toxicity of TMB-4 and LüH6 in rats (table 5.4) show that, depending on the route of administration, LüH6 is 29 to 39 per cent less toxic than TMB-4. The greater toxicity of TMB-4 in relation to LüH6 may be partly explained by the differences in persistence of these oximes in the body found in the present study and in earlier animal

Table 5.4. Acute toxicity of trimedoxime and obidoxime in rats by different routes of administration

Oxime	Route of administration	LD_{50} *mg/kg (95 per cent confidence limits)*
Trimedoxime (TMB-4)	Intravenous	89 (80–99)
	Intramuscular	123 (109–139)
	Intraperitoneal	137 (127–145)
Obidoxime (LüH6)	Intravenous	133 (125–140)
	Intramuscular	172 (150–188)
	Intraperitoneal	225 (170–300)

Table 5.5. Concentrations of trimedoxime and obidoxime in the blood of rats after intramuscular administration (25 mg/kg)

Time after injection of oximes *min*	Concentrations of oximes in blood *μg/ml (mean±SE)* Trimedoxime (TMB-4)	Obidoxime (LüH6)	P[a]
3	5.0±0.4	5.1±0.6	ns
5	12.0±3.0	11.0±2.5	ns
10	32.0±2.0	30.0±2.6	ns
15	30.0±2.5	27.7±3.0	ns
30	23.0±1.7	19.2±0.4	0.05
45	14.7±0.5	10.5±0.25	0.001
60	9.4±0.4	7.7±0.3	0.005
90	6.0±0.4	3.8±0.5	0.005
120	3.8±0.5	2.3±0.25	0.02
180	1.1±0.1	0.5±0.1	0.005

[a] P=probability (ns=non-significant).

and human experiments [3–4, 24]. The results presented in table 5.5 show that there is a rapid absorption of both oximes from the site of injection and that blood levels of at least 2 μg/ml are maintained for about two hours. On a weight basis, TMB-4 and LüH6 are approximately 10 times more potent than monopyridinium oximes (2-PAM, P2S) as reactivators of phosphorylated acetylcholinesterase [2, 17], so that concentrations of about 2 μg/ml should be considered as therapeutic. The shorter persistence of LüH6 in

Table 5.6. Reactivation *in vivo* by trimedoxime and obidoxime of rat-blood acetylcholinesterase inhibited by sublethal doses of Gd-7 and Gd-42 compounds

	Acetylcholinesterase activity, per cent of normal (*mean*[a] *±95 per cent confidence limits*) Gd-7 (dose=0.2 mg/kg, *sc*)	Gd-42 (dose=0.02 mg/kg, *sc*)
Trimedoxime (TMB-4)		
Control	100	100
30 min after poison	51.8±4.7	29.6±2.4
60 min after poison	45.7±5.2	25.1±3.6
60 min after poison and 30 min after TMB-4 (25 mg/kg)	84.8±7.2	86.2±3.3
Obidoxime (LüH6)		
Control	100	100
30 min after poison	45.4±4.5	30.4±4.6
60 min after poison	43.8±4.2	28.6±3.7
60 min after poison and 30 min after LüH6 (25 mg/kg)	82.6±8.1	96.4±3.4

[a] Mean of results from four animals.

Figure 5.1. Protective effects of oximes (25 mg/kg, *im*) in rats poisoned by 2 LD_{50} (0.72 mg/kg) of Gd-7[a]

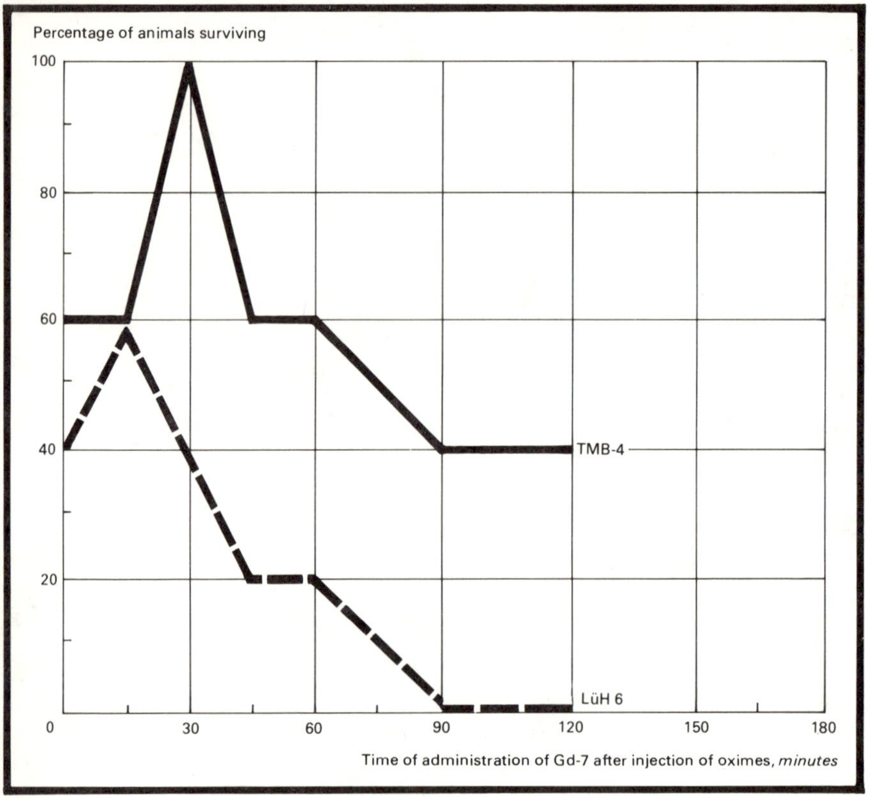

[a] Gd-7=

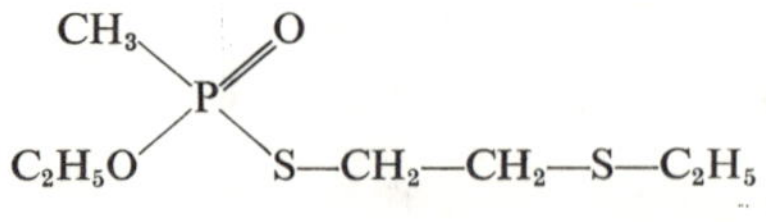

blood in relation to TMB-4 is particularly evident 30–180 minutes after injection. The velocity constants (*k*) characterizing the drug-elimination rate from the bloodstream [25] were 2.057×10^{-2} for TMB-4 and 2.443×10^{-2} for LüH6, with corresponding half-lives ($t/2$) of 33.7 minutes for TMB-4 and 26.4 minutes for LüH6.

Inhibition of acetylcholinesterase in rat blood was more pronounced after poisoning by Gd-42 than after the administration of an equitoxic dose of Gd-7 (table 5.6). In relation to the reactivation of acetylcholinesterase inhibited by these compounds, the application of TMB-4 or LüH6 produced a marked return of enzyme activity, regardless of which particular organophosphorus compound was used. Since there was no substantial difference between the reactivating potencies of TMB-4 and LüH6 after inhibition of acetylcholinesterase in blood by Gd-7 and Gd-42 compounds, it seems

Figure 5.2. Protective effects of oximes (25 mg/kg, *im*) in rats poisoned by 2 LD$_{50}$ (0.064 mg/kg) of Gd-42[a]

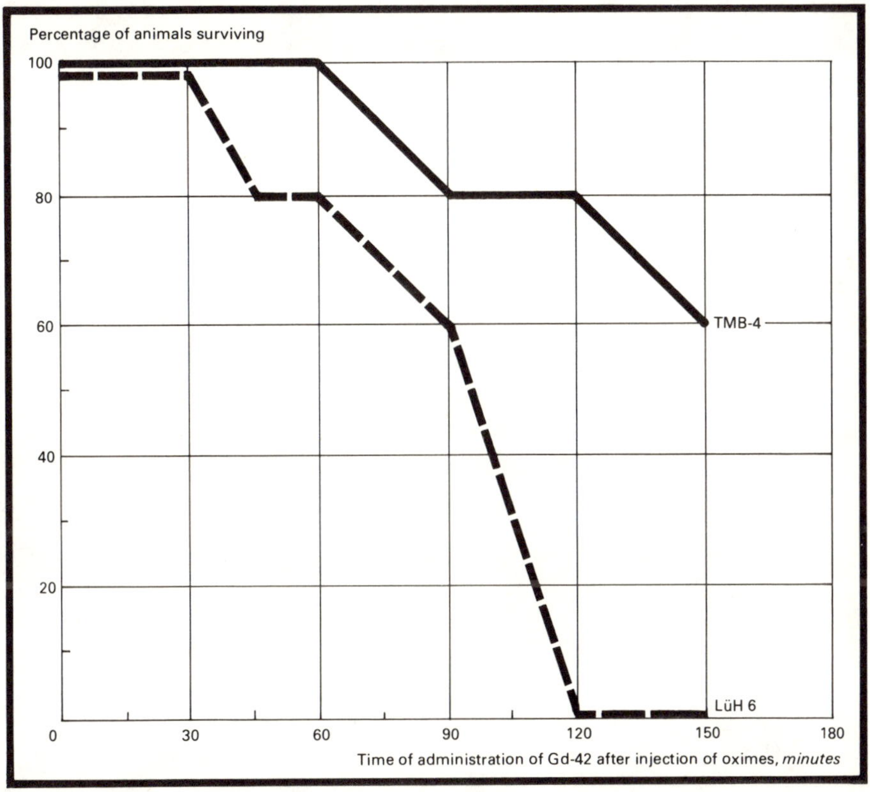

^{a} Gd-42 =

$$\begin{array}{c} CH_3 \\ \diagdown \\ C_2H_5O \end{array} P \begin{array}{c} O \\ \diagup \\ \diagdown \\ S-CH_2-CH_2-\overset{\oplus}{\underset{CH_3}{S}}-C_2H_5 \end{array} \times CH_3SO_4^{\ominus}$$

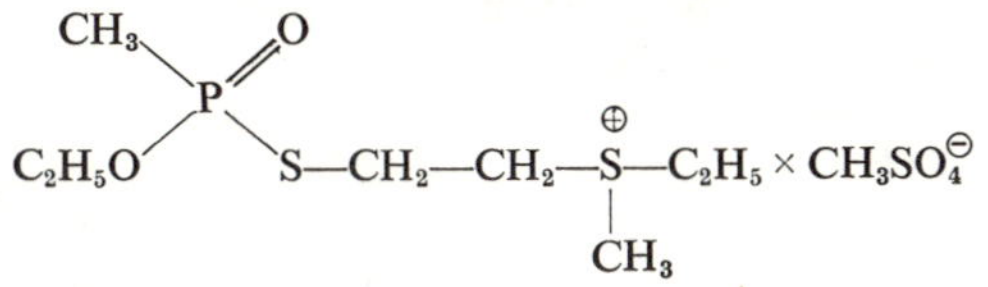

highly probable that the therapeutic effectiveness of both oximes will be at least equal.

However, the protective effect of TMB-4 in relation to LüH6 in rats poisoned by Gd-7 was superior at all times studied (figure 5.1). In poisoning by Gd-42, the protective effect of both oximes was the same only in the groups of animals observed at 0, 15 and 30 minutes, respectively, while after these times the protective effect of TMB-4 was again superior to that of LüH6 (figure 5.2).

In circumstances where the oxime level in blood is a critical factor, any advantage which LüH6 might have due to its lower toxicity in animals is diminished by its shorter persistence in blood. Moreover, in experiments where animals were poisoned by Gd-7 and Gd-42 compounds, producing methylethoxy-phosphorylated acetylcholinesterase, the protective effect of TMB-4 was markedly superior to LüH6. Such a difference was particularly pronounced at intervals of 120 and 150 minutes, when TMB-4 protected more than 50 per cent of poisoned animals while LüH6 was ineffective. This suggests that the toxicity of a particular oxime should not be used as the sole factor for determining the superiority of one oxime over another in cases of poisoning by different organophosphorus compounds.

References

1. Sidell, F. R., Groff, W. A. and Kaminskis, A., "Pralidoxime methanesulphonate: plasma levels and pharmacokinetics after oral administration to man", *J. Pharm. Sci.,* **61** (7), 1136–40 (1972).
2. Karczmar, A. G., ed., "Anticholinesterase agents", in *International Encyclopedia of Pharmacology and Therapeutics* (Oxford, Pergamon Press, 1970).
3. Vojvodić, V. and Grbeša, B., "Farmakodinamski učinci oksima (LüH6) na zdravim ljudima-dobrovoljcima", in *Odabrana poglavlja iz toksikologije.* I Jugoslovenski simpozijum o medicinskoj toksikologiji, Beograd, 1968, pp. 294–98.
4. Vojvodić, V., "Blood levels, urinary excretion and potential toxicity of N,N-Trimethylenebis (Pyridinium-4-aldoxime) dichloride (TMB-4) in healthy man following intramuscular injection of the oxime", *Pharmacol. Clinica,* **2,** 216–20 (1970).
5. Erdmann, W. D. and Engelhard, H., "Pharmakologisch-toxicologische Untersuchungen mit dem Dichlorid des Bis-(4-hydroxyiminomethyl-pyridinium-(1)-methyl) äthers, einem neuen Esterase-Reaktivator", *Arzneimittel-Forsch.,* **14,** 5–11 (1964).
6. Erdmann, W. D. and Clarman, M., "Ein neuer esterasere Aktivator für die Behandlung von Vergiftungen mit Alkylphosphaten", *Deut. Med. Wochschr.,* **45,** 2201–206 (1963).
7. Luznjikov, E. A. and Pankov, A. G., "Iskustva primene reaktivatora holinesteraze pri akutnim trovanjima organofosfornim jedinjenjima" (Translation from Russian). *Klinich. Med.,* **7,** 134–36 (1969).
8. Golikov, S. N. and Zaugolnikov, S. D., "Reaktivatori holinesteraz", (Leningrad, Izdatelstvo, "Medicina", 1970).
9. Jager, B. V., Green, N. and Jager, L., "Studies on distribution and disappearance of pyridine-2-aldoxime methiodide (PAM) and diacetyl monoxime (DAM) in man and in experimental animals", *Johns Hopkins Med. J.,* **102,** 225–34 (1958).
10. Jager, B. V. and Stagg, G. N., "Toxicity of diacetyl monoxime and pyridine-2-aldoxime methiodide in man", *Johns Hopkins Med. J.,* **102,** 203–11 (1958).
11. Sundwall, A., "Minimum concentrations of N-methyl-pyridinium-2-aldoxime ethane sulphonate which reverse neuromuscular block", *Biochem. Pharmacol.,* **8,** 413–17 (1961).
12. Barkman, R., Edgren, B. and Sundwall, A., "Self-administration of pralidoxime in nerve gas poisoning with a note on the stability of the drug", *J. Pharm. Pharmacol.,* **15,** 671–77 (1963).
13. Erdmann, W. D., Bosse, I. and Franke, P., "Absorption and excretion of Toxogonin, an alkyl-phosphate antidote, after intramuscular injection in man", *Germ. Med. Monthly,* **12,** 503–505 (1965).

14. Sidell, F. R., Groff, W. A. and Ellin, R. I., "Blood levels of oxime and symptoms in humans after single and multiple oral doses of 2-pyridine aldoxime methochloride", *J. Pharm. Sci.*, **58** (9), 1093–98 (1969).
15. Sidell, F. R., Groff, W. A. and Kaminskis, A., "Toxogonin and pralidoxime: kinetic comparison after intravenous administration to man", *J. Pharm. Sci.*, **61** (11), 1765–69 (1972).
16. Swartz, R. D. and Sidell, F. R., "Renal tubular secretion of pralidoxime in man", *Proc. Soc. Exp. Biol. Med.*, **146**, 419–24 (1974).
17. Hobbiger, F., "Reactivation of phosphorylated acetylcholinesterase", in Koelle, G. B., ed., *Cholinesterases and Anticholinesterase Agents*, Volume XV of *Handbuch der experimentellen Pharmakologie* (Berlin, Göttingen and Heidelberg, Springer-Verlag, 1963) pp. 921–88.
18. Staudacher, L. H., "Erfolgreiche Behandlung einer E-605 Vergiftung mit einem neuen Cholinesterase-reaktivator", *Arzneimittel-Forsch.*, **17**, 441–43 (1963).
19. Heilbronn, E. and Tolagen, B., "Toxogonin in sarin, soman and tabun poisoning", *Biochem. Pharmacol.*, **14**, 73–77 (1965).
20. Hobbiger, F. and Vojvodić, V., "The reactivating and antidotal actions of TMB-4 and Toxogonin with particular reference to their effect on phosphorylated acetylcholinesterase in the brain", *Biochem. Pharmacol.* **15**, 1677–90 (1966).
21. Hobbiger, F. and Vojvodić, V., "The reactivation by pyridinium aldoximes of phosphorylated acetylcholinesterase in the central nervous system", *Biochem. Pharmacol.*, **16**, 455–62 (1967).
22. Jakovljev, V. A., Brick, I. L. and Volkova, R. I., "The investigation of the active site of cholinesterases by means of organophosphorus compounds", in *Proceedings of the Fifth International Congress of Biochemistry, Moscow, 1961,* Volume 1, pp. 322–25.
23. Aquilonius, S. M., Fredriksson, T. and Sundwall, A., "Studies on phosphorylated thiocholine and choline derivatives. I. General pharmacology and toxicology", *Toxicol. Appl. Pharmacol.*, **6**, 269–79 (1964).
24. Milošević, M. P., Vojvodić, V. and Terzić, M., "Blood concentration of N,N′-trimethylenebis (pyridinium-4-aldoxime) (TMB-4) and N,N′-oxydimethylenebis (pyridinium-4-aldoxime) (Toxogonin) after intravenous and intramuscular administration in the dog", *Biochem. Pharmacol.*, **16**, 2435–38 (1967).
25. Martin, A. N., *Physical Pharmacy: Kinetics of Drug Absorption, Distribution and Elimination* (Philadelphia, Lea and Febiger, 1962) pp. 506–509.

6. Organophosphates and central cholinergic systems

M. P. MILOŠEVIĆ

Square-bracketed numbers, thus [1], *refer to the list of references on page 80.*

I. *Introduction*

Most of the work so far reported on the biochemical lesions produced by organophosphates is concerned with the problem of cholinesterase inhibition. A limited number of attempts have been made to study the changes in acetylcholine level produced by these compounds. However, as Barnes points out in a recent review:

> If we are concerned with factors that decide whether exposure will lead to death or disability and the effects of different forms of therapy, it would be a great help if we knew a little more about the ways in which the delicate balance between enzyme activity, and level of acetylcholine determine the local responses at the periphery and in the central nervous system [1].

This discussion will therefore be limited to three important points: (*a*) the time course of changes in acetylcholine level in the brain in relation to cholinesterase inhibition; (*b*) the possible action of enzyme reactivators on these changes; and (*c*) the effect of atropine on the rise of brain acetylcholine levels produced by organophosphorus anticholinesterases.

In our work, paraoxon (E 600) was used as a standard organophosphate. This so-called "irreversible" inhibitor is extremely toxic and constitutes the active metabolite of the widely used pesticide parathion. One additional reason to select this compound for investigation is that it disappears very rapidly from the brain after administration [2]. Total and "free" brain acetylcholine were measured by biological assay after extraction with or without acidification, respectively [3–4].

II. *Time course of changes in brain acetylcholine level*

The modern concept of the mode of action of organophosphorus anticholinesterases is based on the generally accepted belief that the degree and duration of cholinesterase inhibition are well correlated with the rate of accumulation of acetylcholine above the normal physiological range. An attempt was therefore made to determine the level of "free" acetylcholine in the brains of rats during the course of acute paraoxon intoxication, and to relate the observed changes with the degree of cholinesterase inhibition. In a parallel series of experiments (on rats of the same strain) depression of avoidance reaction—an example of learned behaviour—was tested at various time intervals after paraoxon treatment. The results of these experiments are shown in figure 6.1. These results show that there is a good relationship between severity of behavioural disturbances, reduced brain cholinesterase activity and elevated brain acetylcholine level at about four hours after paraoxon treatment. Therefore, in the early phase of acute intoxication, all data seem to be in good agreement with theoretical hypotheses [5]. However, during the later phase of intoxication, the situation changes completely. In fact, the acetylcholine level returns to normal much faster than the enzyme activity. The disappearance of behavioural depression seems to correlate fairly well with the return of brain acetylcholine to normal, but shows little relationship to cholinesterase activity. Such "dissociation" between enzyme activity and behavioural response is not peculiar to organophosphates: it has also been observed with other compounds, such as tacrine [6].

The relatively rapid restitution of the normal acetylcholine level in spite of "irreversible" inhibition of cholinesterase has also been observed in animals treated with high doses of DFP (diisopropyl phosphorofluoridate). For example, the data of Mayer and Michalek indicate that, only three hours after treatment, brain acetylcholine levels in animals treated with 1.5 mg/kg DFP were practically the same as those found in control animals [7]. The data of Fonnum and Guttormsen show that the high level of brain acetylcholine produced by a dose of DFP corresponding to approximately the LD_{50} was maintained not more than 16 hours after treatment [8]. Similar results were obtained from rabbit cerebral cortex after DFP treatment [9].

Little is known about the mechanism responsible for the rapid restitution of the normal acetylcholine levels after administration of "irreversible" inhibitors. One suggestion is that a high level of acetylcholine in the tissue inhibits the synthesis of the neurotransmitter itself [10], but the evidence is far from clear. Actually, no reduction of cholinesterase activity was observed by Stavinoha *et al* during chronic disolfoton (Demeton-S) intoxication [11]. An alternative hypothesis is offered by the results of Davis and Agranoff, who suggest that some isoenzymes have a half-life of about three hours, that is, that some cholinesterase activity can be restored within a short time, even after treatment with "irreversible" inhibitors [12].

III. *Possible central actions of enzyme reactivators*

The fact that some oximes are strong reactivators of phosphorylated cholinesterase makes them convenient experimental tools for studying neurochemical changes produced by organophosphorus anticholinesterases.

Figure 6.1. Relationship between brain acetylcholine level, active avoidance (behavioural) performance and cholinesterase activity in rats poisoned with paraoxon

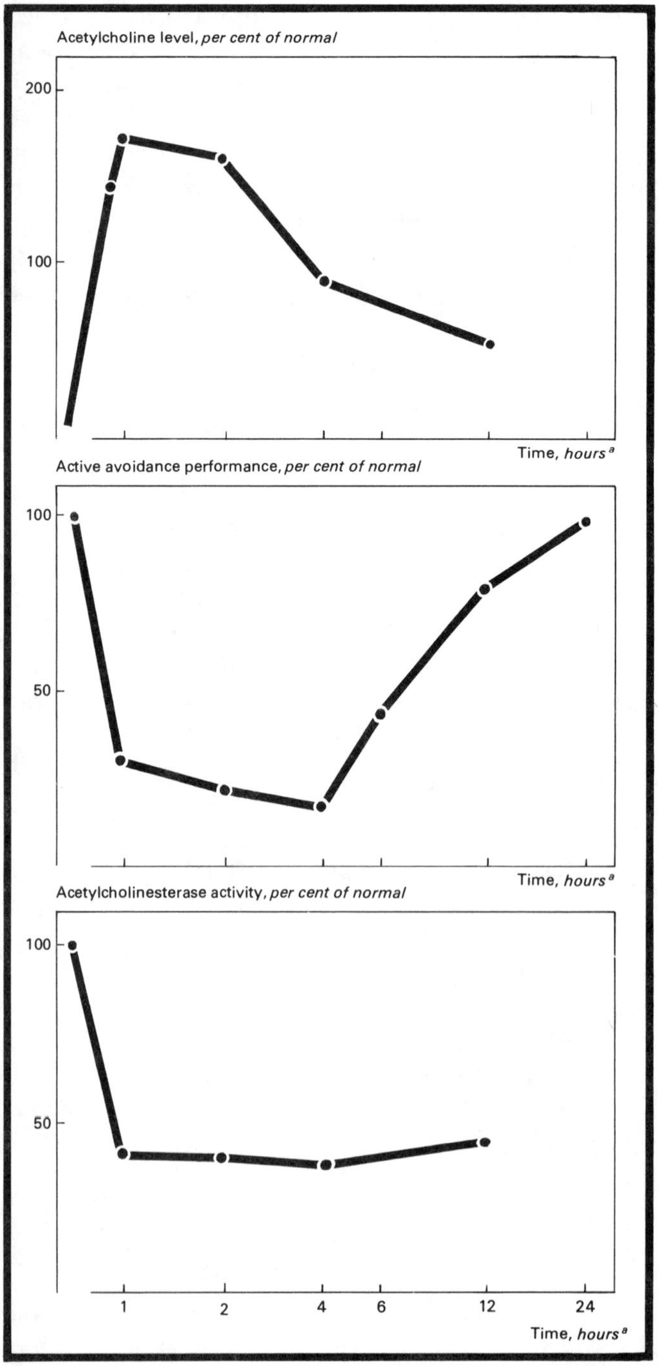

[a] Note log scale.

Source: Rosić, N. and Miloše-vić, M. P., "Two-way (shuttle-box) avoidance in rats after paraoxon treatment", *Activitas Nervosa Superior,* **13,** 241–45 (1971).

Figure 6.2. Total acetylcholine content and cholinesterase activity in brains of paraoxon-intoxicated rats treated with 2-PAM (20 mg/kg, *iv*) 10 minutes after intoxication

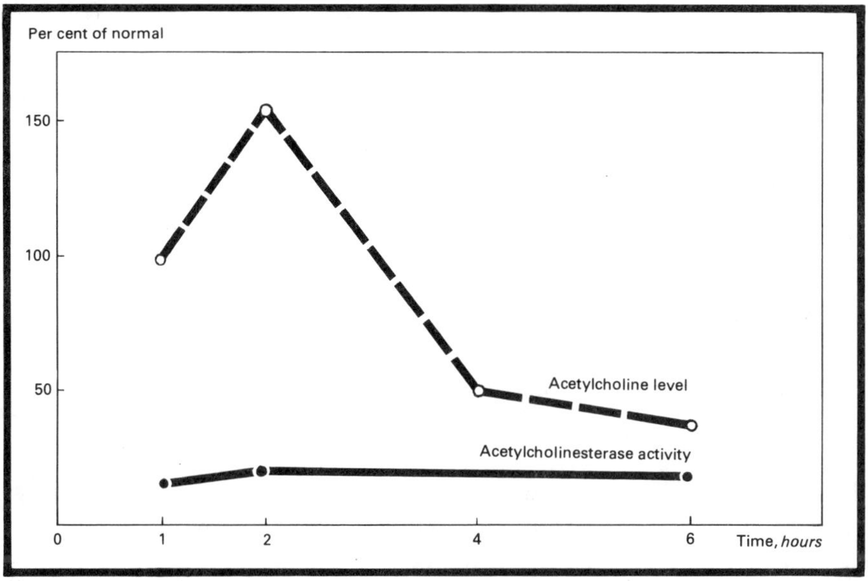

Unfortunately, all the oximes with high reactivating potency are quaternary compounds, and for many years there has been controversy over whether or not the amounts crossing the blood-brain barrier, if any, are sufficient to cause significant reactivation of brain cholinesterase. In fact, recent data show considerable differences in brain oxime level and/or brain enzyme reactivation, depending on the species, on the compound and on the brain area [13]. A few years ago, we showed that reactivation of the so-called "functional" brain cholinesterase, located at the cell surface, is greater than the reactivation of intracellular enzymes [14–15]. This finding, confirmed by Hobbiger and Vojvodić [16], indicates the selectivity of oxime action at the cellular level.

The effects of pralidoxime (2-PAM) and obidoxime (Toxogonin, LüH6) on the rise of brain acetylcholine produced by paraoxon were studied in a series of experiments [3–4]. In a first study, we exploited the protection afforded by pralidoxime to investigate the brain acetylcholine level after subcutaneous administration of a large dose of paraoxon (0.5 mg/kg). Normally this dose very rapidly kills 95 per cent of the animals, thus preventing the measurement of acetylcholine level at several time intervals. The results are shown in figure 6.2. Surprisingly, the increase in brain acetylcholine level in these animals (about 150 per cent above normal) was much larger than those found in unprotected animals immediately after respiration had stopped (70 per cent above normal), which clearly shows

Table 6.1. Effect of obidoxime on acetylcholine content and cholinesterase activity in the pontomedullary region of rat brain after intoxication with armin

Compound	Dose *mg/kg*	Number of rats	Acetylcholine content *µg/kg (mean±SE)*	Per cent above normal	Cholinesterase activity *µl CO_2/30 min/mg (mean±SE)*	Per cent of normal
None (control)	–	12	2.29±0.17	–	0.52±0.04	–
Armin	0.4	20	3.42±0.14	*49*	0.10±0.02	*19*
Armin + obidoxime	0.4 25	20	2.86±0.11	*25*	0.24±0.03	*46*

Source: Vasić, B. and Milošević, M. P., unpublished.

that pralidoxime cannot prevent the increase of brain acetylcholine due to the lethal action of paraoxon. However, in this case too, the level of acetylcholine returned to about 50 per cent above normal only at six hours after treatment, although enzyme activity in whole brain homogenates remained at a very low level.

It is interesting, however, that in spite of an abnormally high concentration of acetylcholine in their brains, the poisoned rats treated with this oxime exhibited no symptoms of central origin, such as convulsions and tremor. It seems, therefore, reasonable to suppose that in the presence of abnormally high concentrations of acetylcholine, the cholinergic receptors in the brain rapidly become less sensitive to acetylcholine. Such an adaptation or tolerance to constant high concentrations of acetylcholine has previously been demonstrated in ganglia [17], and it is likely that it occurs in other parts of the central nervous system as well.

Intravenous injection of 12.5 mg/kg of obidoxime was also without effect on the level of total acetylcholine in the brains of rats one hour after administration of a lethal dose of paraoxon [4]. When a sublethal dose of paraoxon was used, similar increases in brain "free" acetylcholine levels were found, both in the presence, and in the absence, of obidoxime. Somewhat different results were obtained by Mayer and Michalek [7] using a sublethal dose of DFP and twice the dose of obidoxime used in our experiments. In fact, the rise in brain acetylcholine caused by DFP was antagonized by obidoxime only 90 minutes after treatment, although cholinesterase activity in the brain was similar in the presence, and in the absence, of reactivator treatment. Therefore, the effect of obidoxime is difficult to explain. The possibility that obidoxime may act on acetylcholine synthesis, perhaps at the level of a negative feedback mechanism between acetylcholine concentration and rate of synthesis, was recently excluded in experiments *in vitro* [18].

In all these experiments, the brain acetylcholine level and enzyme activity were measured in whole brain homogenates. It is possible, therefore, that some changes in acetylcholine content do occur in some parts of the brain,

Figure 6.3. Effects of atropine (5 mg/kg, *ip*) on brain acetylcholine level of rats intoxicated with paraoxon (E 600)

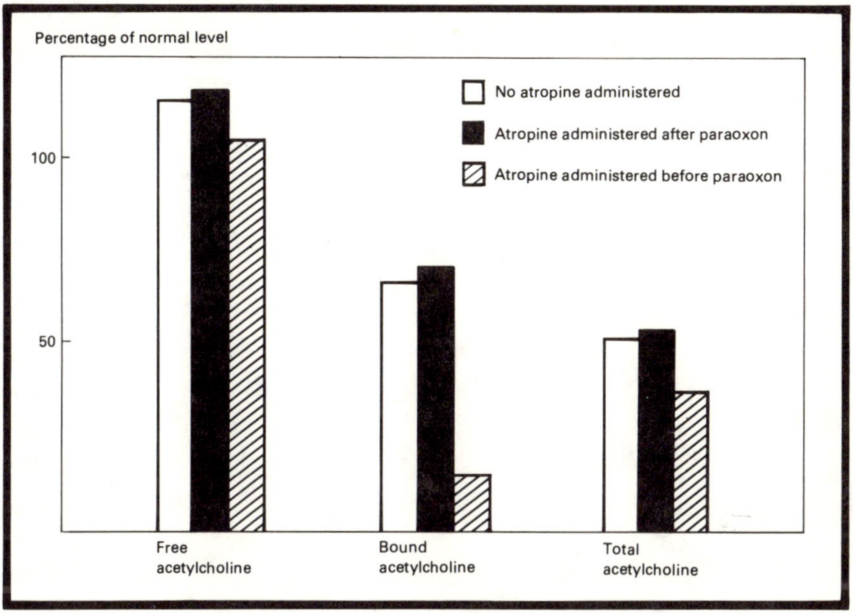

Source: Malobabić, Z., and Milošević, M. P., unpublished.

but that they cannot be detected by measuring the acetylcholine in the whole brain. The results of our experiments with obidoxime and armin, an organophosphate chemically very similar to paraoxon, demonstrate this very clearly. As shown in table 6.1, an injection of 25 mg/kg of obidoxime immediately after a lethal dose of armin effectively prevents the rise of the acetylcholine level in the pons and medulla oblongata regions, but not in the whole brain. This antagonism seems to be in good agreement with the degree of cholinesterase reactivation in these parts of the brain. Similar results with obidoxime were obtained on mice poisoned with sarin [19].

IV. *Effect of atropine on brain acetylcholine*

The protective action of atropine in organophosphate poisoning is attributed exclusively to the blockade of certain actions of accumulated acetylcholine. It is generally accepted that this drug has no action on the fundamental biochemical lesions produced by organophosphates. However, it is well known from the investigations of Giarman and Pepeu [20] that atropine markedly decreases total acetylcholine in the brains of rats. The question arises, therefore, whether this drug has some influence on the accumulation of acetylcholine produced by organophosphorus anticholinesterases.

The previous studies of Michaelis *et al* have shown that the level of "free" acetylcholine in the cerebral cortex of rabbits poisoned with DFP is the same in the presence, and in the absence, of atropine [9]. On the other hand, Holmstedt [21] and Milošević [4] have found that total acetylcholine levels in the brain are lower in rats treated with both organophosphates and atropine than in rats treated with organophosphates alone.

The results of our recent experiments, summarized in figure 6.3, seem to explain these controversies. It may be seen that a relatively small dose of atropine, given 10 minutes before administration of paraoxon, markedly reduces the rise of bound acetylcholine, but has no effect on the rise of "free" acetylcholine in the brains of paraoxon-poisoned rats. It is interesting, however, that the same dose of atropine has no influence on the level of bound (and total) acetylcholine if atropine is given after paraoxon treatment, although it relieves the existing signs of paraoxon intoxication.

Little is known about the mechanism by which atropine exerts this effect, but there is no doubt that such antagonism at the level of brain acetylcholine content may play a role at least as important as the blockade of neurotransmitter effects at the receptor level [21].

References

1. Barnes, J. M., "Anticholinesterases: Some problems in understanding their effects in whole animals", in Ballantyne, B., ed., *Forensic Toxicology* (Bristol, J. Wright & Sons Ltd., 1974) pp. 79–85.
2. Schaumann, W. and Schiller, M., "Inaktivierung von Alkylphosphaten im Gehirn und im Serum", *Arch. Exp. Pathol. Pharmakol.*, **239,** 114–25 (1960).
3. Milošević, M. P., "Acetylcholine content in the brain of rats treated with paraoxon and pyridinium-2-aldoxime methylchloride", *J. Pharm. Pharmacol.*, **21,** 469–70 (1969).
4. Milošević, M. P., "Acetylcholine content in the brain of rats treated with paraoxon and obidoxime", *Brit. J. Pharmacol.*, **39,** 732–37 (1970).
5. Holmstedt, B., Härkönen, M., Lundgren, G. and Sundwall, A., "Relationship between acetylcholine and cholinesterase activity in the brain following an organophosphorus cholinesterase inhibitor", *Biochem. Pharmacol.*, **16,** 404–406 (1967).
6. Rosić, N. and Milošević, M. P., "The effect of Tacrine on cholinesterase activity in brain of rats", *Acta Physiol. Pharmacol. Iugoslav*, **3,** 43–47 (1967).
7. Mayer, O. and Michalek, H., "Effects of DFP and obidoxime on brain acetylcholine levels and on brain and peripheral cholinesterases", *Biochem. Pharmacol.*, **20,** 3029–37 (1971).
8. Fonnum, F. and Guttormsen, D. M., "Changes in acetylcholine content of rat brain by toxic doses of di-isopropyl-phosphoro-fluoridate", *Experientia*, **25,** 505–506 (1969).
9. Michaelis, M., Finesinger, J. E., de Vester, B. and Erickson, R. W., "The effect of the intravenous injection of DFP and atropine on the level of free acetylcholine in the cerebral cortex of the rabbit", *J. Pharmacol. Exp. Ther.*, **111,** 169–75 (1954).

10. Kaita, A. A. and Goldberg, A. M., "Control of acetylcholine synthesis. The inhibition of choline acetyltransferase by acetylcholine", *J. Neurochem.*, **16,** 1185–91 (1069).
11. Stavinoha, W. B., Ryan, L. C. and Smith, P. W., "Biochemical effects of an organophosphorus cholinesterase inhibitor on the rat brain", *Ann. N. Y. Acad. Sci.,* **160,** 378–82 (1969).
12. Davis, G. A. and Agranoff, B. W., "Metabolic behaviour of isoenzymes of acetylcholinesterase", *Nature,* **220,** 277–80 (1968).
13. Bignami, G., Rosić, N., Michalek, H., Milošević, M. P. and Gatti, G. L., "Behavioral toxicity of anticholinesterase agents. Methodological, neurochemical and neuropsychological aspects", in *Proceedings of the Fifth International Conference on Environmental Toxicology (Behavioral Toxicology), Rochester, 1972* (in press).
14. Milošević, M. P. and Andjelković, D., "Reactivation of paraoxon-inactivated cholinesterase in the rat cerebral cortex by pralidoxime chloride", *Nature,* **210,** 206–207 (1966).
15. Andjelković, D. and Milošević, M. P., "Reactivation of phosphoryl cholinesterase in the rat's cerebral cortex following parenteral application of pralidoxime (PAM-2) and Toxogonin (LüH-6)", *Arhiv Hig. Rada,* **17,** 151–57 (1966).
16. Hobbiger, F. and Vojvodić, V., "The reactivation by pyridinium aldoximes of phosphorylated acetylcholinesterase in the central nervous system", *Biochem. Pharmacol.,* **16,** 455–62 (1967).
17. Krivoy, W. A. and Wills, J. H., "Adaptation to constant concentrations of acetylcholine", *J. Pharmacol. Exp. Ther.,* **116,** 220–26 (1956).
18. Michalek, H. and Bonavoglia, F., "Effects of obidoxime on content and synthesis of brain acetylcholine in DFP intoxicated rats", *Biochem. Pharmacol.,* **22,** 3124–27 (1973).
19. Bajgar, J., Jakl, A. and Hrdina, V., "The influence of obidoxime on acetylcholinesterase activity in different parts of the mouse brain following isopropylmethyl phosphonofluoridate intoxication", *Eur. J. Pharmacol.,* **19,** 199–202 (1972).
20. Giarman, N. J. and Pepeu, G., "The influence of centrally acting cholinolytic drugs on brain acetylcholine levels", *Brit. J. Pharmacol.,* **23,** 123–30 (1964).
21. Holmstedt, B., "Mobilization of acetylcholine by cholinergic agents", *Ann. N. Y. Acad. Sci.,* **144,** 433–53 (1967).

7. Reactivation of phosphorylated brain cholinesterase *in vivo*

B. REIFF

Square-bracketed numbers, thus [1], *refer to the list of references on page 86.*

I. *Introduction*

The results of exposing a mammal to cholinesterase-inhibiting organophosphorus compounds can be divided into two distinct components—peripheral effects and central effects. The peripheral effects have been largely elucidated [1]. They are antagonized symptomatically by cholinolytic drugs, particularly atropine—both the tertiary atropine and the quaternary methylatropine being effective [2]—and this antagonism can be reinforced by PAM, P2S and other oximes that reactivate the phosphorylated enzyme before it becomes "aged".

The importance of the central effects of cholinesterase inhibition, however, remains to some extent unresolved. These effects can also be antagonized by the parenteral administration of the tertiary form of atropine (in this case the quaternary form is not effective), but there is controversy over the effects of reactivating oxime therapy on the brain: while some authors consider that oximes play a valuable role in this context [3], others regard their importance as negligible [4]. In order to contribute to this debate, a number of relevant parameters have been investigated with the view to drawing some meaningful conclusions.

II. *Summary of experimental studies*

First, the bimolecular rate constants of inhibition, k_i [5], for a number of dimethoxy-, diethoxy- and diisopropoxy phosphates with rat blood and brain cholinesterases were measured *in vitro*. From table 7.1, in which the compounds, bimolecular rate constants and ratios k_i (brain)/k_i (blood) are listed, it can be seen that in each case the brain cholinesterase had a greater reactivity with the organophosphates than had the blood cholinesterase.

Second, the speed at which the organophosphorus compounds penetrate into the central structures is a factor which affects both the severity and the rapidity of onset of symptoms. To investigate this factor, we anaesthetized rats with urethane, injected the compounds intravenously and measured the rise in blood pressure from the carotid artery [6], and the inhibition of brain

Table 7.1. Rates of inhibition by organophosphates of rat blood and brain acetylcholinesterase

	Bimolecular rate constant (k_i) $M^{-1}min^{-1}$		
	Brain acetylcholinesterase	Blood acetylcholinesterase	$\frac{k_i \text{ (brain)}}{k_i \text{ (blood)}}$
Monocrotophos	1.0×10^4	6.0×10^3	1.7
Dicrotophos	1.3×10^4	1.0×10^4	1.3
Mevinphos	1.0×10^6	4.0×10^4	25
Dichlorvos	9.0×10^4	4.0×10^4	2.25
Crotoxyphos	1.7×10^6	5.0×10^5	3.4
Chlorfenvinphos	3.7×10^5	2.5×10^5	1.5
Paraoxon	7.9×10^6	1.3×10^5	60

cholinesterase 2½ minutes after injection. Both magnitudes of effects were dose-related. The steep rise in blood pressure immediately following the injection of the organophosphorus compounds (see table 7.2) is due to a centrally mediated action [6] and thus indicates a rapid entry of the compounds into the brain.

Third, we ascertained *in vitro* whether the rat brain cholinesterases inhibited by these organophosphorus compounds were indeed sensitive to reactivation by oximes. Table 7.3 displays the experimentally estimated reactivation rates: in all cases, the inhibited enzymes were "oxime sensitive" but the rate of reactivation depended on the phosphorylating moiety; that is, the diethoxy compounds had a greater reactivation rate than the dimethoxy compounds, while the diisopropoxy compounds showed the least sensitivity.

Fourth, the *in vivo* effects of the subcutaneous injection of crotoxyphos (a dimethoxy compound) and chlorfenvinphos (a diethoxy compound) were tested in animals which received atropine sulphate either alone or in combi-

Table 7.2. Inhibition of brain acetylcholinesterase and increase in blood pressure following intravenous injection of organophosphates in rats

Organophosphate compound	ID_{50}[a] *µmol/kg*	Increase in blood pressure due to ID_{50} *mm Hg*
Monocrotophos	25.8	22
Dicrotophos	8.8	14
Mevinphos	0.5	34
Dichlorvos	11.7	>35
Crotoxyphos	3.0	30
Chlorfenvinphos	28.8	55
Paraoxon	0.3	30

[a] ID_{50} denotes the intravenous dose that caused 50 per cent inhibition of brain acetylcholinesterase 2½ minutes after injection.

Table 7.3. Rates of reactivation by P2S of phosphorylated rat brain acetylcholinesterase *in vitro*

Organophosphate compound	Mean reactivation rate constant $M^{-1}min^{-1}$
Dimethoxy	
Monocrotophos, Dicrotophos, Crotoxyphos, Dichlorvos, Mevinphos	2.70×10^2
Diethoxy	
Chlorfenvinphos, SD 7779	6.33×10^2
Diisopropoxy	
SD 9588	0.81×10^2

nation with 0.25 mmol/kg P2S or obidoxime, also subcutaneously, upon the onset of symptoms. Table 7.4 indicates that neither P2S nor obidoxime had any effect on the degree of brain cholinesterase inhibition after crotoxyphos administration, but that both oximes reduced the brain-enzyme inhibition resulting from chlorfenvinphos administration for periods of two and six hours, respectively.

Finally, actual measurement of the concentrations of P2S and obidoxime in the brain [7] after parenteral administration did not reveal any evidence for the penetration of oximes into central structures. However, the lower limit of detection by this method is about 4 μg/ml, and it is therefore possible that smaller concentrations may have been present.

How can the beneficial effects of P2S and obidoxime on brain cholinesterase inhibited by chlorfenvinphos, but the absence of effect after crotoxyphos, be explained?

III. *Discussion of results*

Hobbiger has reported [4] that 2-PAM had a negligible effect on the phosphorylated acetylcholinesterase activity of the brains of mice injected with tetraethyl pyrophosphate (TEPP) or the diethyl phosphate, paraoxon, although the oxime was effective when allowed to act on phosphorylated acetylcholinesterase in brain homogenates, as confirmed in the present study. Milošević and Andjelković, however, showed that rats treated with 2-PAM after intoxication with paraoxon had a significantly higher cholinesterase activity in the brain cortex than had rats that had been treated with paraoxon alone [3]. This report followed the finding of

Table 7.4. Effects of P2S and obidoxime on brain acetylcholinesterase inhibition in atropinized rats

Time after injection *hours*	Per cent acetylcholinesterase inhibition			
	P2S		Obidoxime	
	No oxime	With oxime (dose=0.25 mmol/kg)	No oxime	With oxime (dose=0.25 mmol/kg)
Crotoxyphos (dose=2 LD_{50} (300 μmol/kg) *sc*)				
1	47	42	67	64
2	62	58	73	70
4	53	43	70	68
6	52	55	66	66
Chlorfenvinphos (dose =2 LD_{50} (86 μmol/kg) *sc*)				
1	49	35	44	23
2	77	38	74	11
4	60	55	90	35
6	–	–	96	21

Firemark, Barlow and Roth [8] that after a single intravenous dose of ^{14}C-labelled 2-PAM, the concentration of the oxime was significantly higher in the cortex than in other regions of the brain, while Hobbiger and Vojvodić later suggested that P2S reactivated the surface-located phosphorylated functional cholinesterase but had no effect on the intracellular non-functional enzyme in rats intoxicated with paraoxon [9]. In 1965, Erdmann reported significant reactivation of phosphorylated brain cholinesterase and protection by obidoxime *in vivo* following the intoxication of rats with paraoxon [10]. When obidoxime was given 15 minutes before paraoxon, the results reported by Erdmann may have been due to a direct action of obidoxime on paraoxon, as seen when paraoxon was given after 2-PAM [11].

Erdmann found that central respiratory paralysis in the rat after high doses of paraoxon could be reversed by obidoxime but not by P2S [10]. This is compatible with the greater efficiency of obidoxime compared with P2S in combination with atropine sulphate as an antidote to paraoxon intoxication in the rat [2].

The greater efficiency of obidoxime as a reactivator of phosphorylated cholinesterase appears not to depend on its bispyridinium aldoxime structure: Dirks, Scherer, Schmidt and Zimmer [12] showed that the substitution of one oxime group does not alter the reactivating potency of the compound, indicating that only one oxime group is effective as a reactivator. It seems likely, therefore, that obidoxime owes its superiority over P2S to a slower excretion, to slower metabolism after administration *in vivo,* or to both, as was demonstrated by the measurement of plasma concentrations and the volume of distribution in the rat after the subcutaneous injection of equimolar amounts of the oximes. In addition, at physiological pH the proportion of active oxime anions will be higher in bispyridinium aldoximes than in corresponding monoaldoximes [13]. The oximes were more effective in preventing mortality due to intoxication with diethoxy phosphates than in preventing death due to intoxication with dimethoxy phosphates [2]. The mortality of rats intoxicated with chlorfenvinphos was reduced by administration of either P2S or obidoxime, which, *in vivo,* caused a reduction of 62.5 and 59.3 per cent, respectively, in the inhibition of brain cholinesterase, compared with similarly intoxicated animals which had not also received an oxime. Similar experiments after intoxication with crotoxyphos (a dimethoxy phosphate) did not lead to reactivation of inhibited brain cholinesterase *in vivo.*

Direct spectrophotometric analysis of brain tissue for the presence of oximes has not added to the evidence of their penetration into the brain. Erdmann reported [10] that 20 minutes after the intravenous injection of 50 mg/kg of 2-PAM into rats, the oxime concentration in the brain tissue was 0.4 μg/g, while the same author also found a concentration of obidoxime of 11.0 μg/g in the brain 20 minutes after the intravenous injection of 100 mg/kg of this compound: he admitted, however, that the amounts found may have been due to residual oxime in the cerebral blood vessels.

In agreement with Hobbiger and Vojvodić, who were unable to detect either obidoxime or TMB-4 in the rat brain after intravenous injection [14], the present study did not detect oximes in the brain by the spectrophotometric methods employed, yet brain cholinesterase inhibition by the diethoxy phosphates paraoxon [10] and chlorfenvinphos appeared to be reversed. It has been suggested that anticholinesterase intoxication alters the permeability of the blood-brain barrier [15] without there being a causal relationship between brain cholinesterase activity and permeability. As the oxime concentrations in plasma and brain were determined in animals which had not also received anticholinesterase compounds, the actual concentrations in the brain may have been different from those in intoxicated animals. Our results *in vitro* confirm that a concentration of 0.4 μg/g of brain (approximately 2×10^{-6} M), as reported by Erdmann [10], would be capable of causing reactivation of diethoxy-phosphorylated cholinesterase but would hardly affect the dimethoxy- or diisopropoxy-phosphorylated cholinesterase. This may explain the findings that P2S or obidoxime reactivates some phosphorylated cholinesterase in the brain after chlorfenvinphos (a diethoxy phosphate) intoxication but not after crotoxyphos (a dimethoxy phosphate) intoxication.

References

1. Koelle, G. B., ed., *Cholinesterases and Anticholinesterase Agents,* Volume XV of *Handbuch der experimentellen Pharmakologie* (Berlin, Göttingen and Heidelberg, Springer-Verlag, 1963).
2. Natoff, I. L. and Reiff, B., "Quantitative studies of the effect of antagonists on the acute toxicity of organophosphates in rats", *Brit. J. Pharmacol.,* **40,** 124–34 (1970).

3. Milošević, M. P. and Andjelković, D., "Reactivation of paraoxon-inactivated cholinesterase in the rat cerebral cortex by pralidoxime chloride", *Nature,* **210,** 206–207 (1966).
4. Hobbiger, F., "Protection against the lethal effects of organophosphates by pyridine-2-aldoxime methiodide", *Brit. J. Pharmacol.,* **12,** 438–46 (1957).
5. Aldridge, W. N., "Some properties of specific cholinesterase with particular reference to the mechanism of inhibition by diethyl-*p*-nitrophenyl thiophosphate", *Biochem. J.,* **46,** 451–59 (1950).
6. Varagić, V., "The action of eserine on the blood pressure of the rat", *Brit. J. Pharmacol.,* **10,** 349–53 (1955).
7. Sundwall, A., "Plasma concentration curves of N-methyl pyridinium-2-aldoxime methane sulphonate after i.v., i.m. and oral administration in man", *Biochem. Pharmacol.,* **5,** 225–30 (1960).
8. Firemark, H., Barlow, C. F. and Roth, L. J., "The penetration of 2-PAM-C^{14} into brain and the effect of cholinesterase inhibitors on its transport", *J. Pharmacol. Exp. Ther.,* **145,** 252–65 (1964).
9. Hobbiger, F. and Vojvodić, V., "The reactivation by pyridinium aldoximes of phosphorylated acetylcholinesterase in the central nervous system", *Biochem. Pharmacol.,* **16,** 455–62 (1967).
10. Erdmann, W. D., "Vergleichende Untersuchungen über das Penetrationsvermögen einiger esterase-reaktivierenden Oxime in das zentrale Nervensystem", *Arzneimittel-Forsch.,* **15,** 135–39 (1965).
11. Burow, A. C. (1964), quoted in reference [10].
12. Dirks, E., Scherer, A., Schmidt, M. and Zimmer G., "Beziehung zwischen chemischer Struktur und Cholinesterasereaktivierender Wirkung bei einer Reihe neuer unsymmetrischer Pyridinium-salze", *Arzneimittel-Forsch.,* **20,** 55–62 (1970).
13. Bieger, D. and Wassermann, O., "Ionization of cholinesterase reactivating bispyridinium aldoximes", *J. Pharm. Pharmacol.,* **19,** 844–47 (1967).
14. Hobbiger, F. and Vojvodić, V., "The reactivating and antidotal actions of TMB-4 and Toxogonin with particular reference to their effect on phosphorylated acetylcholinesterase in the brain", *Biochem. Pharmacol.,* **15,** 1677–90 (1966).
15. Paulet, G., Marsol, H. and Coq, H., "Cholinésterase et perméabilité de la barrière hématoencéphalique", *J. Physiol. (Paris),* **49,** 342–45 (1957).

8. Kinetic studies on chemical reactions between acetylcholinesterase, toxic organophosphates and pyridinium oximes

K. SCHOENE

Square-bracketed numbers, thus [1], *refer to the list of references on page 100.*

I. *Introduction*

During the past few years we have been investigating some of the chemical reactions that take place between acetylcholinesterase, organophosphates and pyridinium salts (see figure 8.1). The purpose of these investigations was to discover which of these reactions, and also which particular structural features of the pyridinium-salt molecules, determine the protective, or reactivating, properties, and some of the side-effects, of these compounds *in vivo*. Our method was to study the kinetics of these reactions under several experimental conditions *in vitro* in order to obtain data that could clearly be correlated with observed *in vivo* phenomena.

II. *Reactivation and rephosphorylation*

Inhibition by paraoxon in the absence of substrate

Since the reactivation reaction shown in figure 8.1 is reversible, it is reasonable to suppose that, once reactivation of the inhibited acetylcholinesterase has begun, all subsequent events will be determined by the rephosphorylating activity of the phosphorylated oxime and by its decomposition to non-inhibiting products. The synthesis of the therapeutically relevant phosphorylated oximes proved impossible, and so we attempted to study them indirectly by carrying out kinetic studies on the reactivation/rephosphorylation equilibrium [1].

Acetylcholinesterase inhibited with equimolar amounts of paraoxon was incubated with various concentrations of reactivators in the absence of substrate (acetylcholine). The reaction was followed by withdrawing aliquots of the reaction mixture at appropriate intervals and measuring the enzyme activity by the Michel method [2].

Figure 8.2 shows some typical experimental results. In the upper and middle curves, which show the progress of the reaction with Toxogonin at high (5×10^{-4} M) and low (1×10^{-4} M) concentrations, respectively, it is seen that reactivation is very rapid at first, and that an equilibrium is soon

Figure 8.1. Chemical reactions of acetylcholinesterase, organophosphates and pyridinium oximes

Inhibition of acetylcholinesterase	$EH + PX \rightleftharpoons [EH \cdot PX] \longrightarrow EP + HX$
Reactivation of inhibited acetylcholinesterase	$EP + RH \underset{EH}{\overset{EH}{\rightleftharpoons}} RP \longrightarrow POH + \text{other products}$
"Ageing" of inhibited acetylcholinesterase	$EP_{\text{non-aged}} \longrightarrow EP_{\text{aged}}$
"Direct reaction"	$RH + PX \xrightarrow[HX]{} RP \longrightarrow POH + \text{other products}$

Key:

EH=free acetylcholinesterase
PX=organophosphate
EP =phosphorylated (inhibited) acetylcholinesterase
RH=pyridinium oxime
RP =phosphorylated pyridinium oxime

reached. This equilibrium, however, is not stable: there is a slow shift to higher enzyme activity, a shift that can only be caused by the decomposition of the intermediate inhibitor, the phosphorylated oxime. The rate constant of decomposition could be calculated from the rate of increase of enzyme activity after equilibrium. The rate constant of reactivation was calculated as suggested by Reiner in 1965 [3]. Calculation of the equilibrium constant required knowledge of the concentration of the reactivated enzyme, and we determined the molarity of the enzyme solutions by active-site titration with soman [4]. The rate constant of rephosphorylation could then be calculated from the expression $K_{eq}=k_r/k_i$, where K_{eq} is the equilibrium constant, k_r is the reactivation rate constant and k_i the rate constant of rephosphorylation.

The lowest curve in figure 8.2 shows the course of a reaction (in this case with HS-6) in which no equilibrium is achieved, the reaction following exactly first-order kinetics. Such results mean that the rate of decomposition of the phosphorylated oxime is higher than the rate of reactivation of the inhibited acetylcholinesterase.

Calculated data for a number of pyridinium oximes are presented in table 8.1. No equilibrium could be achieved with the pyridinium-2-oximes 2-PAM

Figure 8.2. Rate of reactivation of paraoxon-inhibited acetylcholinesterase by Toxogonin and HS-6

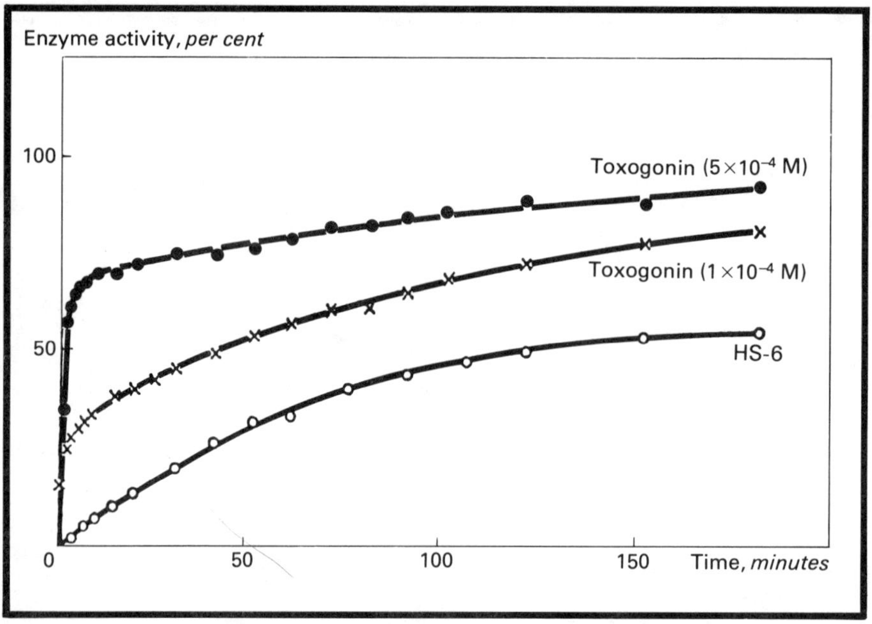

and HS-6 or the pyridinium-4-oxime LüH-40. As mentioned above, this indicates that the decomposition of the phosphorylated oxime proceeds faster than the reactivation reaction, and this can be the result of a poor reactivation potency (HS-6), of a high decomposition rate (2-PAM) or of both (LüH-40). Among the bisquaternary compounds, the rate of decomposition of the phosphorylated oximes decreases with increasing length of the methylene bridge (compare IV and R-21 with TMB-4), but is enhanced by the introduction of an oxygen atom into the bridge (compare Toxogonin with TMB-4, and HI-1 with HS-7). Phosphorylated ketoximes (such as R-23) show relatively low decomposition rates.

A comparison of the rephosphorylation and reactivation rate constants shows that the highest anticholinesterase potencies are exhibited by Toxogonin and TMB-4, compounds that are also among the best reactivators. Moreover, the decomposition rates of the phosphorylated derivatives of these compounds are relatively low, far too low, in fact, to be consistent with the excellent reactivating potency of Toxogonin and TMB-4 *in vivo*. Thus while these results are interesting, they clearly do not provide a suitable explanation for the observed *in vivo* effects of these compounds. In other words, in the case of paraoxon poisoning at least, the toxicity and stability of the phosphorylated oximes cannot be the factors that govern the effectiveness of the reactivators *in vivo*. Thus, another factor must be involved *in vivo* which has not been taken into account in these *in vitro* studies.

Table 8.1. Kinetic data for the *in vitro* reactivation and rephosphorylation of paraoxon-inhibited acetylcholinesterase in the absence of substrate

General formula:

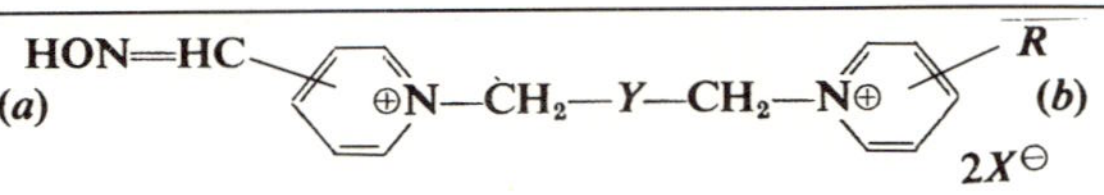

Compound	Substituents[a] a	Y	R	b	X	Oxime concentration ($\times 10^3$) M	Equilibrium constant[b], K_{eq} ($\times 10^6$)	Reactivation rate constant, k_r ($\times 10^{-2}$) $M^{-1}\ min^{-1}$	Rephosphorylation rate constant[c], k_i ($\times 10^{-6}$) $M^{-1}\ min^{-1}$	Decomposition rate constant, k_z ($\times 10^3$) min^{-1}
2-PAM	2	H	–[d]		I	0.1		1.0		≥10
						0.5		0.7		
						1.0		0.5		
4-PAM	4	H	–[d]		I	1.0	6.1	0.04	0.7	<1
LüH-40	4	O-CH_3	–[d]		Cl	1.0		0.06		≥6
HS-6	2	O	$CONH_2$	3	Cl	1.0		0.01		≥1
Toxogonin	4	O	CHNOH	4	Cl	0.1	41.6	11.8	28.4	
						0.5	31.7	10.1	31.8	9.6
TMB-4	4	CH_2	CHNOH	4	Br	0.5	69.9	12.2	17.4	7.0
						1.0	63.6	8.4	13.2	
IV	4	$(CH_2)_2$	CHNOH	4	Br	0.5	38.9	3.1	8.0	
						1.0	35.0	2.6	7.4	<1
R-21	4	CH(OH)-CH(OH)	CHNOH	4	Br	1.0	21.3	2.6	12.2	<1
HS-7	4	CH_2	$CONH_2$	3	Br	1.0	22.4	1.1	4.9	2.7
HI-1	4	O	$CONH_2$	3	Cl	1.0	13.0	2.6	20.0	8.2
HI-4	4	O	H		Cl	1.0	13.2	2.3	17.4	7.4
R-23[e]						1.0	30.0	0.6	1.9	1.7

[a] a and b refer to the positions of the oxime group and R, respectively, in the pyridine rings.

[b] The equilibrium constant, K_{eq}, is defined by $K_{eq}=\frac{[EH]_{eq}[RP]_{eq}}{[RH]\,[EP]_{eq}}$, where $[EH]_{eq}$, $[RP]_{eq}$ and $[EP]_{eq}$ are the concentrations of free enzyme, phosphorylated oxime and inhibited enzyme, respectively, at equilibrium, and [RH] is the concentration of the oxime.

[c] The rephosphorylation rate constant, k_i is derived from $K_{eq}=k_r/k_i$.

[d] Monopyridinium compounds.

[e] Bis-(4-acetoxypyridinium-(1)-methyl)-ether-dioxime dichloride.

Inhibition by paraoxon in the presence of substrate

It is well known that acetylcholine, if present in sufficient concentration, protects acetylcholinesterase against attack by acylating inhibitors *in vitro:* it is possible that this effect is also operative, and of some importance, *in vivo*. However, reactivation in the presence of substrate is possible *in vitro,* provided that the reactivator is present in sufficient concentration. So we continued our studies by investigating the reactivation of paraoxoninhibited acetylcholinesterase in the presence of acetylcholine [5].

The course of the reaction was followed by pH-stat titration, as described by Kitz, Ginsburg and Wilson [6]. We determined the first-order rate constants k_{obs} for various concentrations of reactivator. The ratio k_{obs} : reactivator concentration was found not to be a constant, as might have been expected, but to decrease with increasing reactivator concentration. This behaviour is consistent with the idea that, before reactivation can take place, a complex must be formed between the phosphorylated acetylcholinesterase and the reactivator [7]:

$$\mathrm{EP} + \mathrm{RH} \rightleftharpoons [\mathrm{EP} \cdot \mathrm{RH}] \rightarrow \mathrm{EH} + \mathrm{RP} \rightarrow \ldots$$

(In this case, rephosphorylation is prevented by the presence of substrate.)

The fact that the ratio k_{obs} : reactivator concentration is not a constant can be used to calculate the dissociation constant K_D of the complex and a "reactivity rate constant" k_2; this is done by plotting $1/k_{obs}$ against 1/reactivator concentration from the expression:

$$\frac{1}{k_{obs}} = \frac{K_D}{k_2} \cdot \frac{1}{[\mathrm{RH}]} + \frac{1}{k_2} \quad \text{where } K_D = \frac{[\mathrm{EP}][\mathrm{RH}]}{[\mathrm{EP} \cdot \mathrm{RH}]}$$

Since k_2 is the first-order rate constant at zero reactivator concentration, it is an appropriate measure for the reactivity term. The dissociation constant K_D is a measure of the affinity of the reactivator to the phosphorylated acetylcholinesterase: the larger the value of K_D, the smaller the affinity.

Thus the effectivity of the reactivator *in vitro* can be described by two terms—affinity and chemical reactivity. The combination of the two terms in the expression k_2/K_D is a measure of the overall reactivating potency *in vitro,* a measure which can then be compared with the effectivity *in vivo* [8], the latter being expressed as the reciprocal of the ED_{50} value of the reactivator. Such a comparison is presented in figure 8.3. The fact that there is a good correlation between the *in vivo* and the *in vitro* results means that both the affinity and the reactivity terms are suitable criteria for analysing the effectivity of such oximes against paraoxon poisoning.

Table 8.2 lists the experimental results obtained for some oximes. The data show that lengthening the methylene bridge between the pyridinium nuclei lowers the reactivity of the compound, while the affinity reaches a

Figure 8.3. Relationship between *in vivo* effectivity and *in vitro* reactivating potency of oximes with paraoxon-inhibited acetylcholinesterase

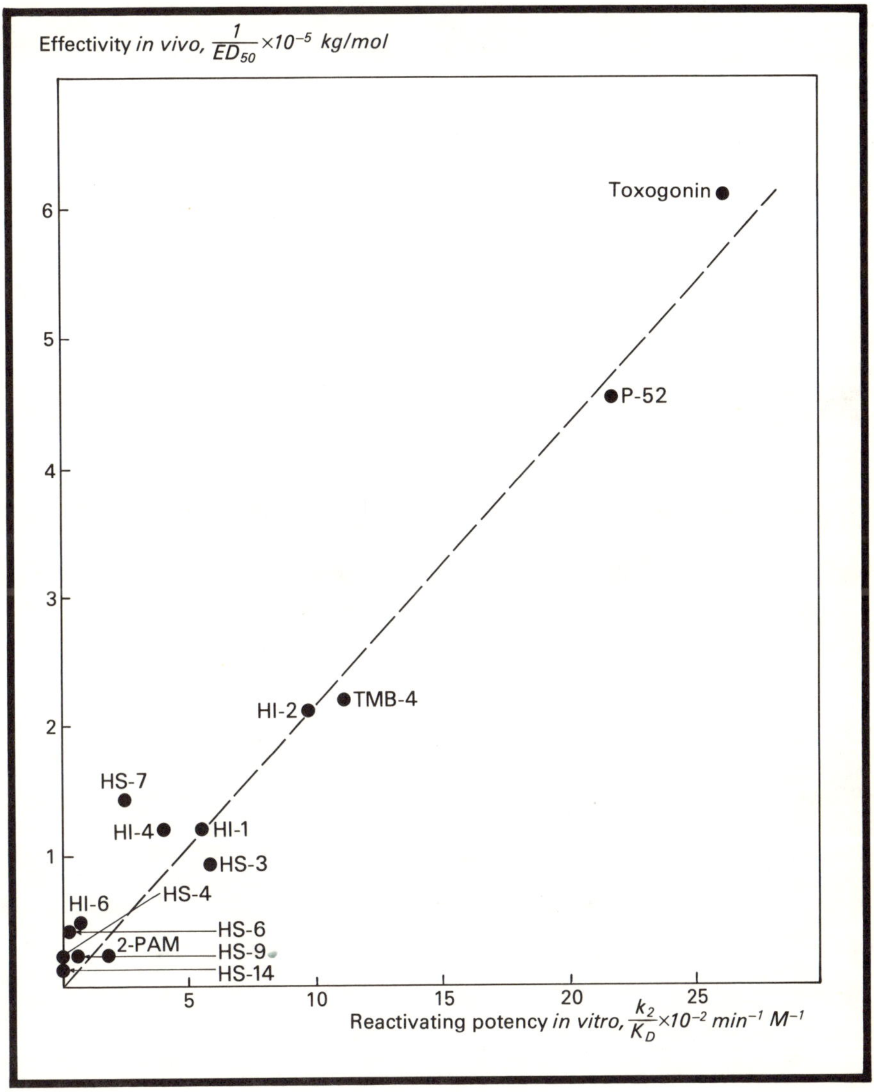

maximum with a bridge composed of three methylene groups (as in TMB-4). Moreover, substitution of the trimethylene bridge (as in TMB-4) with an acetal-aminal bridge (as in Toxogonin) results in an enhancement of the affinity but a lowering of the reactivity. But perhaps the most important and interesting conclusion that can be drawn from these data comes from a comparison of the affinity and reactivity values of compounds with either one or two oxime groups. Hence, a comparison of TMB-4 with HS-7 and

Table 8.2. Kinetic data for the *in vitro* reactivation and rephosphorylation of paraoxon-inhibited acetylcholinesterase in the presence of substrate

General formula:

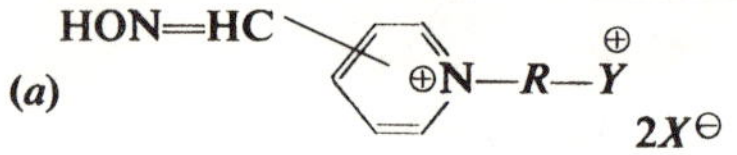

	Substituents[a]				Reactivity rate constant, k_2 ($\times 10^2$) min^{-1} ($\pm$ SE)	Dissociation constant, K_D ($\times 10^4$) M ($\pm$ SE)
Compound	*a*	*R*	*Y*	*X*		
HS-4	2	CH_2-O-CH_2	Pyridine-2-aldoxime	Cl	0.43±0.01	0.88±0.16
3,3-LüH6	3	CH_2-O-CH_2	Pyridine-3-aldoxime	Cl	2.16±0.25	6.91±1.43
Toxoginin	4	CH_2-O-CH_2	Pyridine-4-aldoxime	Cl	10.9±1.8	0.42±0.08
P-52	4	CH_2-O-CH_2	Pyridine-4-aldoxime	HF_2	10.4±0.9	0.48±0.05
R-23[b]					4.82±0.37	3.48±0.85
S-47	2	CH_2-O-CH_2	Pyridine	Cl	2.65±0.42	17.8±4.00
HS-5	2	CH_2-O-CH_2	Pyridine-3-aldoxime	Cl	3.33±0.31	3.58±0.50
HS-6	2	CH_2-O-CH_2	Nicotinamide	Cl	3.20±0.07	18.4±0.8
HS-9	2	CH_2-O-CH_2	Nicotinamide-N-methylamide	Cl	2.76±0.13	19.4±0.2
HI-6	2	CH_2-O-CH_2	Iso-nicotinamide	Cl	4.69±0.29	10.3±0.9
HI-4	4	CH_2-O-CH_2	Pyridine	Cl	10.1±1.3	2.54±0.37
HI-1	4	CH_2-O-CH_2	Nicotinamide	Cl	11.6±1.7	2.11±0.39
HI-2	4	CH_2-O-CH_2	Iso-nicotinamide	Cl	10.6±0.9	1.09±0.10
HS-3	4	CH_2-O-CH_2	Pyridine-2-aldoxime	Cl	10.4±0.3	1.78±0.08
2-PAM	2	CH_3	–[c]	I	4.06±0.10	2.20±0.32
4-PAM	4	CH_3	–[c]	I	1.06±0.07	15.8±2.0
LüH-40	4	CH_2-O-CH_3	–[c]	Cl	1.43±0.06	3.08±0.50
I	4	CH_2	Pyridine-4-aldoxime	Br	36.1±4.2	11.1±2.1
II	4	$(CH_2)_2$	Pyridine-4-aldoxime	Br	43.3±0.8	4.33±1.16
III (TMB-4)	4	$(CH_2)_3$	Pyridine-4-aldoxime	Br	21.3±3.1	1.72±0.45
IV	4	$(CH_2)_4$	Pyridine-4-aldoxime	Br	12.7±1.6	2.16±0.33
V	4	$(CH_2)_5$	Pyridine-4-aldoxime	Br	8.11±0.06	2.73±0.23
R-21 (meso)	4	CH_2-CH(OH)-CH(OH)-CH_2	Pyridine-4-aldoxime	Br	4.44±0.68	0.43±0.09
S-27 (racem)	4	CH_2-CH(OH)-CH(OH)-CH_2	Pyridine-4-aldoxime	Br	4.36±0.25	1.45±0.20
HS-7	4	$(CH_2)_3$	Nicotinamide	Br	17.8±2.5	7.23±1.43
P-18	4	$(CH_2)_3$	Iso-nicotinamide	Br	21.7±3.6	1.82±0.42

[a] *a* refers to the position of the oxime group in the pyridine ring.
[b] Bis-(4-acetoxypyridinium-(1)-methyl)-ether-dioxime dichloride.
[c] Monopyridinium compounds.

P-18, and of Toxogonin with HI-4, HI-1 and HI-2, shows that although the reactivities within each series are almost identical, the affinity values vary widely, the highest affinities in each series being exhibited by TMB-4 and Toxogonin themselves. Both of these compounds have two reactive oxime groups, while the other compounds have only one. This suggests that, in the bisoximes, only one oxime group contributes to the reactivity properties, the second oxime group being mainly responsible for the attachment of the reactivator to the enzyme: in other words, the affinity characteristics of these reactivators are localized mainly in the so-called second pyridine ring.

Table 8.3. Kinetic data for the *in vitro* reactivation and rephosphorylation of tabun-inhibited acetylcholinesterase in the presence of substrate

Reactivator[a]	Reactivity rate constant, k_2 ($\times 10^2$) min^{-1} ($\pm SE$)	Dissociation constant, K_D ($\times 10^3$) M ($\pm SE$)
TMB-4	2.37±0.07	0.68±0.07
HS-7	2.05±0.29	6.56±0.14
P-18	1.89±0.26	2.50±0.15
Toxogonin	2.01±0.37	1.06±0.10
P-52	1.74±0.49	0.80±0.07
HI-4	0.48±0.13	0.94±0.08
HI-2	0.96±0.06	4.98±0.35

[a] The chemical formulae of these compounds are shown in table 8.2.

Inhibition by tabun

The experiments in the presence of substrate were repeated with acetylcholinesterase inhibited with tabun [9], and data from these studies are presented in table 8.3. The reactivities in this case are significantly lower than those found with paraoxon-inhibited acetylcholinesterase, and it is probable that the amido group in tabun lowers the electrophilicity of the phosphorus atom so that attack by the oxime is more difficult. Moreover, the affinity values found with tabun-inhibited acetylcholinesterase are considerably lower than was the case with paraoxon inhibition. But these results are not really surprising: they simply indicate, as might have been expected, that the affinity characteristics of the reactivator are determined by the nature of the phosphoryl residue attached to the active site of the enzyme.

If the *in vivo* effectivity is plotted against the reactivating power *in vitro*, as in figure 8.4 [9], it is seen that there is no correlation. This suggests that, unlike the case of paraoxon inhibition, affinity and reactivity are not suitable criteria for analysing the effectivity of oximes against tabun inhibition. But a detailed study of the graph shows that in all cases the effectivity *in vitro* is higher than should be expected from the *in vivo* results, indicating that some additional toxic process takes place *in vivo*, but not *in vitro*. This process may in some way be related to the "direct reaction" between an organophosphate and an oxime (see figure 8.1): perhaps a phosphorylated oxime is formed in this reaction that is more toxic than the original organophosphate compound.

III. *The direct reaction: inhibition by soman*

The direct reaction was investigated using soman as an inhibitor of acetylcholinesterase [10] since this compound is more convenient for this purpose than tabun. The soman molecule, like tabun, has an asymmetric

Figure 8.4. Relationship between *in vivo* effectivity and *in vitro* reactivating potency of oximes with tabun-inhibited acetylcholinesterase

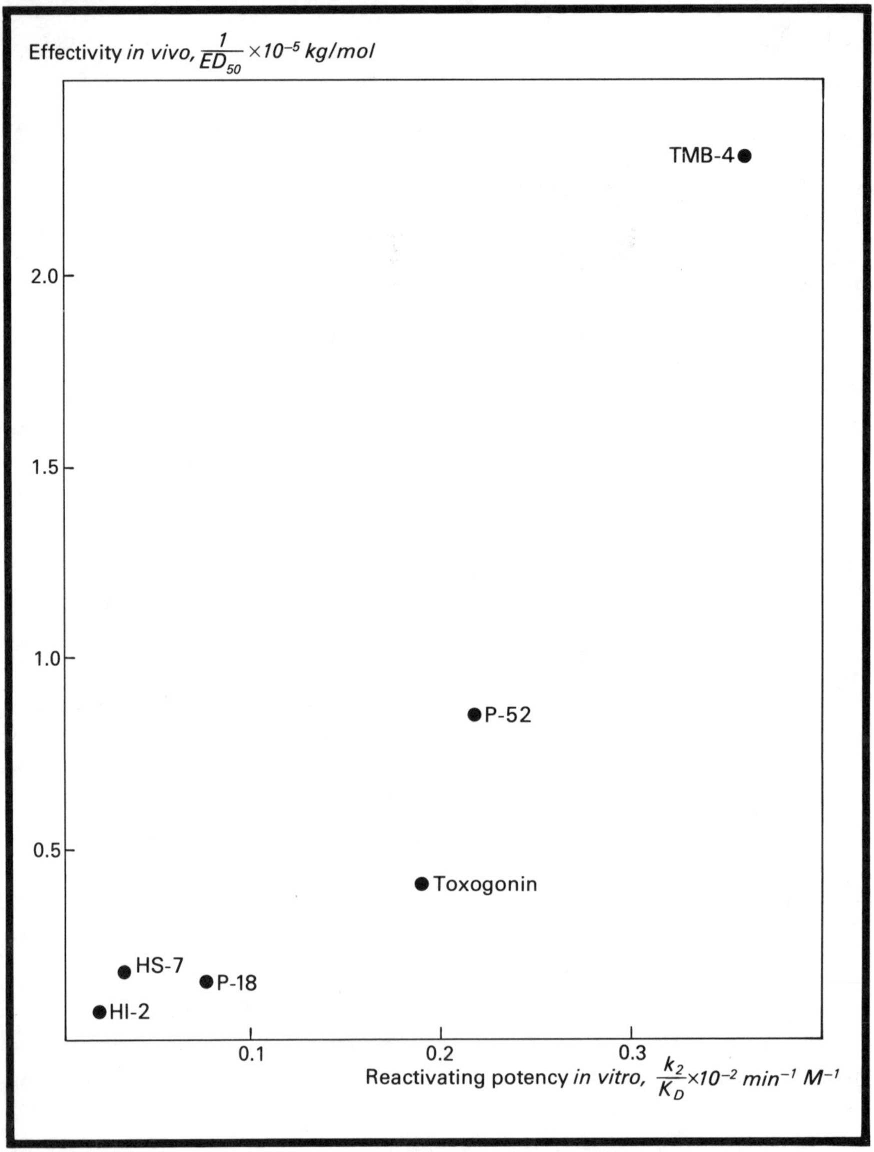

phosphorus atom, but it also has an asymmetric carbon atom, and it therefore exists as four stereoisomers. As shown by Keijer and Wolring [11], two isomers with identical configuration around the phosphorus atom—here called the R_p-configurated isomers—are extremely potent inhibitors of acetylcholinesterase (having inhibition rate constants of the order of 10^7 M^{-1} min^{-1}), while the other two isomers with opposite configuration around the phosphorus atom—the so-called S_p-configurated isomers—are

Figure 8.5. Relationship between oxime concentration and degree of additional acetylcholinesterase inhibition due to the formation of toxic phosphonylated oximes in a "direct reaction" between oxime and soman

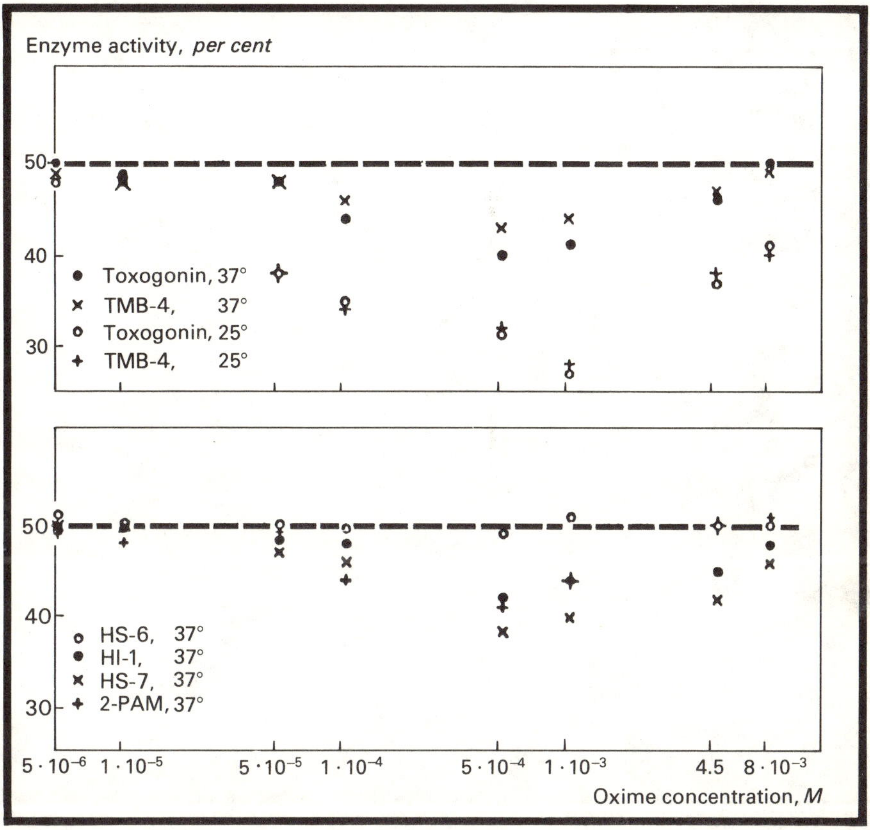

considerably less potent inhibitors (with inhibition rate constants of the order of 10^4 M^{-1} min^{-1}).

Acetylcholinesterase was reacted with a stoichiometric quantity of total soman (which was assumed to contain equal concentrations of each of the four stereoisomers). The rapid inhibition of the enzyme was due almost entirely to the R_p soman (the S_p-configurated isomers, because of their low inhibition rate constants, contributed only 0.1 per cent of the total inhibitory effect) and when it was complete, the enzyme activity had decreased to 50 per cent of the original activity. The reaction was carried out at 37°C and pH 7.6 so that ageing of the inhibited acetylcholinesterase would be rapid, and the reaction mixture was left for 90 minutes to ensure that ageing was complete. At this time, therefore, the reaction mixture contained equal

Figure 8.6. Possible chemical reactions arising from a "direct reaction" between an organophosphate and a pyridinium oxime

1. "Direct reaction"	$(S_p)-PX + RH \longrightarrow RP$
2. Inhibition of acetylcholinesterase	$RP + EH \longrightarrow EP_{non\text{-}aged}$
3. Reactivation of inhibited acetylcholinesterase	$EP_{non\text{-}aged} + RH \underset{?}{\rightleftharpoons} EH + RP$
4. Decomposition of organophosphate	$(S_p)-PX \longrightarrow$ decomposition products
5. Decomposition of phosphorylated oxime	$RP \longrightarrow$ decomposition products
6. "Ageing" of inhibited acetylcholinesterase	$EP_{non\text{-}aged} \longrightarrow EP_{aged}$

Key:

$(S_p)-PX$ = organophosphate (S_p-configurated isomers of soman)
RH = pyridinium oxime
RP = phosphorylated pyridinium oxime
EH = free acetylcholinesterase
EP = phosphorylated (inhibited) acetylcholinesterase

concentrations of aged, non-reactivatable inhibited acetylcholinesterase, uninhibited acetylcholinesterase and unreacted S_p soman. Oxime was then added to this reaction mixture, and any further effect on the enzyme activity could only be the result of a reaction between the oxime and the S_p soman, that is, of a "direct reaction".

The addition of Toxogonin, TMB-4, 2-PAM and some other oximes with similar chemical structures led to a further decrease in enzyme activity: in other words, these oximes reacted with S_p soman to form toxic acetylcholinesterase inhibitors. The addition of HS-6, however, did not result in any further decrease in enzyme activity. The experiments were repeated with varying concentrations of oximes, and the maximum additional decrease in enzyme activity, reached after 30 minutes, was plotted against oxime concentration, as shown in figure 8.5. Clearly, the degree of additional inhibition depends on the concentration of the oxime.

Table 8.4. Rate constants of formation of phosphorylated oximes formed in a "direct reaction" between the oxime (2×10^{-4}M) and soman (5.5×10^{-3}M) at 37°C and pH 7.6

Oxime[a]	Rate constant of formation[b] M^{-1} min^{-1} *(mean ±SE)*
TMB-4	17.2±0.3
Toxogonin	19.0±0.2
HS-7	17.3±0.1
HI-1	19.4±0.3
HS-6	14.9±0.2
2-PAM	17.3±0.1

[a] The chemical formulae of these compounds are shown in table 8.2.
[b] Each value is the mean and standard error of three calculations.

This dependence may be explained by considering the several reactions that can be involved here (see figure 8.6). Reaction 1 was studied with total soman: using the 340-nm maximum of the oxime to follow the course of the reaction, we calculated the rate constants of formation of the phosphorylated oximes (see table 8.4). The phosphorylated derivative of HS-6 has the lowest rate of formation. But furthermore, table 8.1 shows that the paraoxon-phosphorylated derivative of HS-6 decomposed very rapidly, and it is reasonable to suppose that the same would be true for the phosphorylated derivative produced from soman. Thus HS-6 causes no additional inhibition of acetylcholinesterase (at any concentration) because its phosphorylated derivative decomposes very rapidly (reaction 5 in figure 8.6).

The relatively minor effect of the other oximes at low concentrations can also be explained on this basis: the rate of formation of the phosphorylated oxime is so slow that their decomposition rates would be sufficient to ensure that high concentrations of these inhibitors did not accumulate. The minor effect of the oximes at high concentrations, however, must be explained in another way. Probably the reactivation reaction (reaction 3 in figure 8.6) prevents ageing of the inhibited enzyme (reaction 6 in figure 8.6) and hence a lasting inhibition. This could be shown by reactivation experiments with non-aged, R_p-soman-inhibited acetylcholinesterase: high oxime concentrations (5×10^{-3} M to 5×10^{-2} M) produced very rapid reactivation, while low oxime concentrations led to a further decrease in enzyme activity, except in the case of HS-6, which reactivated the inhibited acetylcholinesterase at all concentrations down to 5×10^{-5} M.

The results presented in figure 8.5 can now be summarized. High concentrations of oxime produce rapid reactivation and hence the degree of additional inhibition is small. At low oxime concentrations, the rate of formation of the phosphorylated oxime is too low to produce any significant degree of additional inhibition. And therefore, the highest degree of additional inhibition should be expected, as indeed is shown in figure 8.5, with medium oxime concentration. The degree of inhibition is, of course, temperature-dependent: at lower temperatures than those used in these investigations, the inhibition rate increases.

The practical conclusion that emerges from these latter experiments is that in the case of soman poisoning, the use of oximes such as Toxogonin and TMB-4 as antidotes is contra-indicated, because of the formation of additional toxic compounds as a result of a reaction between the oxime and the less toxic isomers of soman.

References

1. Schoene, K., "Reaktivierung von O,O-Diäthylphosphorylacetylcholinesterase; Reaktivierungs-Rephosphorylierungs-Gleichgewicht", *Biochem. Pharmacol.*, **21,** 163–70 (1972).
2. Michel, H. O., "An electrometric method for the determination of red blood cell and plasma cholinesterase activity", *J. Lab. Clin. Med.*, **34,** 1564–68 (1949).
3. Reiner, E., "Oxime reactivation of erythrocyte cholinesterase inhibited by ethyl-*p*-nitrosophenyl ethylphosphonate", *Biochem. J.*, **97,** 710–14 (1965).
4. Schoene, K., "'Titration' of acetylcholinesterase with soman", *Biochem. Pharmacol.*, **20,** 2527–29 (1971).
5. Schoene, K. and Strake, E. M., "Reaktivierung von O,O-Diäthylphosphorylacetylcholinesterase; Affinität und Reaktivität einiger Pyridiniumoxime", *Biochem. Pharmacol.*, **20,** 1041–51 (1971).
6. Kitz, R. J., Ginsburg, S. and Wilson, J. B., "Activity-structure relationships in the reactivation of diethylphosphoryl acetylcholinesterase by phenyl-1-methylpyridinium-ketoximes", *Biochem. Pharmacol.*, **14,** 1471–77 (1965).
7. Green, A. L. and Smith, H. J., "The reactivation of cholinesterase inhibited with organophosphorus compounds", *Biochem. J.*, **68,** 28–35 (1958).
8. Oldiges, H. and Schoene, K., "Pyridinium- und Imidazoliumsalze als Antidote gegenüber Soman- und Paraoxonvergiftungen bei Mäusen", *Arch. Toxikol.*, **26,** 293–305 (1970).
9. Schoene, K. and Oldiges, H., "Die Wirkungen von Pyridinium-salzen gegenüber Tabun- und Sarinvergiftungen *in vivo* und *in vitro*", *Arch. Int. Pharmacodyn. Ther.*, **204,** 110–23 (1973).
10. Schoene, K., "Phosphonyloxime aus Soman; Bildung und Reaktion mit Acetylcholinesterase *in vitro*", *Biochem. Pharmacol.*, **22,** 2997–3003 (1973).
11. Keijer, J. H. and Wolring, G. J., "Stereospecific aging of phosphonylated cholinesterases", *Biochim. Biophys. Acta*, **185,** 465–68 (1969).

9. Comparative studies of the protective effects of pyridinium compounds against organophosphate poisoning

H. OLDIGES

Square-bracketed numbers, thus [1], *refer to the list of references on page 108.*

I. *Introduction*

Although the highly toxic nature of organophosphorus compounds has been known for many years, there are still serious limitations in the antidotal therapy available against poisoning by these compounds. Symptomatic therapy with atropine [1] or centrally acting cholinolytics [2–3] is useful, but against some organophosphates—the most important examples being the chemical-warfare nerve agent soman and the ordinary commercial compound dimethoate—there is a lack of causally acting antidotes that can support this therapy by reactivating the inhibited acetylcholinesterase.

The monopyridinium oxime 2-PAM (pralidoxime) was the first compound to be used as a reactivator of inhibited acetylcholinesterase [4]. Subsequent systematic investigations resulted in the development of other reactivators, the dioximes TMB-4 [5] and Toxogonin (obidoxime) [6]. But even good reactivators, such as Toxogonin and TMB-4, which have been used successfully in treating poisoning by parathion, show no antidotal effect against soman intoxication in animal experiments, and have even been found to have negative effects [7]. In other words, although poisoning by other organophosphates, including the chemical-warfare agents tabun and sarin, can be treated therapeutically [8], none of the known reactivating agents can reverse the effects of soman intoxication by reactivating the inhibited enzyme *in vivo*. On the other hand, certain oxime-free bispyridinium salts do exhibit an antidotal effect, but this effect is not based on enzyme reactivation, and the mechanism of action is still unclear.

One of the aims of the search for new reactivating antidotes is to find agents with a sufficiently high reactivity and affinity to the inhibited acetylcholinesterase to reactivate it before it becomes aged. This requirement is of primary importance for those organophosphate intoxications in which the phosphonylated (inhibited) acetylcholinesterase is dealkylated (aged), and thus made resistant to reactivation, within a few minutes, as is the case with soman intoxication. Another aim is to develop antidotes able to penetrate the blood-brain barrier and thus reactivate inhibited acetyl-

Table 9.1. Chemical structures of monopyridinium compounds tested as antidotes against organophosphate intoxication

General formula:

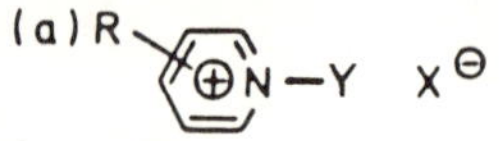

Compound	Substituents[a] *a*	*R*	*Y*	*X*
HP 20	2	NHCHO	CH_3	I
HP 27	4	CH=NOH	$CH_2CH_2C(CH_3)_3$	I
HP 28	2	$CH{=}NNHCONH_2$	CH_3	I
HP 32	2	CH=NOH	$CH_2O(CH_2)_{11}CH_3$	I
HP 33	3	CH=NOH	$CH_2O(CH_2)_{11}CH_3$	I
HP 34	4	CH=NOH	$CH_2O(CH_2)_{11}CH_3$	I
HP 36	3	$NHCOCH_3$	CH_3	I
HH 24	3	$NHCONH_2$	CH_3	I
HH 25	2	$NHCONH_2$	CH_3	I
HH 30	4	$CH{=}CHC_6H_5$	CH_3	I
HH 32	2	$CH{=}CHC_6H_5$	CH_3	I
HH 34	4	$CH{=}CHCONH_2$	CH_3	I
HH 35	2	$NHCONH(\alpha)C_5H_4N$	CH_3	I
HH 36	4	CH=NOH	$CH_2OCHCH_3C(CH_3)_3$	Cl
HH 37	3	$CONH_2$	$CH_2OCHCH_3C(CH_3)_3$	Cl
HH 50	3	$CH{=}CHCONH_2$	CH_3	I
HH 53	3	$NHCONH(\alpha)C_5H_4N$	CH_3	I
HH 55	3	$NHCONH(\gamma)C_5H_4N$	CH_3	I

[a] *a* refers to the position of *R* in the pyridine ring.

cholinesterase in the central nervous system. It is known that after organophosphate poisoning, the acetylcholinesterase level in the brain remains extremely low for several weeks, which might lead to delayed effects. Passage through the blood-brain barrier can only be achieved by increasing the lipophilic character of the antidotes so that they can be effective in therapeutically practicable doses. However, in experimental studies, lipophically substituted aliphatic oximes failed to have the expected success [9].

Another possible approach to protection against soman intoxication is to find chemical compounds which accelerate the hydrolysis of soman before it is able to react with the acetylcholinesterase. One promising example of such compounds is the agent HS-6—an asymmetrical bispyridinium aldoxime with a nicotinamide group on the second pyridine ring—which is able to react with soman very quickly under physiological conditions. Such antidotes show good results when given prophylactically, because of their ability to produce a rapid direct reaction.

II. *Material and methods*

This paper presents the results of investigations into the antidotal effects of 18 monopyridinium and 25 bispyridinium compounds (these compounds are listed in tables 9.1 and 9.2) against intoxications with the organophosphates

Table 9.2. Chemical structures of bispyridinium compounds tested as antidotes against organophosphate intoxication

General formula: 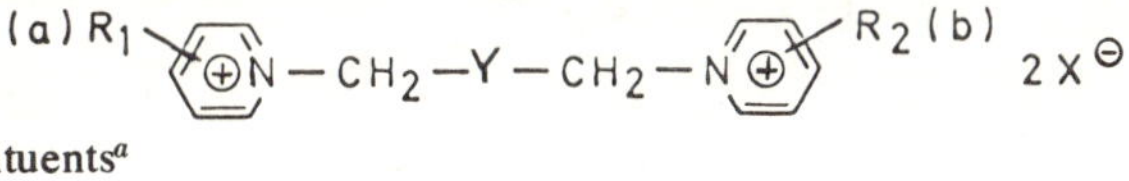

Compound	Substituents[a] *a*	R_1	Y	*b*	R_2	X
HP 9	2	CH=NOH	O	2	NH_2	Cl
HP 15	4	CH=NOH	CONHCO	4	CH=NOH	Cl
HP 23	2	CH=NOH	O	4	NH_2	Cl
HP 35	4	CH=NOH	O	2	$CONH_2$	Cl
HP 42	3	$CONHCH_2CH_2OH$	O	3	$CONHCH_2CH_2OH$	Cl
HP 44	4	$CONHCH_2CH_2OH$	O	4	$CONHCH_2CH_2OH$	Cl
HP 45	4	CH=NOH	O	4	$CH{=}NNHCONH_2$	Cl
HP 48	2	CH=NOH	O	3	$CH{=}NNHCONH_2$	Cl
HP 49	2	CH=NOH	O	2	$CH{=}NNHCONH_2$	Cl
HP 50	2	CH=NOH	O	3	NHCHO	Cl
HP 51	4	CH=NOH	O	4	NHCHO	Cl
HP 70	3	$CH{=}NNHCONH_2$	O	3	$CH{=}NNHCONH_2$	Cl
HP 71	4	$CH{=}NNHCONH_2$	O	4	$CH{=}NNHCONH_2$	Cl
HP 73	3	$NHCOCH_3$	O	3	$NHCONH_2$	Cl
HP 74	2	CH=NOH	O	3	$CONHCH_2CH_2OH$	Cl
HP 75	2	CH=NOH	O	4	$CONHCH_2CH_2OH$	Cl
HH 8	2	CH=NOH	O	3	$NHCONH_2$	Cl
HH 9	4	CH=NOH	O	3	$NHCONH_2$	Cl
HH 20	3	$NHCONH_2$	O	3	$NHCONH_2$	Cl
HH 21	2	CH=NOH	O	4	$CH{=}CHC_6H_4(p)CH{=}NOH$	Cl
HH 27	3	$CONH_2$	–	3	$CONH_2$	Br
HH 28	4	$CH{=}CHC_6H_5$	O	4	$CH{=}CHC_6H_5$	Cl
HH 29	3	$CONH_2$	OC_2H_4O	3	$CONH_2$	I
HH 31	4	$CONH_2$	OC_2H_4O	4	$CONH_2$	Cl
HH 33	4	CH=NOH	CH_2	4	$CH{=}CHC_6H_5$	Br

[a] *a* and *b* refer to the positions of R_1 and R_2, respectively, in the pyridine rings.

paraoxon, tabun, sarin and soman. The experiments were performed on female NMRI mice with an average body weight of 23 grams. The animals were housed in Macrolon cages at a temperature of 22°C and were fed with standard-diet pellets. Drinking water was given *ad libitum*.

Solutions of the organophosphates were prepared from standard solutions of the pure compounds in absolute ethanol by mixing with 0.9 per cent NaCl solution immediately before use. The compounds tested as antidotes were supplied by Professor I. Hagedorn, Freiburg, FR Germany, and fresh solutions in distilled water were prepared every day. The organophosphates were administered subcutaneously, and the antidotes intramuscularly.

Tests involving paraoxon poisoning were carried out without atropine protection: intoxication was induced simply by administering 2 LD_{50} of the compound. In the experiments on intoxication with tabun, sarin and soman, on the other hand, atropine (10 mg/kg) was given together with the antidote to be tested, and in order to eliminate the protection due to atropine from the results, the organophosphates were administered in doses which, in the absence of any other antidote, would just overcome the antidotal effects of the atropine and guarantee the death of the animals: for tabun, this dosage was estimated as 3 LD_{50} (1.53 mg/kg), for sarin 2 LD_{50} (0.64 mg/kg) and for soman 1.2 LD_{50} (0.28 mg/kg). The antidotes were given either prophylactically (five minutes prior to intoxication) or therapeutically (one minute after intoxication).

As a criterion of the antidotal effects, we calculated the ED_{50} value of the antidote against the chosen dose of the organophosphate. A group of eight animals was used for each test, and evaluation of the results was carried out 24 hours after commencing the experiments.

III. *Results and discussion*

Monopyridinium compounds

Of the 18 monopyridinium compounds, tested, only two (HP 32 and HP 34) showed any protective effect against soman intoxication. In both of these compounds, the substituent on the pyridinium nitrogen is a methoxydodecyl residue and the aldoxime group is in position 2 or 4. In fact, the experimental results, shown in table 9.3, indicate that an aldoxime group in position 4, together with a methoxydodecyl residue on the pyridinium nitrogen, is the most advantageous molecular arrangement (as in compound HP 34). Even minor differences in structure appear to destroy the effect of these compounds. Compound HP 33, for example, which has a methoxydodecyl group on the pyridinium nitrogen, but in which the aldoxime group is at position 3, had no effect against soman. And compounds with the aldoxime group at position 4, but with a shorter-chain substitutent on the pyridinium nitrogen, also had no effect, as in compounds HH 36, in which the substituent is a methylpinacolether residue, and HP 27, which has a 3-dimethylbutyl residue at the nitrogen. Compound HP 27, however, was found to have an effect against sarin intoxication. None of the compounds tested showed any protective effect against intoxication with paraoxon or tabun.

Bispyridinium compounds

Better results were obtained with the bispyridinium derivatives. Of the 25 compounds tested, 10 were effective against soman intoxication, eight against sarin, two against tabun and 11 against paraoxon.

The experimental results, shown in table 9.4, indicate that the aldoxime group in position 2 of the pyridine ring is the structural feature most favourable for antidotal effect against soman (as in compounds HP 75, HP 74, HP 50 and HH 8). Moreover, a carboxamide or formamide group in position 3 of the so-called second pyridine ring is especially advantageous (as in compounds HP 74, HP 50 and HH 8). The results obtained with

Table 9.3. Monopyridinium compounds: antidotal effects against organophosphate intoxication in female NMRI mice

Antidote	Molecular weight	LD_{50} *mg/kg*	Type of application[a]	ED_{50} against organophosphate intoxication *mg/kg*			
				Soman[b]	Sarin[c]	Tabun[d]	Paraoxon[e]
HP 20	264	0	Proph	–	0	–	–
			Ther	–	0	–	–
HP 27	334	419.84	Proph	–	27.21	–	–
			Ther	–	26.87	–	–
HP 28	306.1	0	Proph	–	–	–	–
			Ther	–	–	–	–
HP 32	356.9	0	Proph	46.44	–	–	–
			Ther	35.13	–	–	–
HP 33	356.9	0	Proph	–	–	–	–
			Ther	–	–	–	–
HP 34	356.9	0	Proph	31.20	–	–	–
			Ther	30.75	–	–	–
HP 36	278.1	0	Proph	–	0	0	–
			Ther	–	0	0	–
HH 24	279.1	0	Proph	–	–	–	–
			Ther	–	–	–	–
HH 25	272.1	0	Proph	–	–	–	–
			Ther	–	–	–	–
HH 30	323.2	0	Proph	–	–	–	–
			Ther	–	–	–	–
HH 32	323.2	0	Proph	–	–	–	–
			Ther	–	–	–	–
HH 34	290.1	218.70	Proph	–	0	0	–
			Ther	–	0	0	–
HH 35	356.2	0	Proph	–	0	0	–
			Ther	–	0	0	–
HH 36	261	0	Proph	–	0	0	–
			Ther	–	0	0	–
HH 37	272.8	0	Proph	–	0	0	–
			Ther	–	0	0	–
HH 50	290.1	0	Proph	–	–	–	–
			Ther	–	–	–	–
HH 53	356.2	0	Proph	–	–	–	–
			Ther	–	–	–	–
HH 55	355.2	0	Proph	–	–	–	–
			Ther	–	–	–	–

Key:
0 = not tested
– = without effect

[a] Proph=prophylactic administration, intramuscularly, five minutes before the intoxication. Ther=therapeutic administration, intramuscularly, one minute after the intoxication.
[b] Intoxicating dose of soman=1.2 LD_{50} subcutaneously, given together with atropine, 10 mg/kg intramuscularly.
[c] Intoxicating dose of sarin=2 LD_{50} subcutaneously, given together with atropine, 10 mg/kg intramuscularly.
[d] Intoxicating dose of tabun=3 LD_{50} subcutaneously, given together with atropine, 10 mg/kg intramuscularly.
[d] Intoxicating dose of paraoxon=2 LD_{50}, given without atropine.

Table 9.4. Bispyridinium compounds: antidotal effects against organophosphate intoxication in female NMRI mice

Antidote	Molecular weight	LD_{50} *mg/kg*	Type of application[a]	ED_{50} against organophosphate intoxication *mg/kg*			
				Soman[b]	Sarin[c]	Tabun[d]	Paraoxon[e]
HP 9	331	0	Proph	–	0	–	21.67
			Ther	–	0	–	21.04
HP 15	414	0	Proph	–	0	–	–
			Ther	–	0	–	–
HP 23	349	129.00	Proph	–	0	–	36.64
			Ther	–	0	–	33.84
HP 35	359.2	0	Proph	–	0	–	23.89
			Ther	–	0	–	17.73
HP 42	447.1	0	Proph	–	–	–	–
			Ther	–	–	–	–
HP 44	447	0	Proph	–	–	–	–
			Ther	–	–	–	–
HP 45	401	0	Proph	–	10.84	17.38	2.17
			Ther	–	12.54	18.90	1.44
HP 48	401	0	Proph	–	4.66	21.94	2.54
			Ther	–	4.65	25.55	2.47
HP 49	401	0	Proph	–	4.05	0	2.93
			Ther	–	3.76	0	2.82
HP 50	359	92.45	Proph	29.86	5.57	–	19.39
			Ther	27.61	5.85	–	14.97
HP 51	359	0	Proph	27.79	6.77	0	4.17
			Ther	29.31	7.15	0	3.93
HP 70	443	37.55	Proph	21.41	–	–	–
			Ther	19.17	–	–	–
HP 71	443	30.85	Proph	15.22	–	–	–
			Ther	14.67	–	–	–
HP 73	387	0	Proph	39.74	–	–	–
			Ther	33.43	–	–	–
HP 74	403	522	Proph	6.50	9.92	–	–
			Ther	9.98	8.87	–	–
HP 75	400	0	Proph	21.64	3.24	–	26.95
			Ther	18.27	3.38	–	24.68
HH 8	392.2	103.16	Proph	12.17	3.06	–	21.67
			Ther	11.74	2.25	–	20.38
HH 9	374.2	87.83	Proph	32.60	0	0	2.67
			Ther	28.73	0	0	2.46
HH 20	407.3	0	Proph	–	0	0	–
			Ther	–	0	0	–
HH 21	515.4	17.20	Proph	12.66	0	0	–
			Ther	12.81	0	0	–
HH 27	450.1	344.00	Proph	–	–	–	–
			Ther	–	–	–	–
HH 28	471.4	215.00	Proph	–	–	–	–
			Ther	–	–	–	–
HH 29	586.2	344.00	Proph	–	–	–	–
			Ther	–	–	–	–
HH 31	403.3	0	Proph	–	–	–	–
			Ther	–	–	–	–
HH 33	541.3	0	Proph	–	0	0	–
			Ther	–	0	0	–

Key:
0 = not tested
– = without effect

compound HP 74 are remarkable: this compound has a low toxicity and exhibits a good antidotal effect against soman and sarin intoxication.

A positive effect against soman was also seen with bis-semicarbazones (compounds HP 71 and HP 70). However, the replacement of one of the two semicarbazone residues with an aldoxime group (as in compounds HP 45, HP 48 and HP 49) destroys the antidotal effect against soman. On the other hand, these compounds showed good effects against sarin, tabun and paraoxon intoxication. A styrylpyridinium oxime (compound HH 21) showed a low ED_{50} against soman but its toxicity was so high that it is without any practical importance.

These investigations confirm our previous findings [7] that even oxime-free agents (compounds HP 73, HP 71 and HP 70) can be effective antidotes against soman intoxication.

The only compounds to show an antidotal effect against sarin were those with one oxime group on a pyridine ring (compounds HP 75, HP 74, HP 51, HP 50, HP 49, HP 48, HP 45 and HH 8) [10]. Against tabun, only two semicarbazone derivatives (compounds HP 48 and HP 45) were effective, and each had one oxime group on the other pyridine ring.

Recently a number of biochemical investigations have been carried out into the nature of the phosphorylated and phosphonylated oximes formed as intermediates during the acetylcholinesterase-reactivation process [11–14]. It was found that phosphorylated oximes formed by good reactivators such as Toxogonin and TMB-4 during reactivation of paraoxon-inhibited acetylcholinesterase can themselves be potent inhibitors of the enzyme: in fact, their inhibition potencies can exceed that of paraoxon by a factor of up to 10.

Phosphonylated oximes formed by Toxogonin, TMB-4 and other similar compounds have also been found to have a considerable inhibitory effect on acetylcholinesterase. Thus the failure, and the negative effects, of treatment with Toxogonin or TBM-4 *in vivo* following soman intoxication can be explained by the formation of highly toxic phosphonylated oximes. But the phosphonylated oximes formed between soman-inhibited acetylcholinesterase and bispyridinium-2-aldoximes did not show any inhibitory effect on the enzyme. These findings agree well with our *in vivo* results: compounds HP 75, HP 74, HP 50, HH 21 and HH 8, all of which are bispyridinium-2-aldoximes, were found to be effective against soman intoxication.

Notes to table 9.4:

[a] Proph=prophylactic administration, intramuscularly, five minutes before the intoxication. Ther=therapeutic administration, intramuscularly, one minute after the intoxication.

[b] Intoxicating dose of soman=1.2 LD_{50} subcutaneously, given together with atropine, 10 mg/kg intramuscularly.

[c] Intoxicating dose of sarin=2 LD_{50} subcutaneously, given together with atropine, 10 mg/kg intramuscularly.

[d] Intoxicating dose of tabun=3 LD_{50} subcutaneously, given together with atropine, 10 mg/kg intramuscularly.

[e] Intoxicating dose of paraoxon=2 LD_{50}, given without atropine.

IV. *Conclusions*

Our results demonstrate that the protective effect of a substance against an organophosphate intoxication depends both on the structure of the antidote and on the structure of the organophosphate. This suggests that research aimed at developing antidotes with a broad range of application together with a high effectiveness is unlikely to be very fruitful, and this presents a serious problem for antidote research.

References

1. Wills, J. H., "Pharmacological antagonists of the anticholinesterase agents", in Koelle, G. B., ed., *Cholinesterases and Anticholinesterase Agents,* Volume XV of *Handbuch der experimentellen Pharmakologie* (Berlin, Göttingen and Heidelberg, Springer-Verlag, 1963) pp. 883–920.
2. Coleman, I. W., Little P. E., Patton G. E. and Bannard, R. A. B., "Cholinolytics in the treatment of anticholinesterase poisoning. IV. The effectiveness of five binary combinations of cholinolytics with oximes in the treatment of organophosphorus poisoning", *Can. J. Physiol. Pharmacol.,* **44,** 745–64 (1966).
3. Jović, R. and Vojvodić, V., "Akutna taksičnost; terapijske mogućnosti pri eksperimentalnim trovanjima somanom", *Vojnosanitet. Pregl.,* **28,** 186–89 (1971).
4. Wilson, I. B. and Ginsburg, S., "A powerful reactivator of alkylphosphate-inhibited acetylcholinesterase", *Biochim. Biophys. Acta,* **18,** 168–70 (1955).
5. Hobbiger, F., O'Sullivan, D. B. and Sadler, P. W., "New potent reactivators of acetocholinesterase inhibited by tetraethyl pyrophosphate", *Nature,* **182,** 1498–99 (1958).
6. Lüttringhaus, A. and Hagedorn, I., "Quartäre Hydroxyiminomethyl-pyridiniumsalze", *Arzneimittel-Forsch.,* **14,** 1–5 (1964).
7. Oldiges, H. and Schoene, K., "Pyridinium- und Imidazoliumsalze als Antidoten gegenüber Soman- und Paraoxonvergiftungen bei Mäusen", *Arch. Toxikol.,* **26,** 293–305 (1970).
8. Heilbronn, E. and Tolagen, B., "Toxogonin in sarin, soman and tabun poisoning", *Biochem. Pharmacol.,* **14,** 73–77 (1965).
9. Chwalinski, S., Sawicki, K. and Gorski, A., "Poszukiwanie nowych reaktywatorow cholinesterazy unieczynnionej zwiazkami fosforoorganicznymi", *Rocz. Chem.,* **38,** 919–24 (1964).
10. Oldiges, H. and Schoene, K., "Antidote gegen Alkylphosphatvergiftungen; Struktur-Wirkungs-Beziehungen *in vivo* und *in vitro*", *Forschungsbericht Wehrtechnick,* **72** (8), 1–33 (1972).
11. Schoene, K., "Phosphonyloxime aus Soman; Bildung und Reaktion mit Acetylcholinesterase *in vitro*", *Biochem. Pharmacol.,* **22,** 2997–3003 (1973).
12. Hagedorn, I., Gündel, W. H. and Schoene, K., "Reaktivierung phosphorylierter Acetylcholinesterase mit Oximen: Beitrag zum Studium des Reaktionsablaufes", *Arzneimittel-Forsch.,* **19,** 603–606 (1969).
13. Schoene, K., "Reaktivierung von O,O-Diäthylphosphorylacetylcholinesterase; Reaktivierungs-Rephosphorylierungs-Gleichgewicht", *Biochem. Pharmacol.,* **21,** 163–70 (1972).
14. Nenner, M., "Phosphonylierte Aldoxime. Hemmwirkung auf Acetylcholinesterase und hydrolytischer Abbau", *Biochem. Pharmacol.,* **23,** 1255–62 (1974).

10. Limitations of pharmacotherapy in organophosphate intoxications

S. RUMP and J. FAFF

Square-bracketed numbers, thus [1], *refer to the list of references on page 115.*

I. *Introduction*

Three general factors largely determine the efficacy of pharmacotherapy in organophosphate intoxication: (*a*) the time interval between intoxication and the start of treatment; (*b*) the particular organophosphate involved; and (*c*) the strength and mode of action of the drug used in the treatment. The first two factors are reasonably well understood and require no detailed explanation: only the third one will be discussed in this chapter.

Chemicals may be used to antagonize the toxic effects of organophosphates in many ways, for example, by destroying the organophosphate in the body before it reaches functional sites, by reducing the rate of synthesis and release of acetylcholine at nerve endings, by protecting the means of access of acetylcholine to receptor sites, or by reactivating inhibited acetylcholinesterase. At present, only the last two have any practical importance, although recently there have been attempts to include in experimental pharmacotherapy chemicals with other modes of action, namely anti-convulsant drugs and veratrine-like agents.

II. *Pharmacotherapy*

The toxic effects of organophosphate anticholinesterase agents can be classified as muscarinic, nicotinic or central neuronal.

Cholinolytic compounds

Among the drugs used to combat the muscarinic effects of organophosphates, atropine is the most popular, although when used alone, its efficacy in experimental therapy is rather poor. Administration of atropine elevates the LD_{50} of organophosphates 1.5–4 times, depending on the time when therapy is started, the kind of organophosphate involved and the experimental animal used. However, it has been reported that some other cholinolytic drugs multiply the LD_{50} of organophosphates even more than atropine. The most interesting of these are derivatives of glycollic acid, such

Table 10.1. Effects of various cholinolytics (used in conjunction with P2S (30 mg/kg)) on the toxicity of sarin in the mouse

Drug	Dose *μmol/kg*	Elevation of LD_{50} of sarin	Efficacy relative to atropine
Atropine sulphate	50	2.03	1
l-N′-diethylaminoethyl α-cyclohexyl-α-(N-thineyl) glycollate d-bitartrate (Win 5779-6)	50	3.7	1.8
l-tropyl-α-methyltropate	50	2.8	1.4
N-2′-diethylaminoethyl-1-phenyl-cyclopentane carboxylate HCl (parpanit)	50	3.2	1.6
4′-N-methylpiperidyl-l-phenyl-cyclopentane carboxylate HCl (G-3063)	50	4.7	2.3

Source: Coleman, I. W., Little, P. E. and Bannard, R. A. B., "Cholinolytics in the treatment of anticholinesterase poisoning. I. The effectiveness of certain cholinolytics in combination with an oxime for treatment of sarin poisoning", *Can. J. Biochem. Physiol.*, **40,** 815–26 (1962).

as parpanit and N-ethyl-2-pyrrolidylmethyl cyclopentylphenyl glycollate (PMCG) [1], and derivatives of aromatically substituted carboxylic acids, such as 4′-N-methylpiperidyl-1-phenylcyclopentane carboxylate (G-3063) [2]. The efficacy of these drugs, however, does not exceed five LD_{50} of organophosphate [3] (see table 10.1). And, unfortunately, therapeutic doses of all these compounds elicit psychotomimetic action.

The degree of protection afforded by different cholinolytics varies according to the organophosphate involved and the experimental animal used. Jović and Milošević reported that for mice poisoned with Gd-42, the drugs scopolamine, atropine and methylatropine were much more effective than other cholinolytics which have predominantly central action, such as parpanit and benactyzine [4]. In contrast, the most effective cholinolytics against poisonings with soman, sarin and tabun were parpanit and benactyzine. In a series of animal experiments, Coleman *et al* demonstrated that the superiority of parpanit over atropine is highest in the mouse, that it is lower in the rat and the hamster, and that there is no difference in the protection afforded by the two drugs in guinea-pigs or rabbits [5].

The effectiveness of treatment with cholinolytics increases with increasing dosage of the drug, but only within certain limits. According to Coleman *et al* [2] the protection afforded by atropine (in combination with P2S) in animals poisoned with sarin reaches its maximum at a dose of about 10 μmol/kg. In contrast, there was a steady increase in protective potency with increased dosage of parpanit at all tested doses up to 100 μmol/kg. These results are in agreement with those of Jović and Milošević who studied amiton intoxication in mice [4].

Table 10.2. Effects of various oximes, given as adjuncts to atropine, on the toxicity of DFP in the rat

Drug	Elevation of LD_{50} of DFP
None	–
Pralidoxime	12
Trimedoxime	35
Obidoxime	41

Sources: Fleisher, J. H., Michel, H. O., Yates, L. and Harrison, C. S., "1, 1′-trimethylene bis (4-formylpyridinium bromide) dioxime (TMB-4) and 2-pyridine aldoxime methiodide (2-PAM) as adjuvants to atropine in the treatment of anticholinesterase poisoning", *J. Pharmacol. Exp. Ther.*, **129,** 31–35 (1960); Rump, S. and Grudzińska, E., "Investigations on the effects of diazepam in acute experimental intoxication with fluostigmine", *Arch. Toxicol.*, **31,** 223–32 (1974); Askew, B. M., "Oximes and hydroxamic acids as antidotes in anticholinesterase poisoning", *Brit. J. Pharmacol.*, **11,** 417–23 (1956).

Ganglia-blocking and enzyme-reactivating compounds

The principal limitation to the effectiveness of the above-mentioned anti-muscarinic compounds in treating organophosphate intoxication is their inability to restore neuromuscular transmission. Some quaternary analogues, however, do have this action, so that they are valuable as adjuncts to atropine: N-benzyl-atropinium chloride, for example, has been found to increase the survival ratio significantly when administered in conjunction with atropine [6].

The limited effectiveness of anti-muscarinic drugs has led to a search for adjunctive compounds. Because the ganglia are among the structures in which abnormal activity is induced by nicotinic-like phenomena, one obvious possibility was compounds with the ability to modify ganglionic transmission. Wills reported [7] that azomethonium or pentamethonium given as adjuncts to atropine enhanced its effectiveness. Similarly Fleisher *et al* stated that mecamylamine has an adjunctive effect to atropine [8]. However, the effects of these drugs are also rather small. A more pronounced action is elicited by hexane 1,6-bis-(N,N-dimethyl-N-3′-phthalimidopropyl ammonium), originally synthetized by Ohnesorge [9]. This drug, given together with atropine 10 minutes before the intoxication, elevated the LD_{50} of DFP in the rat 22 times [10]. However, the prophylactic effect of this drug is probably due more to its cholinesterase-protecting action than to its ganglia-blocking properties. Unfortunately, this drug is very toxic and its ED_{50} is higher than one-half of its LD_{50} [11].

The most important nicotinic effect of organophosphates is paralysis of skeletal muscles. The muscarinic and ganglia-blocking compounds have comparatively little effect on neuromuscular transmission. It has been reported that some curare-like agents, such as *d*-tubocurarine and gallamine, enhance the rate of recovery of responsiveness of the muscle to repetitive stimulation of the motor nerve after some organophosphates [12–13]. This action has also been observed with some local anaesthetics, such as cinchocaine and lidocaine [14–15] and anti-parkinsonian drugs [16]. Unfortunately, these drugs only exert these effects at near-toxic doses, so that they only have theoretical importance.

The development of effective reactivators of inhibited acetylcholinesterase was the most crucial event in the history of pharmacotherapy of organophosphate intoxication. Oximes of the monoquaternary (for example, pralidoxime) or the bisquaternary (for instance, trimedoxime and obidoxime) types are the most potent reactivators known, and are the most effective chemical adjuncts to atropine in the treatment of organophosphate poisoning. As shown in table 10.2, pralidoxime given together with atropine elevated the LD_{50} of DFP in the mouse 12 times and obidoxime 40 times [17]. Similar effects have been reported in rats [18].

There is evidence that mono- and bisquaternary oximes exert their major effects at the neuromuscular junction [19]. However, oximes afford very little, if any, protection to animals poisoned with soman, methylfluorophosphorylcholine, OMPA or dimethoate [20–22]. According to Oldiges and Schoene [23] and Kisieliński *et al* [24], some protection against soman and dimethoate was obtained with HS-6 and SAD-128, although these drugs have only prophylactic, and not therapeutic, action.

Treatment of central effects

Although the penetration of oximes across the blood-brain barrier has been extensively studied, none of the usable oxime reactivators known today has been found to have a striking effect *in vivo* on phosphorylated brain acetylcholinesterase. Oximes are therefore of little value in treating central effects. The effects of organophosphates on the central respiratory systems and on several other functions of the central nervous system have been mentioned by many authors. Among other symptoms, convulsions play a large part in the mechanism of death in these intoxications. Anticonvulsant drugs, such as mepazine, phenytoin, trimethadione and paramethadione, when given in conjunction with atropine, were of little, if any, value in treating these symptoms [7], but experiments conducted in our laboratory have shown the effectiveness of some benzodiazepines when given as adjuncts to atropine and obidoxime. Diazepam, for example, when given together with atropine and obidoxime, elevated the LD_{50} of DFP in the rat 80 times [18]. (See table 10.3.) Given alone, on the other hand, diazepam had a much smaller effect, although it quickly stopped the convulsive activity in the cortex induced by DFP [25–26] and soman [27–28]. Paralysis of striated muscles, especially those associated with respiratory activity, is also a serious cause of mortality in organophosphate intoxication. Recently it was reported that simple derivatives of benzoic acid, such as 3-chloro-2,5,6,-trimethyl benzoate, which show a veratrine-like action, pre-

Table 10.3. Effects of various drugs on the toxicity of DFP in the rat

Drug	Elevation of LD_{50} of DFP	
	After 2 hours	After 24 hours
Atropine	4.1	3.7
Obidoxime	25.4	6.5
Diazepam	1.1	1.0
Atropine + obidoxime	41.0	13.1
Atropine + diazepam	14.4	8.6
Obidoxime + diazepam	38.2	9.3
Atropine + obidoxime + diazepam	80.6	15.6

Source: Rump, S. and Grudzińska, E., "Investigations on the effects of diazepam in acute experimental intoxication with fluostigmine", *Arch. Toxicol.*, **31**, 223–32 (1974).

vented paralysis of striated muscle [29] and elevated the LD_{50} of DFP 74 times when given together with atropine and obidoxime in the rat [10]. Germine monoacetate [29] and 9-anthroic acid [30] have similar action.

Repetitive administration of drugs

In discussing the problem of the effectiveness of pharmacotherapy, the question arises whether treatment actually preserves life or merely prolongs it. Most of the toxicological data cited above were obtained from experiments in which the observation time was only two hours, and recently we reported that, using such a short observation period, it is possible to demonstrate an extremely high efficacy of pharmacotherapy. For example, a combined treatment consisting of atropine, obidoxime, diazepam and the above-mentioned derivatives of benzoic acid and hexamethonium results in the elevation of the LD_{50} of DFP in the rat by some 300 times after two hours (see table 10.4). However, 24 hours after treatment, the LD_{50} of this organophosphate is only 29 times higher than in an untreated control group, indicating that this therapy actually only prolongs the survival time.

These data show the importance of using adequate observation periods in assessing the effectiveness of pharmacotherapy. They also raise the important question of whether it is possible to enhance the effectiveness of treatment by a second administration of these drugs, or some of them, or by the sequenced multiple administration of these drugs. Some clinical observations [31–32] have been encouraging, and recent experiments conducted in our laboratory have provided some interesting data on this question.

We found that when atropine and obidoxime were administered in suf-

Table 10.4. Effects of combined therapy on the toxicity of DFP in the rat

Drugs	Elevation of LD_{50} of DFP	
	After 2 hours	After 24 hours
Atropine +obidoxime	41	13
Atropine +obidoxime +diazepam	80	24
Atropine +obidoxime +diazepam +chlorotrimethylbenzoate	157	35
Atropine +obidoxime +diazepam +hexane bis (dimethylphthalimido-propylammonium)	251	28
Atropine +obidoxime +diazepam +chlorotrimethylbenzoate +hexane bis (dimethylphthalimido-propylammonium)	304	29

Source: Rump, S., Galecka, E., Grudzińska, E., Ilczuk, I. and Rabsztyn, T., "New trends in experimental therapy of organophosphate intoxications", in *Proceedings of the Third International Congress of Pesticide Chemistry, Helsinki, 3–9 July 1974,* abstract no. 302.

ficient doses after intoxication, repetitive administration of these drugs did not enhance the final result. Only when atropine had been given alone at the start of the therapy did a second administration of atropine and obidoxime, up to 90 minutes after the intoxication, protect against death all those animals which were still alive at that time; in other words, this procedure enhanced the efficacy of atropine given alone. A second administration of the other adjunctive drugs cited above was without effect [33].

The lack of effectiveness of repeated doses of obidoxime or of atropine is rather surprising, especially since we found that the administration of a second dose of obidoxime up to 90 minutes after DFP intoxication markedly elevated acetylcholinesterase activity and restored some of the abnormalities of neuromuscular transmission due to that organophosphate [3].

III. *Conclusions*

Under experimental conditions, it is possible to save the lives of animals intoxicated with 30–40 LD_{50} of DFP or other irreversible acetylcholinesterase inhibitors [10, 17] or even higher doses of those organophosphates that result in an enzyme/inhibitor complex that is more susceptible to spontaneous reactivation. However, it was not possible to save animals intoxicated with more than 90 LD_{50} of an organophosphate, and so this value seems to represent the limit of the efficacy of experimental pharmacotherapy of organophosphate intoxications at the present time.

References

1. Brimblecombe, R. W. and Green, D. M., "The peripheral and central actions of some anticholinergic substances", *Int. J. Neuropharmacol.,* **7,** 15–21 (1968).
2. Coleman, I. W., Little, P. E. and Bannard, R. A. B., "Cholinolytics in the treatment of anticholinesterase poisoning. I. The effectiveness of certain cholinolytics in combination with an oxime for treatment of sarin poisoning", *Can. J. Biochem. Physiol.,* **40,** 815–26 (1962).
3. Faff, J., Bak, W. and Ziolkowska, G., unpublished.
4. Jović, R. and Milošević, M. P., "Effective doses of some cholinolytics in the treatment of anticholinesterase poisoning", *Eur. J. Pharmacol.,* **12,** 85–93, (1970).
5. Coleman, I. W., Patton, G. E. and Bannard, R. A. B., "Cholinolytics in the treatment of cholinesterase poisoning. V. The effectiveness of parpanit with oximes in the treatment of organophosphorus poisonings", *Can. J. Physiol. Pharmacol.,* **46**, 109–17 (1968).
6. Kunkel, A. M., Wills, J. H. and Oikemus, A. M., "Effect of a quaternary derivative of atropine, N-benzyl atropinium chloride", *Proc. Soc. Exp. Biol. (N.Y.),* **96,** 791–94 (1957).
7. Wills, J. H., "Pharmacological antagonists of the anticholinesterase agents", in Koelle, G. B., ed., *Cholinesterases and Anticholinesterase Agents,* Volume XV of *Handbuch der experimentellen Pharmakologie* (Berlin, Göttingen and Heidelberg, Springer-Verlag, 1963) pp. 883–920.
8. Fleisher, J. H., Harris, L. W., Miller, G. R., Thomas, N. C. and Cliff, W., "Antagonism of sarin poisoning in rat and guinea-pigs by atropine, oximes and mecamylamine", *Toxicol. Appl. Pharmacol.,* **16,** 40–47 (1970).
9. Ohnesorge, F. K., "Wirkungen und Wirkungsmechanismen von Alkan-bis-ammonium-derivaten bei der Organophosphatvergiftungen", *Naunyn-Schmiedebergs Arch. Pharmakol. Exp. Pathol.,* **263,** 72–88 (1969).
10. Rump, S., Galecka, E., Grudzińska, E., Ilczuk, I. and Rabsztyn, T., "New trends in experimental therapy of organophosphate intoxications", in *Proceedings of the Third International Congress of Pesticide Chemistry, Helsinki, 3–9 July 1974,* abstract no. 302.
11. Galecka, E., unpublished.
12. Kunkel, A. M., Wills, J. H. and Monier, J. S., "Antagonists to neuromuscular block produced by sarin", *Proc. Soc. Exp. Biol. (N.Y.),* **92,** 529–32 (1956).
13. Rump, S., Kaliszan, A. and Edelwein, Z., "Actions of curare-like agents on the neuromuscular abnormalities caused by an organophosphate in the rat", *Arch. Int. Pharmacodyn. Ther.,* **173,** 173–81 (1968).
14. Rump, S., "Some effects of cinchocaine on sarin-induced abnormalities of neuromuscular transmission in the rat", *Arch. Int. Pharmacodyn. Ther.,* **164,** 91–95 (1966).
15. Rump, S. and Kaliszan, A., "Anticonvulsive effects of some local anaesthetics in organic phosphate intoxications", *Arch. Int. Pharmacodyn. Ther.,* **182,** 178–81 (1969).

16. Rump, S., "Wplyw zwiazków antycholinoesterazowych na przekaźnictwo nerwowo-mieśniowe", *Postepy Hig. Med. Dośw.*, **26,** 225–49 (1972).
17. Faff, J., Kaliszan, A. and Rump, S., "Badania wplywu 2-PAM, toksogoniny i atropiny w zatruciach myszy estrem dwuizopropylowym kwasu fluorofosforowego (DFP)", *Med. Pracy,* **17,** 112–15 (1966).
18. Rump, S. and Grudzińska, E., "Investigations on the effects of diazepam in acute experimental intoxication with fluostigmine", *Arch. Toxikol.,* **31,** 223–32 (1974).
19. Wills, J. H., "Recent studies on organic phosphate poisoning", *Federation Proc.,* **18,** 1020–25 (1959).
20. Kewitz, H., Wilson, I. B. and Nachmansohn, D., "A specific antidote against lethal alkylphosphate intoxication. II. Antidotal properties", *Arch. Biochem. Biophys.,* **64,** 456–65 (1956).
21. Jović, R. and Bošković, B., "Antidotal action of pyridinium oximes in poisoning by O,O-diethyl-S-(3)-N-methyl-N-phenylamino (ethyl) thiophosphonate methyl-sulfomethylate (GT-45) and its two new analogues", *Toxicol. Appl. Pharmacol.,* **16,** 194–200 (1970).
22. Faff, J., "Badania nad wartościa lecznicza toksogoniny w zatruciach somanem", *Med. Pracy,* **22,** 626–32 (1971).
23. Oldiges, H. and Schoene, K., "Pyridinium- und Imidazoliumsalze als Antidoten gegenüber Soman- und Paraoxonvergiftungen bei Mäusen", *Arch. Toxikol.,* **26,** 293–305 (1970).
24. Kisieliński, T., Gajewski, D., Owczarczyk, H. and Sońta, J., unpublished.
25. Rump, S., Grudzińska, E. and Edelwein, Z., "Effects of diazepam on abnormalities of bioelectrical activity of the rabbit's brain due to fluostigmine", *Act. Nerv. Sup. (Prague),* **14,** 176–77 (1972).
26. Rump, S., Grudzińska, E. and Edelwein, Z., "Effects of diazepam on epileptiform patterns of bioelectrical activity of the rabbit brain induced by fluostigmine", *Neuropharmacol.,* **12,** 815–19 (1973).
27. Lipp, J. A., "Effects of diazepam on soman-induced seizure activity and convulsions", *Electroencephalog. Clin. Neurophysiol.,* **32,** 557–69 (1972).
28. Lipp, J. A., "Effects of benzodiazepine derivatives on soman-induced seizure activity and convulsions in the monkey", *Arch. Int. Pharmacodyn. Ther.,* **202,** 244–51 (1973).
29. Wolthuis, O. L. and Postel-Westra, K. B., "Germine monoacetate and 3-chloro-2,5,6-trimethylbenzoic acid, therapeutic possibilities against inhibition of neuromuscular transmission by organophosphorus anticholinesterase compounds", *Eur. J. Pharmacol.,* **14,** 93–97 (1971).
30. Nickolson, V. J. and Wolthuis, O. L., "Therapy of anticholinesterase intoxication using compounds with veratrine-like action and the role of calcium", in *Proceedings of the Third International Congress of Pesticide Chemistry, Helsinki, 3–9 July 1974,* abstract no. 310.
31. Kränzle, H., "Zur Therapie der E-605 Vergiftung", *Deut. Med. Wochschr.,* **79,** 1756–57 (1954).
32. Namba, T. and Hiraki, K., "PAM (pyridine-2-aldoxime methiodide) therapy for alkylphosphate poisoning", *J. Am. Med. Assoc.,* **166,** 1834–39 (1958).
33. Szymańska, T., Ziólkowska, G., Faff, J. and Rump, S., unpublished.

11. The possibility of complex therapy in acute dimethoate poisoning

T. KISIELIŃSKI, D. GAJEWSKI, H. OWCZARCZYK and J. SOŃTA

Square-bracketed numbers, thus [1], *refer to the list of references on page 119.*

I. *Introduction*

Data from clinical and other experimental studies on the efficacy of oximes in treating poisoning by organophosphorus insecticides and chemical-warfare agents show that these compounds can be classified into three groups according to sensitivity to oxime therapy: (*a*) those compounds that induce an intoxication that shows a good response to oxime therapy, such as paraoxon, parathion, dipterex and sarin; (*b*) those that induce an intoxication that is only moderately responsive to oximes, such as diazinon; and (*c*) those that induce an intoxication that is not responsive to oxime therapy, such as soman and dimethoate. The resistance of soman poisoning to oxime therapy is known to be due primarily to rapid ageing of the inhibited acetylcholinesterase. In the case of dimethoate poisoning, however, another mechanism seems to be responsible for the resistance. The purpose of this chapter is to show the possibilities of therapy against dimethoate poisoning by means of oximes, cholinolytics and other compounds.

II. *Methodology*

The experimental animals used were male BALB mice which had been kept on a standard diet and had a mean weight of 25 g. Dimethoate (98 per cent pure) was dissolved in propylene glycol and then in distilled water, and was injected into the mice intraperitoneally. The LD_{50} of dimethoate was determined by the method of Thompson-Weil. The drugs used for treatment in these tests—atropine sulphate, Toxogonin (Merck), SAD-128, HS-6, PMCG and diazepam (Valium)—were administered by subcutaneous injection: prophylactic injections were carried out five minutes before the administration of dimethoate, and therapeutic injections in the first minute after dimethoate administration.

Table 11.1. Effects of the prophylactic and therapeutic administration of some drugs on the LD_{50} of dimethoate (intraperitoneally) in mice

Drug (and dose (*mg/kg*))									
Prophylactic administration		Therapeutic administration							
HS-6 (86.2)	SAD-128 (27)	Atropine sulphate (10)	Toxogonin (40)	HS-6 (86.2)	SAD-128 (27)	Valium (1)	PMCG (5.4)	LD_{50} of dimethoate *mg/kg*	Elevation of LD_{50}
								209 (162–269)	–
●		●	●					1 123 (1 059–1 195)	5.4
	●	●	●					1 454 (1 423–1 480)	7.0
		●						1 440 (1 327–1 564)	6.9
		●	●					1 729 (1 567–1 906)	8.3
		●		●				2 261 (2 075–2 464)	10.8
		●			●			1 836 (1 728–1 951)	8.8
		●	●			●		1 542 (1 351–1 760)	7.4
		●		●		●		1 667 (1 440–1 930)	8.0
		●			●	●		1 952 (1 745–2 182)	9.3
		●	●				●	1 512 (1 495–1 685)	7.2
			●				●	1 330 (1 152–1 540)	6.3

III. *Discussion of results*

The prophylactic and therapeutic effects of various combinations of drugs on dimethoate poisoning are presented in table 11.1.

Atropine sulphate given alone elevated the LD_{50} by almost seven times, an effect which differs from that seen in sarin poisoning, where the LD_{50} was elevated only 1.38 times [1]. The use of Toxogonin in conjunction with atropine sulphate resulted in a further elevation of the LD_{50}, to almost 8.5 times higher than in untreated animals, and again these effects differ from those seen in other cases of organophosphate poisoning: in sarin poisoning, the addition of Toxogonin to atropine sulphate elevated the LD_{50} by 19.4 times, and in DFP poisoning, atropine sulphate alone elevated the LD_{50} by 5.4 times while the addition of Toxogonin elevated the LD_{50} by 41 times [2]. Thus the improvement in therapeutic effect obtained by adding Toxogonin to atropine sulphate is much more marked in the treatment of sarin or DFP poisoning than in the treatment of dimethoate poisoning.

In our experiments, the most effective therapeutic mixture was found to be HS-6 with atropine sulphate, a combination that elevated the LD_{50} of dimethoate by almost 11 times. Another very effective combination was SAD-128 with atropine sulphate, and since SAD-128 has no nucleophilic group, this interesting result seems to suggest that this compound has a different therapeutic mode of action from that of other compounds. Moreover, these observations lend support to earlier results of Oldiges and Schoene, who demonstrated the effectiveness of SAD-128 in soman poisoning [3].

However, in contrast to the results of Oldiges and Schoene, who also found that SAD-128 and HS-6 show a significant prophylactic effect in soman poisoning, our results show that prophylactic injections of these two compounds have only marginal effects in dimethoate poisoning.

The addition of PMCG to atropine sulphate had little effect, and we found no evidence to support reports by other authors that an additional therapeutic effect can be obtained by using two cholinolytic drugs [4].

Surprisingly little additional therapeutic effect was obtained by the use of Valium in conjunction with oxime and atropine sulphate. Again, these results contrast with those of other authors who have been able to demonstrate a marked improvement in therapeutic effect with Valium in DFP poisoning [5].

IV. *Conclusions*

Our studies have shown that atropine sulphate is an effective therapeutic agent against dimethoate poisoning, and that its therapeutic effect is improved by the addition of Toxogonin, HS-6 or SAD-128. They have also shown that HS-6 and SAD-128 have little value as prophylactic agents in this poisoning, and that the addition of Valium to atropine sulphate and oxime has little additional therapeutic value. Clearly there is a need for further research aimed at discovering new therapeutic or prophylactic compounds with different modes of action from these compounds.

References

1. Coleman, I. W., Little, P. E. and Bannard, R. A. B., "Cholinolytics in the treatment of anticholinesterase poisoning. I. The effectiveness of certain cholinolytics in combination with an oxime for treatment of sarin poisoning", *Can. J. Biochem. Physiol.*, **40,** 815–26 (1962).
2. Rump, S., Galecka, E., Grudzińska, E., Ilczuk, I. and Rabsztyn, T., "New trends in experimental therapy of organophosphate intoxications", in *Proceedings of the Third International Congress of Pesticide Chemistry, Helsinki, 3–9 July 1974,* abstract no. 302.
3. Oldiges, H. and Schoene, K., "Pyridinium- und Imidazoliumsalze als Antidoten gegenüber Soman- und Paraoxonvergiftungen bei Mäusen", *Arch. Toxikol.,* **26,** 293–305 (1970).
4. Jović, R. and Milošević, M. P., "Effective doses of some cholinolytics in the treatment of anticholinesterase poisoning", *Eur. J. Pharmacol.,* **12,** 85–93 (1970).
5. Rump, S. and Grudzińska, E., "Investigations on the effects of diazepam in acute experimental intoxication with fluostigmine", *Arch. Toxikol.,* **31,** 223–32 (1974).

12. The prophylactic value of oximes against organophosphate poisoning

H. P. BENSCHOP, L. R. A. DE JONG, J. A. J. VINK,
H. KIENHUIS, F. BERENDS, D. M. W. ELSKAMP,
L. A. KEPNER, E. MEETER and R. P. L. S. VISSER

Square-bracketed numbers, thus [1], *refer to the list of references on page 131.*

I. *Introduction*

For several reasons, therapeutic treatment of organophosphate poisoning with atropine and oximes is not always successful. In severe intoxications, the rapid action of the inhibitor requires the almost instantaneous administration of antidotes, which is usually impossible in practice. Moreover, with several inhibitors, the intoxication rapidly becomes resistant to the oxime therapy due to the "ageing" of the inhibited enzyme, and this also necessitates prompt treatment. And with some other organophosphates, for instance, tabun, oxime therapy fails for other reasons. Frequently it can be attributed to the stability of the phosphorylated enzyme with regard to oxime reactivation, which can only be overcome by the administration of unacceptably high doses of the antidote. In view of these limitations of therapy, a prophylactic treatment against organophosphate intoxication would be highly desirable.

In addition to physical means of protection, such as protective clothing, the best protection would be obtained with antidotes which could inactivate organophosphate in the body before inhibition of the acetylcholinesterase could take place. Such an antidote should be able to compete successfully with the enzyme for the organophosphate, but because of the extremely high affinity of acetylcholinesterase for organophosphates, this is a difficult requirement to meet. Only few attempts in this direction have been described. In an immunological approach, Cuculis and co-workers [1] obtained some positive results by vaccinating animals with the reaction product of an organophosphate and a carrier protein. This approach, however, does not appear very promising: the antibodies produced have a very narrow specificity and are only effective against compounds structurally related to the antigen used in the vaccination. A different approach was tried in our laboratories when we investigated the feasibility of removing organophosphates from the bloodstream by inclusion in injected cyclodextrins. These cycloamyloses are very good complexing agents for organophosphates, as has been demonstrated by van Hooidonk and co-workers

[2–6], but in preliminary experiments, the administration of cyclodextrins to mice prior to an injection of sarin or soman did not raise the LD_{50} [7].

Another possible means of prophylaxis would be to protect the enzyme against organophosphates by shielding it with certain compounds. For this approach, reversible acetylcholinesterase inhibitors have been tried: by pretreatment with these agents, a fraction of the functional acetylcholinesterase in the body is blocked and the activity of the blocked enzyme is either restored gradually by spontaneous reactivation or, when necessary, can be restored rapidly by additional oxime treatment. Although it might be expected that the presence of a second acetylcholinesterase inhibitor—even a reversible one—would enhance the toxicity of the organophosphate, it does appear that, by carefully selecting conditions and compounds, significant protection can be obtained in this way.

Berry and Davies [8] have extended earlier work by Koster [9], and by Callaway and Barnes (see reference [8]) using carbamates and atropine for protecting different species against poisoning by soman. Berry and co-workers [10] also investigated the protective effect against soman of a prophylactic treatment with oxime-responsive organophosphates in conjunction with a therapeutic administration of oximes. In both studies, the maximal effect obtained was an elevation of the LD_{50} by a factor of seven to nine. It is not yet clear whether this method will be applicable in practice, but it has the great advantage that, in principle, it can be used against any type of organophosphate.

A third means of protection against organophosphate intoxication is the prophylactic use of therapeutically active oximes. Strictly speaking this is not prophylaxis, but a method for securing instantaneous therapy. In this approach, the reactivator circulates in the body before the organophosphate enters the organism and the reactivation process can start at almost the same moment the inhibition of acetylcholinesterase takes place. Investigations into this approach were reported by Davies and co-workers [11] and by Edery and Schatzberg-Porath [12] in 1959. Both groups reported that N-methyl-pyridine-2-aldoxime salts (2-PAM, P2S) showed promising prophylactic effects in various species against sarin, tetraethyl pyrophosphate or guthion. This was confirmed in 1967 by Svirblis and Kondritzer [13]. A number of other pyridinium derivatives, such as obidoxime (Toxogonin) and trimedoxime (TMB-4), show therapeutic properties that are comparable with, or even better than, 2-PAM or P2S, and might therefore also be considered promising prophylactic agents. But it appears that, in general, the pyridinium oximes are not suitable as prophylactic antidotes because of their short half-lives in the body, mainly resulting from rapid renal excretion [14–16].

We decided to investigate the possibility of designing oximes which combine low toxicity and therapeutic effectiveness with a prolonged half-life in the mammalian body, and which therefore might be suitable as prophylactic agents. So far, only a limited insight has been obtained into the relationship between biological half-life and chemical structure of drugs. It is known that, in general, quaternary ammonium compounds are rapidly excreted whereas lipophilic compounds are better retained in the body. Until now, the majority of drugs with long biological half-lives have been selected by pharmacological screening. The structural characteristics of these compounds may also provide guidance in the design of new oximes. In the selection of new compounds to be synthesized and tested we followed three different approaches: (*a*) the introduction of lipophilic groups at the quaternary-nitrogen atom of pyridinium aldoximes, in order to compensate for the effect of the positive charge present at this atom; (*b*) the replacement of the pyridinium ring by the non-quaternary, but also highly electron-withdrawing, thiadiazole ring systems; and (*c*) the structural modification of uncharged aliphatic oximes such as monoisonitrosoacetone (MINA) and certain derivatives of oximinoacetic acid. The work on the thiadiazole derivatives can be regarded as an extension of our previous studies on isothiazole oximes [17].

It was expected that among the more lipophilic oximes synthesized, compounds might be obtained which are better able to penetrate into the central nervous system than the oximes which are presently employed. Although this is not a criterion for prophylactic action, an oxime with such a property might be interesting for therapeutic application. Therefore, some of the more promising reactivators were also tested for central activity.

II. *Experimental methods*

Materials

The new oximes were synthesized at the Chemical Laboratory TNO according to methods described in the literature [18–25]. P2S was purchased from Dr F. Raschig GmbH, FR Germany and obidoxime from E. Merck, FR Germany. The organophosphates were synthesized at the Chemical Laboratory TNO. All other chemicals were of an analytical grade.

Reactivation of phosphonylated acetylcholinesterase *in vitro*

Inhibited acetylcholinesterase was obtained by incubating the enzyme with either 0.1 μM sarin at pH 9.0 and 0°C for 100 minutes, or 0.1 μM tabun at pH 7.5 and 25°C for 60 minutes. Excess inhibitor was removed by repeated extraction with ether [17], and after the removal of residual ether by keeping the enzyme solution at reduced pressure for 30 minutes, the pH was adjusted to 7.5. Immediately thereafter, one volume of an oxime solution in 0.04 M phosphate buffer (pH 7.5) was added to four volumes of the enzyme solution. The resulting solution was incubated at 25°C for 24 hours and after various intervals the restored enzyme activity was measured. In general, 1 mM of the oximes was used. Pyridinium-2-aldoximes and bispyridinium-4-aldoximes used in this concentration, however, restore the activity of inhibited acetylcholinesterase too fast to allow an evaluation of the influence of structural variations on reactivating potency, and so these oximes were also tested at a lower concentration.

The restored enzyme activity is expressed as percentage reactivation, which has been calculated in the usual manner after correction for spontaneous reactivation and for effects due to the presence of oxime during the activity determinations.

Biological half-life in rats and rabbits

To evaluate the biological half-life of oximes, a method was required for the assay of oximes of varying structures at concentrations down to 1 μg/ml in small quantities of plasma. The method of choice appeared to be measurement, in alkaline medium, of the absorption in the ultraviolet at the wavelength of maximum absorption, which ranges between 250 and 360 nm [26–27]. The plasma had to be deproteinized first, which was done by precipitation in 12 per cent trichloroacetic acid, or by ultrafiltration (with Amicon filtercones) when the λ_{max} was near 260 nm. For each procedure, calibration experiments were performed with known quantities of oximes.

In the animal experiments, the oximes were injected into the ear vein of rabbits or into the tail vein of rats. In the standard procedure, a dose of 50 mg/kg was used, but with the more toxic oximes the amount was reduced according to the toxicity. The decrease of the blood concentration was determined by measurement of the oxime content of blood samples, taken at intervals from the other ear (rabbits) or obtained by decapitation (rats). The results were expressed as biological half-lives, that is, the time required for a 50 per cent reduction of the blood concentration. Half-lives given for rabbits are the mean of the results from at least three animals; the oxime concentration at the end of each time interval in rats was obtained by averaging the values for four animals.

Toxicity in mice

Toxicity was determined as LD_{50} in mice (♀♀C57 black) by injecting the oxime intraperitoneally in aqueous solution (10 ml/kg), using at least 50 mice for each determination. The LD_{50} values were calculated by the probit method. Values in excess of 400 mg/kg were not determined.

Prophylactic activity against sarin in mice

Prophylactic activity was determined by intraperitoneally injecting groups of 10 mice with either the $LD_{0.1}$ or 100 mg/kg of the oxime, whichever was

Table 12.1. Pyridinium oximes: chemical structures, pK_a values, toxicities and reactivating potencies[a]

Compound	Substituent	pK_a	LD_{50}[b] *mg/kg*	Relative reactivating potency[c]: Sarin-inhibited acetyl-cholinesterase[d]	Relative reactivating potency[c]: Tabun-inhibited acetyl-cholinesterase[e]
Monopyridinium compounds					
General formula:	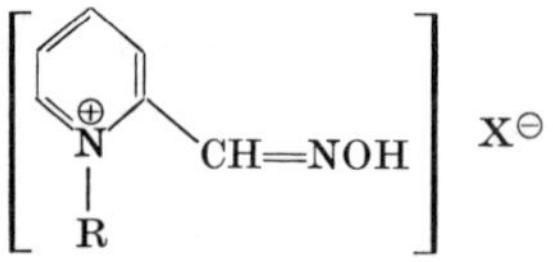				
1	R=CH_3—	7.9	173	++	+
2	R=CH_5O—	7.6	284		+
3	R=C_2H_5—		81	++	+
4	R=n-C_3H_7—		36	++	+
5	R=i-C_3H_7—		62		
6	R=C_7H_{15}—		169	+	+
7	R=$C_{12}H_{25}$—		49	+++	++
8	R=$C_6H_5CH_2$—		31	+	++++
9	R=$(C_6H_5)_2CH$—	7.9	123	+	++
Bispyridinium compounds					
General formula:	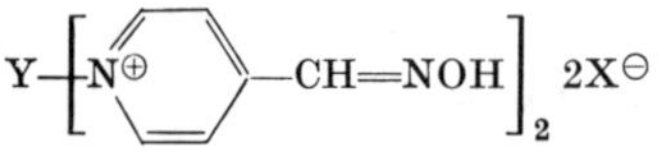				
10	Y=—CH_2OCH_2—		130	+++	+++
11	Y=—$CH_2CH_2CH_2$—	7.6 8.3		+++	++++
12	Y=—CH_2—	7.3 8.1	>400	++++	+

[a] In order to facilitate the evaluation and comparison of the data, the reactivating-potency results are presented in a comparative manner. The original data are available from the authors on request.
[b] In mice by intraperitoneal administration.
[c] Relative reactivating potency refers to the percentage reactivation found after specific periods of incubation. For *sarin-inhibited acetylcholinesterase* the incubation periods were 100 minutes and 300 minutes:
+ denotes <20 per cent and <40 per cent reactivation respectively;
++ denotes 20–35 per cent and 40–60 per cent reactivation respectively;
+++ denotes 35–55 per cent and 60–75 per cent reactivation respectively;
++++ denotes 55–75 per cent and 75–95 per cent reactivation respectively.
+++++ denotes >75 per cent and >95 per cent reactivation respectively.
For *tabun-inhibited acetylcholinesterase* the incubation periods were 160 minutes and 480 minutes, and the same system of signs is used to show the percentage reactivation after these periods.
[d] Oxime concentration used was 5 μM: pH 7.5 and 25°C.
[e] Oxime concentration used was 30 μM: pH 7.5 and 25°C.

the lower, 60 minutes before administration of a challenge dose of sarin (1 mg/kg, subcutaneously).

A control group was injected with P2S, either at a dose level equimolar to that of the test oxime if the $LD_{0.1}$ was used, or at 100 mg/kg otherwise, 60 minutes before sarin. Atropine was administered (37.5 mg/kg, intraperitoneally) $1\frac{1}{2}$ minutes after sarin to all mice. The challenge dose of sarin corresponded to 2.4 LD_{50} (with atropine).

Activity in the central nervous system

The central effectiveness of oximes was determined as described by Meeter and co-workers [28] by measuring the hypothermia-reducing effect in rats pretreated intravenously with DFP, soman or paraoxon.

III. *Results and discussion*

Monopyridinium and bispyridinium oximes

The structures of the investigated oximes, their pK_a values, toxicities and *in vitro* reactivating potencies are summarized in table 12.1.

Most of the mono- and bispyridinium oximes appeared to be potent reactivators *in vitro* of sarin- and tabun-inhibited acetylcholinesterase. However, in order to attain substantial reactivation of the tabun-inhibited enzyme, a considerably higher concentration of the oximes was required than with acetylcholinesterase inactivated by sarin; this was not unexpected in view of the known results obtained with conventional oximes.

For the reactivation of sarin-inhibited acetylcholinesterase, compounds 3 and 4 are comparable in activity with P2S (compound 1), whereas compounds 6, 8 and 9 are less active. The bispyridinium compounds 10–12 are significantly more effective than P2S. For the reactivation of the tabun-inhibited enzyme, compounds 3–6 and 12 equal P2S in activity and compounds 7–11 are more powerful than P2S. In particular, the N-benzyl derivative (compound 8) proved to be remarkably effective. It is surprising that compound 12, which is the superior reactivator for sarin-inactivated acetylcholinesterase, scores very poorly with the tabun-inhibited enzyme.

Obviously, large variations in the lipophilicity of the N-substituent in pyridinium oximes are possible, without adverse effect on the reactivating potency of these compounds.

The *in vivo* toxicity determinations showed that, in contrast to the minor effect on the reactivating potency, the introduction of more lipophilic groups into the monopyridinium oximes appeared to have a considerable influence on the toxicity of these compounds in mice. Compound 6 seems to be exceptional in this respect, but additional experiments with rats and rabbits indicate that this exception does not hold. Lack of sufficient data prevents a conclusion being drawn on the cause of the increased toxicity. It has been found, however, that a number of the more toxic compounds show a considerable anticholinesterase activity *in vitro,* but a relationship between this activity and the cause of death of the animals has not been established.

Figure 12.1. Rate of decrease of P2S and obidoxime concentration in the blood of rabbits after intravenous administration of the oximes

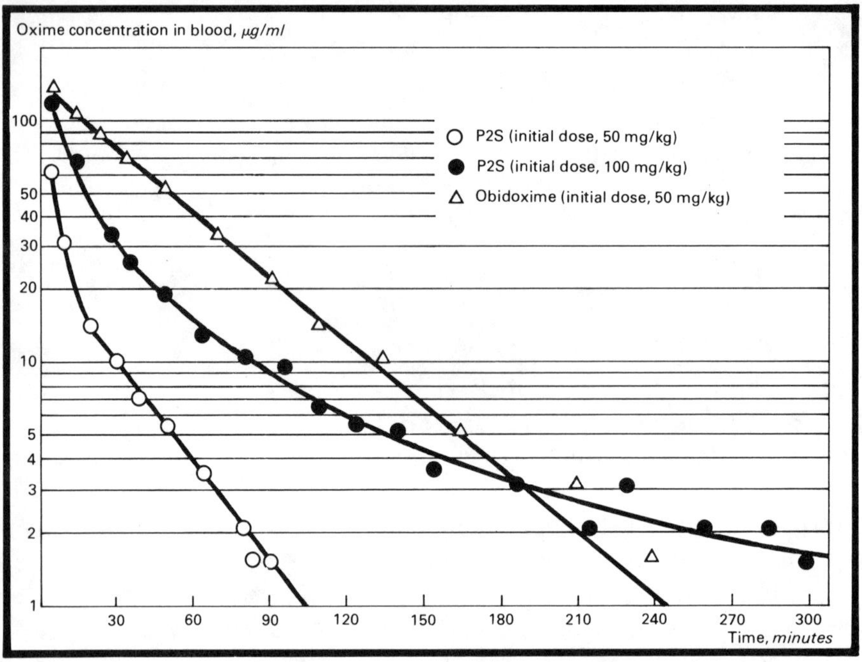

The low toxicity of compound 12 deserves attention. Since this oxime appears to be a rather good reactivator, it might be of therapeutic interest, as already suggested by Yakl and co-workers [29].

In the course of the determination of the biological half-lives it was observed that the concentration of the pyridinium oximes in the blood of rats and rabbits did not decrease according to first-order kinetics. Figure 12.1 shows the results, obtained in rabbits, with two doses of P2S; the plots are clearly non-linear for periods exceeding by far the time needed for distribution of the injected oxime in the body. At the lower dose, the curve eventually tends to become linear but at the higher dose the graph remains curved. Consequently, a true biological half-life value cannot be obtained, since this quantity not only depends on the part of the curve used for the determination, but also varies with the initial dose. For instance, the decrease from 10 to 5 μg of P2S per ml blood takes 22 minutes after the administration of 50 mg/kg, but 60 minutes at twice this dose. This phenomenon was also observed with the other monopyridinium oximes, and with N-methyl-pyridine-4-aldoxime iodide (4-PAM). This effect should be borne in mind when considering data from the literature on the biological half-lives of these compounds.

Strikingly, as also shown in figure 12.1, the phenomenon is not observed with the structurally related compound 10, obidoxime, which follows first-order kinetics throughout ($t/2=30$ minutes). In this case the half-life does not depend on the initial dose. Half-lives of the other two bispyridinium oximes have not yet been determined. The difference in behaviour of obidoxime and monopyridinium oximes is a subject of further study.

Because of the relatively high toxicity of a number of the P2S homologues, the dose used for the half-life studies had to be varied. Since the decrease of the oxime level of the blood with time depends on the initial dose, the results were compared with those obtained with an equal dose (by weight) of P2S. On the basis of this comparison, no significant differences were found between P2S and its homologues. To our disappointment, the introduction of lipophilic groups evidently does not lead to a longer biological half-life.

Only a rough first screening for prophylactic activity against sarin was carried out, since the principal objective was to select oximes with a considerable prophylactic activity (at least comparable with that of P2S), not to detect marginal differences. Therefore, only a limited number of animals were used for the test, with the consequence that the results obtained show rather large statistical variations. The possibility, however, of a really effective oxime going unnoticed is negligible.

Because of the high toxicity of many of the oximes, varying doses, usually the $LD_{0.1}$, were used for the test. Each result was compared with that obtained with an equimolar dose of P2S. At each of the doses of P2S used, ranging from 17 to 100 mg/kg, some prophylaxis was seen, varying between one to six surviving animals out of 10. In general, the effects of the other monopyridinium oximes were somewhat poorer but the differences were not significant because of the statistical variations. The bisquaternary oximes, however, appeared to give a somewhat better protection than P2S.

Since the P2S homologues are, in general, more toxic than P2S itself, without possessing a remarkably good prophylactic capacity, these compounds are not considered likely candidates for prophylactic application. Compound 12, however, combines a low toxicity with good reactivating, and fair prophylactic, properties, and deserves further attention.

Thiadiazole oximes

Table 12.2 lists the structures and properties of the three thiadiazole derivatives investigated. The electron-withdrawing potency of these heterocyclic ring systems appeared sufficiently strong to lower the pK_a of the oxime group to the desired range. The reactivating capability, however, was poor. A concentration of 1 mM was required to obtain results, with sarin-inhibited acetylcholinesterase, comparable with those obtained with the well-studied oxime MINA (compound 22). At the same concentration, none of these oximes was able to restore the enzyme activity of tabun-inhibited acetylcholinesterase.

Table 12.2. Thiadiazole oximes: chemical structures, pK_a values, toxicities, reactivating potencies and biological half-lives[a]

Compound	Chemical structure	pK_a	LD_{50}[b] *mg/kg*	Relative reactivating potency for sarin-inhibited acetylcholinesterase[c]	Relative biological half-life[d]	
					Rabbit	Rat
29	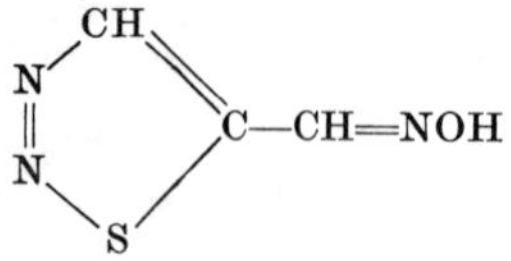	7.6	>400	+	+	+
30	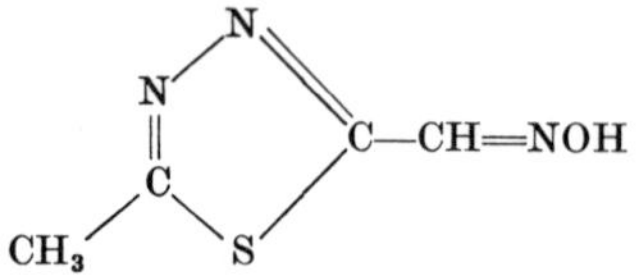	8.4	>400	+	+	+
31	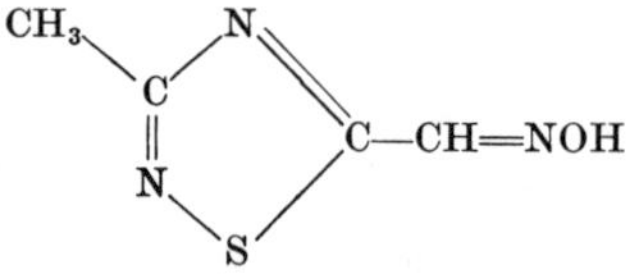	7.0	>400	+++	+	+
22	$CH_3C(O)—CH{=}NOH$	8.3		++		

[a] In order to facilitate the evaluation and comparison of the data, the reactivating-potency and biological half-life results are presented in a comparative manner. The original data are available from the authors on request.
[b] In mice by intraperitoneal administration of the sodium salts.
[c] Oxime concentration used was 1 mM: pH 7.5 and 25°C. For explanation of the signs, see the description for sarin-inhibited acetylcholinesterase in footnote *c* to table 12.1.
[d] The number of + signs indicates the approximate ratio between the half-life of the oxime and the half-life calculated for the linear part of the curve obtained with P2S at 50 mg/kg in the same species.

Because of the low toxicity of the three oximes, the half-lives could be measured with the standard dose of 50 mg/kg. The oxime concentration in the blood decreased according to first-order kinetics. The half-lives are hardly different from those measured for P2S and its homologues at 50 mg/kg (about 20 minutes in rabbits), although the thiadiazole compounds do not contain the positively charged quaternary-nitrogen atom, which usually contributes to rapid excretion.

At a dose of 100 mg/kg, no prophylactic activity against sarin could be observed with these compounds.

Aliphatic oximes

The structures, pK_a values and further results obtained with the investigated aliphatic oximes are collected in table 12.3. Although the pK_a values

Table 12.3. Aliphatic oximes: chemical structures, pK_a values, toxicities, reactivating potencies and biological half-lives[a]

General formula: 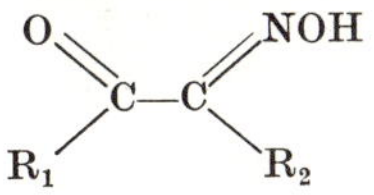

Compound	Substituents R_1	R_2	pK_a	LD_{50}[b] *mg/kg*	Relative reactivating potency for sarin-inhibited acetylcholinesterase[c]	Relative biological half-life in rats[d]
13	$(C_2H_5)_2N(CH_2)_2NH—$	H	8.8	>400	+++++	++
14	$(C_2H_5)_2N(CH_2)_3NH—$	H	8.6	>400	++++	++
15	$(C_2H_5)_2N(CH_2)_4NH—$	H	8.9	370	+++	++
16	$(C_2H_5)_2N(CH_2)_3O—$	H	8.1	>400	+++++	++
17	$C_7H_{15}NH(CH_2)_3NH—$	H	8.9	144	++++	++
18	$i\text{-}C_3H_7NH(CH_2)_3NH—$	H	8.9	>400	++++	++
19	$C_6H_{11}NH(CH_2)_3NH—$	H	9.0	328	+++++	++
20	$C_6H_5CH_2NH(CH_2)_3NH—$	H	8.9	>400	+++++	++
21	$C_6H_5NH(CH_2)_3NH—$	H	9.3	>400	+	++
22	$CH_3—$	H	8.3	163	++	
23	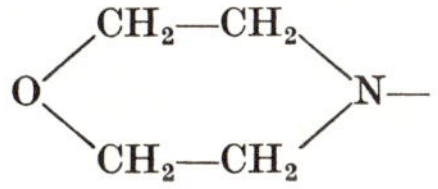	H	9.2	>400	–	+++++
24	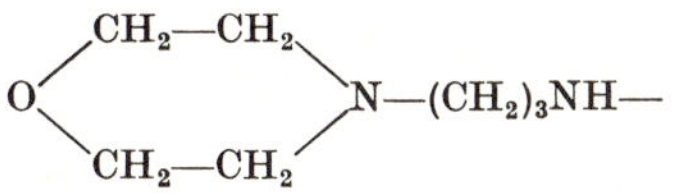	H	7.1 9.2	>400	++++	++++
25	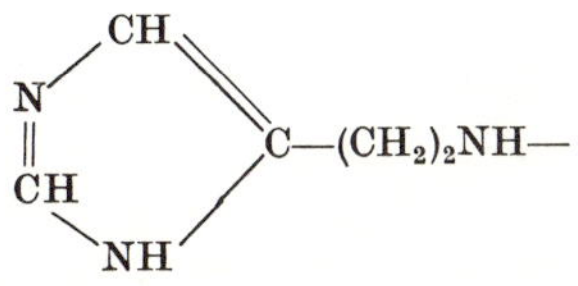	H	7.2 9.5		++	++++
26	$CH_3—$	$(CH_3)_2NCH_2—$	7.2	>400	+	++++[e]
27	$CH_3—$	$(C_2H_5)_2N(CH_2)_2$	8.0	124	+	+++[e]
28	$CH_3—$	$CH_3—$	9.3		–	++[e]

[a] In order to facilitate the evaluation and comparison of the data, the reactivating-potency and biological half-life results are presented in a comparative manner. The original data are available from the authors on request.
[b] In mice by intraperitoneal administration.
[c] Oxime concentration used was 1 mM: pH 7.5 and 25°C. For explanation of the signs, see the description for sarin-inhibited acetylcholinesterase in footnote *c* to table 12.1.
[d] For explanation of the signs, see footnote *d* to table 12.2.
[e] Half-lives of these compounds were measured in rabbits instead of rats.

of the majority of these oximes are rather high, many of them are moderately good reactivators of sarin-inhibited acetylcholinesterase, although fairly high concentrations are needed. Used at 1 mM, most of the derivatives of oximinoacetic acid—compounds 13–20 and 24—are superior to the well-known aliphatic oxime MINA (compound 22). Against tabun-inhibited acetylcholinesterase, however, none of these oximes showed

Figure 12.2. Effect of intraperitoneal injection of an aliphatic oxime[a] on the hypothermia induced in rats by intravenous administration of soman and paraoxon

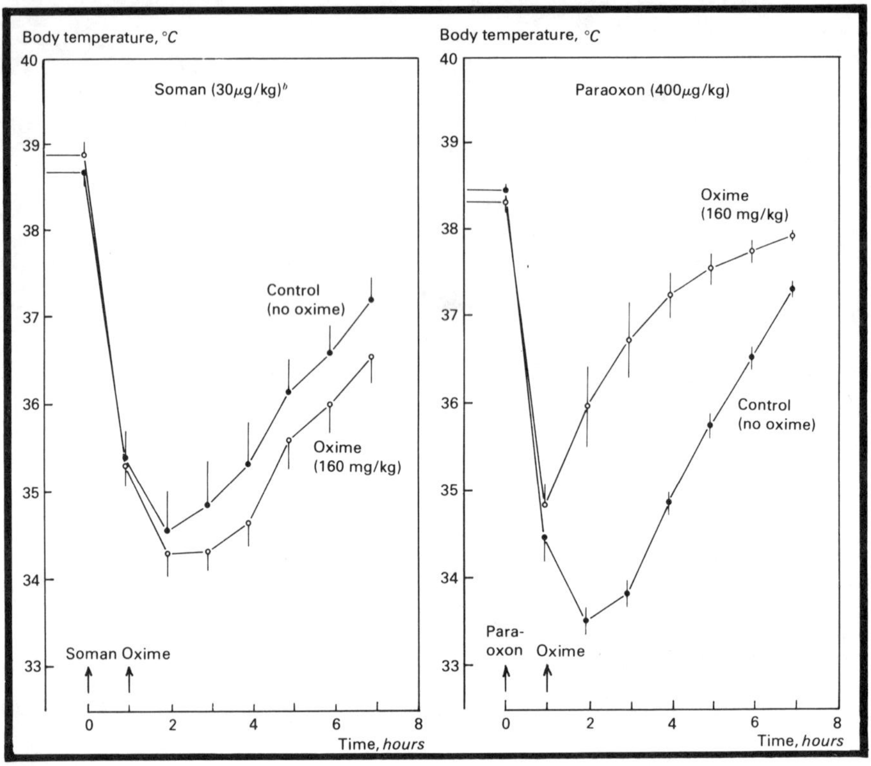

Note: Each point plotted represents the mean ± SE of results from eight animals.

[a] The aliphatic oxime used was compound 16 of table 12.3.

[b] In the case of soman intoxication, the oxime had no effect on the induced hypothermia because the inhibited acetylcholinesterase had aged before the oxime was administered, and hence could not be reactivated.

interesting activity at 1 mM. Compounds 13 and 17 were better than the others, but even with these two, reactivation did not exceed 15 per cent after 12 hours.

Most of the aliphatic oximes are relatively non-toxic, and all compounds could be administered at a dose of 50 mg/kg for determination of their biological half-lives. In general, first-order kinetics were obeyed. All compounds in this series showed longer half-lives than P2S at the same dose. Rather encouraging results were obtained with the compounds 23–27, which showed half-lives four or five times longer than that of P2S. Of these oximes, however, only compound 24 is a reasonably effective reactivator *in vitro*. Unfortunately, neither this compound, nor any of the other aliphatic oximes, showed any prophylactic activity.

Central activity of the investigated oximes

It was previously shown [28] that in DFP-poisoned rats, P2S does not reduce the hypothermia evoked by this anticholinesterase, whereas obidoxime has a significant hypothermia-reducing action. This is in accordance with Erdmann and Engelhard [30] who reported central reactivating activity of obidoxime but not of P2S. Among the aliphatic oximes, compound 16 showed the most pronounced central effectiveness against DFP and paraoxon, as is demonstrated in figure 12.2. Also two thiadiazole oximes, compounds 29 and 31, were found to be centrally active, particularly against paraoxon. Of these two, the former was also rather effective against DFP.

IV. *Conclusions*

Although our investigations produced valuable information about the biochemical and biological properties of known and new oximes, the results are not very promising in view of our main objective—to find an oxime with superior properties for prophylactic application. An evaluation of the properties of the three main groups of oximes studied in this context leads to the following conclusions.

1. The pyridinium aldoximes are in general very potent reactivators, but introduction of lipophilic groups, which makes the compounds more toxic, does not improve their biological half-lives nor their prophylactic activity.
2. The bispyridinium oxime, compound 12, shows both low toxicity and reasonable prophylactic activity and deserves further attention.
3. Among the thiadiazole oximes, only one moderately good reactivator has been found. The compounds have low toxicities, but short half-lives and no prophylactic value.
4. Most of the aliphatic oximes derived from oximinoacetic acid are moderately good reactivators, and in this respect are superior to MINA. They are of very low toxicity and some have a remarkable central activity while other members of this series have significantly longer half-lives than P2S. Their prophylactic properties, however, are very disappointing.

On the basis of these results it has been decided that continuation of our investigations should be concentrated on aliphatic oximes and bispyridinium oximes. It is hoped that new candidate agents may be derived from drugs which are known to have long biological half-lives.

References

1. Cuculis, J. J., Meyer, H. G., Sim, V. M. and Sternberger, L. A., (US Army) "Vaccines comprising the reaction product of a carrier with an aromatic compound for protecting mammals against poisoning by an anti-cholinesterase com-

position", US Patent 3642981, (app. May 1970), *Chemical Abstracts,* **76**, 131472 (1972).
2. Van Hooidonk, C. and Breebaart-Hansen, J. C. A. E., "Stereospecific reaction of isopropyl methylphosphonofluoridate (Sarin) with α-cyclodextrin", *Rec. Trav. Chim. Pays-Bas,* **89,** 291–99 (1970).
3. Van Hooidonk C. and Groos, C. C., "Model studies for enzyme inhibition. Part II. The stereospecific reaction of isopropyl p-nitrophenyl methylphosphonate with α-cyclodextrin in aqueous alkaline media", *Rec. Trav. Chim. Pays-Bas,* **89**, 845–56 (1970).
4. Van Hooidonk, C. and Breebaart–Hansen, J. C. A. E., "Model studies for enzyme inhibition. Part III. Kinetics and thermodynamics of the reaction of diisopropyl phosphorofluoridate with α-cyclodextrin in aqueous alkaline media", *Rec. Trav. Chim. Pays-Bas,* **90**, 680–86 (1971).
5. Van Hooidonk, C. and Breebaart-Hansen, J. C. A. E., "Model studies for enzyme inhibition. Part IV. The association of some alkyl methylphosphonates with α-cyclodextrin in an aqueous medium", *Rec. Trav. Chim. Pays-Bas,* **91**, 958–64 (1972).
6. Van Hooidonk, C., "Model studies for enzyme inhibition. Part V. Reactions of organophosphorus compounds with α-cyclodextrin. A quantitative approach of model activity and stereospecificity", *Rec. Trav. Chim. Pays-Bas,* **91**, 1103–109 (1972).
7. Cohen, E. M. and Mobach, E., unpublished.
8. Berry, W. K. and Davies, D. R., "The use of carbamates and atropine in the protection of animals against poisoning by 1,2,2-trimethylpropyl methylphosphonofluoridate (GD)", *Biochem. Pharmacol.,* **19,** 927–34 (1970).
9. Koster, R., "Synergisms and antagonisms between physostigmine and diisopropyl fluorophosphate in cats", *J. Pharmacol. Exp. Ther.,* **88,** 39–46 (1946).
10. Berry, W. K., Davies, D. R. and Gordon, J. J., "Protection of animals against soman (1,2,2-trimethylpropyl methylphosphonofluoridate) by pretreatment with some other organophosphorus compounds, followed by oxime and atropine", *Biochem. Pharmacol.,* **20,** 125–34 (1971).
11. Davies, D. R., Green, A. L. and Willey, G. L., "2-Hydroxyiminomethyl-N-methylpyridinium methanesulphonate and atropine in the treatment of severe organophosphate poisoning", *Brit. J. Pharmacol.,* **14**, 5–8 (1959).
12. Edery, H. and Schatzberg-Porath, G., "Prophylactic and therapeutic effects of pyridine-2-aldoxime methiodide and diacetyl monoxime against poisoning by organophosphorus compounds", *Arch. Int. Pharmacodyn.,* **121** (1–2), 104–109 (1959).
13. Zvirblis, P. and Kondritzer, A. A., "Prophylaxis against sarin poisoning in the rat by oral administration of pralidoxime chloride", *J. Pharmacol. Exp. Ther.,* **157,** 432–34 (1967).
14. Sidell, F. R., Groff, W. A. and Ellin, R. I., "Blood levels of oxime and symptoms in humans after single and multiple oral doses of 2-pyridine aldoxime methochloride", *J. Pharm. Sci.,* **58** (9), 1093–98 (1969).
15. Sidell, F. R., Groff, W. A. and Kaminskis, A., "Pralidoxime methansulfonate: plasma levels and pharmacokinetics after oral administration to man", *J. Pharm. Sci.,* **61** (7), 1136–40 (1972).
16. Berglund, F., Elwin, C.-E. and Sundwall, A., "Studies on the renal elimination of N-methylpyridinium-2-aldoxime", *Biochem. Pharmacol.,* **11**, 383–88 (1962).
17. Benschop, H. P., van Oosten, A. M., Platenburg, D. H. J. M. and van Hooidonk, C., "Isothiazolecarboxaldoximes and methylated derivatives as therapeutic agents in poisoning by organophosphorus compounds", *J. Med. Chem.,* **13**, 1208–12 (1970).

18. Hobbiger, F., Pitmann, M. and Sadler, P. W., "Reactivation of phosphorylated acetocholinesterases by pyridinium aldoximes and related compounds", *Biochem. J.*, **75**, 363–72 (1960).
19. Poziomek, E. J., Hackley, B. E. and Steinberg, G. M., "Pyridinium aldoximes", *J. Org. Chem.*, **23**, 714–17 (1958).
20. Wilson, I. B., "Designing of a new drug with antidotal properties against the nerve gas sarin", *Biochim. Biophys. Acta*, **27**, 196–99 (1958).
21. Schnekenburger, J., "Potentielle Reaktivatoren der Acetylcholinesterase. 1. Mitt. N-Alkoxy-pyridiniumcarbaldoxime", *Arch. Pharm. (Weinheim)*, **302**, 815–22 (1969).
22. Kuznetsov, S. G. and Somin, I. N., "Cholinesterase reactivators I. Synthesis of aminoalkyl esters of oximinoacetic acid", *Khim.-Farm. Zh.*, **1** (7), 30–34 (1967).
23. Somin, I. N. and Kuznetsov, S. G., "Cholinesterase reactivators II. Hydroxyiminoacetic acid amides", *Khim.-Farm. Zh.*, **2** (8), 39–44 (1968).
24. Bachman, G. B. and Welton, D. E., "Oximes of dialkylaminobutanediones", *J. Org. Chem.*, **12**, 221–25 (1947).
25. Goerdeler, J. and Hammen, H. W., "Ueber 1,2,4-Thiodiazole XVIII. 5-Methylthiodiazole", *Chem. Ber.*, **97**, 1134–46 (1964).
26. Creasey, N. H. and Green, A. L., "2-Hydroxyiminomethyl-N-methylpyridinium methanesulphonate (P2S), an antidote to organophosphorus poisoning. Its preparation, estimation, and stability", *J. Pharm. Pharmacol.*, **2**, 485–90 (1959).
27. May, J. R., Zvirblis, P. and Kondritzer, A. A., "Technical requirements and identification of pralidoxime chloride and its determination in biological material", *J. Pharm. Sci.*, **54**, 1508–12 (1965).
28. Meeter, E., Wolthuis, O. L. and van Benthem, R. M. J., "The anticholinesterase hypothermia in the rat: its practical application in the study of the central effectiveness of oximes", *Bull. World Health Organ.*, **44**, 251–57 (1971).
29. Yakl, A., Grdina, V. and Bajgar, I., "Therapeutic action of some dioximes of the pyridine series in an experimental O-isopropyl-methyl-fluorophosphonate poisoning", *Farmakol. Toksikol. (Moscow)*, **36**, 721–24 (1973).
30. Erdmann, W. D. and Engelhard, H., "Pharmakologisch-toxikologische Untersuchungen mit dem Dichlorid des Bis-(4-hydroxyiminomethyl-pyridinium-(1)-methyl) äthers, einem neuen Esterase-Reaktivator", *Arzneimittel-Forsch.*, **14**, 5–11 (1964).

13. An alternative therapy against organophosphate poisoning

O. L. WOLTHUIS

Square-bracketed numbers, thus [1], *refer to the list of references on page 141.*

I. *Limitations of oxime therapy*

About 20 years ago, when the therapeutic value of oximes in the treatment of poisoning by organophosphorus compounds first became known [1–4], it was thought that the existing, unsatisfactory therapy consisting of atropine and artificial respiration had become obsolete. It soon became clear, however, that this view was far too optimistic: not only was atropine still indispensable in therapy against organophosphates, but the desired effect of oxime therapy—complete restoration of the activity of the inhibited cholinesterase *in vivo*—could, in practice, only be partially achieved, and even then only under certain conditions. It was also discovered that, with some cholinesterase inhibitors, the interval between the moment of poisoning and the administration of an oxime largely determines the therapeutic effect. This phenomenon was found to be due to the so-called "ageing" of the phosphorylated cholinesterase [5–8]—dealkylation of the organophosphorus component of the enzyme/inhibitor complex [9–10], which leaves the enzyme resistant to reactivation. With some organophosphates, even a very rapid administration of oximes was unsuccessful [11–14].

The question arose [14] whether the failure of oxime therapy could always be explained by rapid ageing of the enzyme/inhibitor complex. In some cases of organophosphate intoxication, for example, with soman [10, 15] and benzyl methylphosphonofluoridate [16], rapid ageing did in fact prove to be the cause of the failure of the therapy. Intoxications with some other organophosphates, such as tabun and soman-Y (1,2-dimethylpropyl methylphosphonofluoridate), however, showed a resistance to oxime therapy that could not be due to ageing. Van der Meer and Wolthuis found that, in isolated preparations, very high concentrations of such oximes as PAM chloride and MINA were able to restore the function of the cholinesterase inhibited by these latter organophosphates, regardless of the interval between poisoning and therapy [15]. These authors investigated in detail the reactivation of a number of inhibitors by the oximes PAM and MINA, and were able to classify inhibitors according to the oxime-sensitivity and rate of ageing of the resulting inhibited enzymes (see table 13.1). Clearly, with some organophosphates *in vivo,* therapy with oximes failed not because of ageing, but because of the impossibility of achieving a sufficiently high oxime concentration in the body. These results justified a search for more active and less toxic reactivators. In fact, very effective oximes have been developed, for example, trimedoxime (TMB-4), obidoxime (Toxogonin) and HS-6 (2-hydroxyimino-methylpyridinium)-1-methyl-3-((carbamoyl)-pyridinium-1-methyl) ether dichloride. However, even disregarding those instances where rapid ageing is the problem, the type of oxime producing optimal results was found to differ from one inhibitor to another [17–18].

The symptoms of organophosphate poisoning are partly of peripheral, and partly of central, origin. But because most reactivating oximes do not readily penetrate the blood-brain barrier they will be of little value in counteracting central symptoms, even in a case of poisoning by an inhibitor that is sensitive to oximes [19–21]. This means that a disturbance of the function of the respiratory centres cannot effectively be antagonized by oxime administration.

The future possibilities for oxime therapy will therefore remain limited unless a universally active, extremely potent oxime of low toxicity is found that readily penetrates the blood-brain barrier. Even equipped with such a dream oxime, the therapist would have to inject the patient within seconds after intoxication to be sure of success.

The unsatisfactory nature of the presently available therapy with oximes and atropine is illustrated by the attempts of many investigators to supplement this therapy with additional medication. In animal experiments, the effectiveness of the therapy has been somewhat improved with the aid of drugs such as *d*-tubocurarine [22], hexamethonium [23], methylatropine [24], benzodiazepines [25–27] and so on.

II. *An alternative approach: chemotherapy against respiratory paralysis*

In 1969, an investigation was started in our laboratory aimed at a therapy in which an entirely different principle is applied. The approach is based on the following considerations.

1. It is well known that after blockade of the neuromuscular junction by organophosphates, only the first (few) nerve impulse(s) of a train of impulses will be transmitted to the muscle fibres [28–29].

2. Even after a profound disturbance of the respiratory centres by organophosphate poisoning, a few nerve impulses per respiratory cycle still travel down the phrenic nerve [30].

3. The experiments of Bezold in 1867 demonstrated that veratrum alkaloids are able to change the response of striated muscle fibres to a single

Table 13.1. Variations in rapidity of ageing and sensitivity to oxime reactivation of cholinesterases inhibited by various organophosphorus compounds

Characteristics of inhibited cholinesterase		
Oxime concentration required for effective reactivation	Rate of ageing	Examples of organophosphorus compounds
Low	Slow	Sarin, DFP, S4
High	Slow	Tabun, soman-Y
Low	Fast	Benzyl methylphosphonofluoridate
High	Fast	Soman, S12

stimulus—from a single twitch into a prolonged contracture. More recently, a number of semisynthetic compounds such as germine monoacetate [31–33], and a number of synthetic compounds such as 3-chloro-2,5,6-trimethylbenzoic acid (U23223) and 9-anthroic acid (ANCA) [34–35], appeared to induce the same type of action in muscle cells without showing the side-effects of the veratrum alkaloids.

4. If artificial respiration is applied over a sufficiently long period, the poisoned victim resumes spontaneous respiration [36–42]. In a study by Meeter and Wolthuis [19], the rate of recovery of respiration in the rat after poisoning with various organophosphates was found to be dose-dependent. The results of this study, supplemented with hitherto unpublished data, are shown in figure 13.1. The mechanism of recovery differed from one inhibitor to another. In some instances, spontaneous reactivation of the cholinesterase at the neuromuscular junction was involved (low lethal doses, such as 4 LD_{50}, of sarin or ethyl-S-2-diisopropylaminoethyl methylphosphonothioate (S4)). In others (low lethal doses of DFP and cyclopentyl-S-2-trimethylaminoethyl methylphosphonothioate (S54)) this could not be the explanation of the recovery, and an adaptation of the postjunctional membrane might have been responsible [43]. And in a third category of organophosphates (soman and cyclopentyl-S-2-diisopropylaminoethyl methylphosphonothioate (S12)), which had a predominantly central action, recovery of respiration might have been due to a rapid *de novo* synthesis of cholinesterase in the brain [44].

Our present attempts are aimed at bridging the period of respiratory failure with the aid of a medication that converts single twitches in respiratory muscles into contractures of sufficient duration for adequate respiratory movements to occur. Such a therapy would have the advantage of being independent of the peripheral or central nature of the respiratory block. This is illustrated schematically in figure 13.2.

Initially, we tried to maintain respiration in DFP-poisoned, anaesthetized, atropinized rats by the administration of the semisynthetic veratrum derivative, germine monoacetate (GMA) [45]. By itself, this compound was almost ineffective in preventing respiratory failure: it even showed a tendency to

Figure 13.1. Relationship between dose of several organophosphate anticholinesterases administered to rats and time during which artificial respiration was required before animals could breathe unaided for one hour

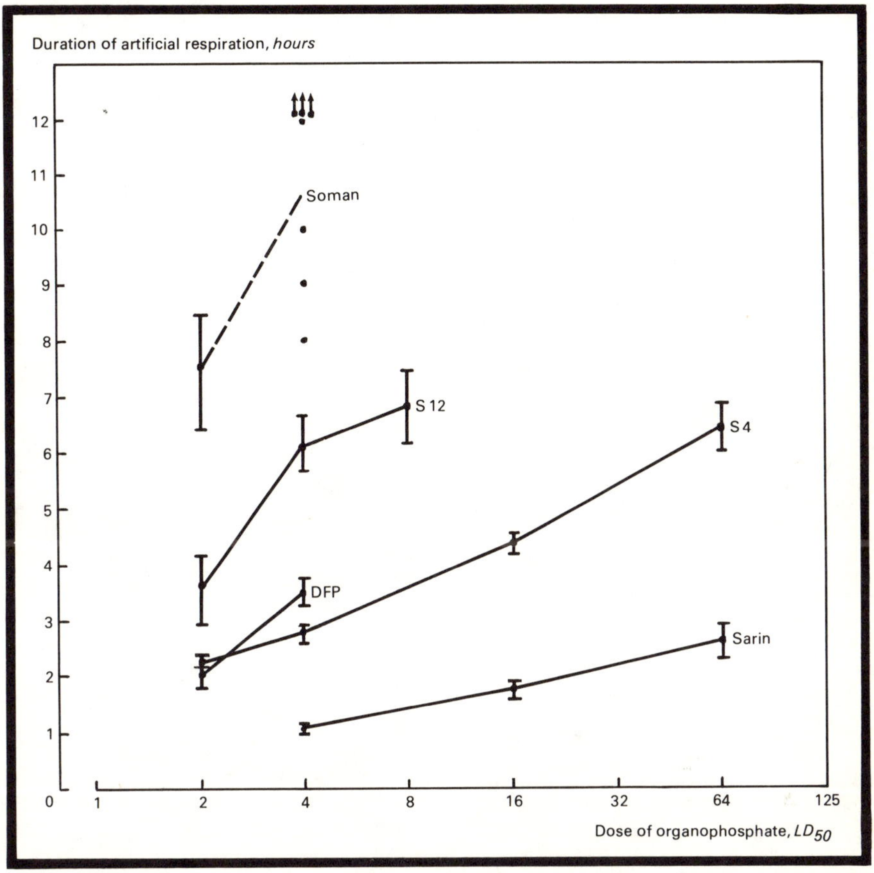

Notes: Each point plotted represents the mean ± SE of results from at least six animals. In the case of the administration of 4 LD_{50} of soman, however, values for individual animals are shown, since three out of seven animals were still unable to breathe unaided for one hour at the termination of the experiment.

prolong the respiratory failure if administered within 30 minutes after DFP. This might have been due to an undesirable interaction between the effect of GMA and the repetitive response of the muscles soon after organophosphate poisoning [29, 46], so in another series of experiments, a very small dose of *d*-tubocurarine was given together with GMA in order to suppress the organophosphate-induced repetitive firing of the muscle fibres. This treatment prevented respiratory paralysis in the majority of the rats intoxicated with 2 LD_{50} DFP. The rather unpredictable results obtained with GMA, and the fact that we were never able to save all animals, prompted us to try the

Figure 13.2. Events during normal respiration (left), after intoxication with a predominantly peripherally acting anticholinesterase (centre) and with a centrally acting anticholinesterase (right), and effects, in each case, of additional administration of ANCA on contractions of the diaphragm

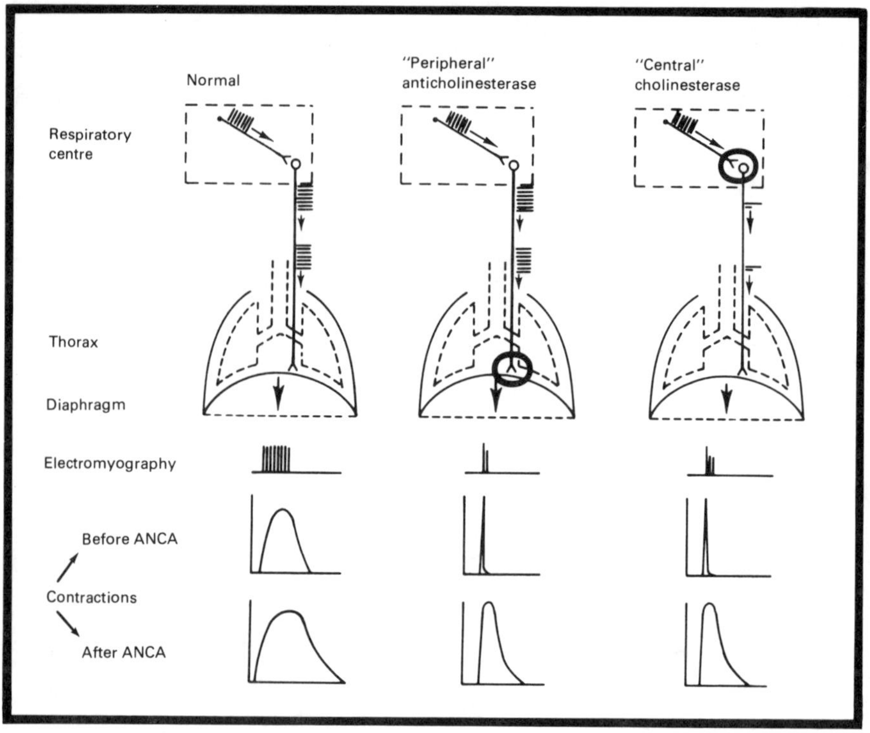

above-mentioned substituted benzoic acids U23223 and ANCA. Since both these compounds are practically insoluble in water, we used the sodium salts.

Treatment with U23223 (see table 13.2) was found to prevent respiratory paralysis in all anaesthetized, atropinized rats intoxicated with 2 LD_{50} DFP or 4 LD_{50} paraoxon [45]. Moreover, it could be shown [47] that after intoxication with the predominantly centrally acting organophosphate soman (4 LD_{50}), this treatment postponed respiratory failure by about 2½ hours. To our disappointment, however, a second injection of U23223 to the soman-poisoned animals, administered just before the respiratory minute volume became insufficient, only postponed the onset of respiratory failure by about 10 minutes. In contrast to the animals treated with one injection of U23223, some of those that received two injections ultimately died, notwithstanding artificial respiration. The reasons for this effect are not known, but it is unlikely that it can be ascribed to a toxic metabolite of U23223, since similar results were obtained with ANCA, a compound with the same pharmacological action but a different chemical structure.

Table 13.2. The effects of U23223 on the respiratory paralysis caused by DFP, paraoxon or soman in anaesthetized, atropinized rats

Organophosphate		Treatment		Interval between injection of organophosphate and onset of respiratory paralysis	Duration of artificial respiration required to restore spontaneous respiration
Compound	Dose LD_{50}	Compound	Dose *mg/kg*	*min*	*min (mean ±SE)*
DFP	2	Saline	–	6–9	105±34
DFP	2	Na-U23223	32 (*sc*)	–	0
Paraoxon	4	Saline	–	1–2	55±3
Paraoxon	4	Na-U23223	8 (*iv*)+ 32 (*sc*)	–	0
Soman	4	Saline	–	1–2	>360[a]
Soman	4	Na-U23223	16 (*iv*)	151±11	>360[a]

[a] Artificial respiration discontinued after 360 minutes without restoration of spontaneous respiration. The criterion in these experiments was one hour of uninterrupted spontaneous breathing.

Subsequent experiments were carried out with ANCA because this substance is commercially available and because its spectrophotometric detection in blood is much easier than that of U23223. Postmortem examination of rats which died from soman and ANCA revealed a very rapid development of rigor mortis (see plate 13.1) and extremely contracted ventricles of the heart combined with atrial and pulmonary congestion. This raised the question whether an accumulation of calcium in the muscles might be involved in the abnormal rigidity of the muscles and the unexpected death of the animals. We therefore investigated whether calcium did accumulate in the muscles, and, if so, to what extent [48]. It appeared that resting muscles did not accumulate calcium, whether the animal was treated with ANCA or not. Indirect stimulation increased the calcium content by 28 per cent in untreated rats as well as in those which had received either soman or ANCA. If, however, soman and ANCA were combined, the accumulation increased significantly, from 28 per cent to 70 per cent. In the same series of experiments, we tried to reduce the influx of calcium into the muscle fibres by lowering the concentration of free calcium in the blood with EDTA. EDTA diminished the calcium accumulation in the muscles of the rats treated with soman and ANCA from 70 per cent to 44 per cent. In these EDTA-treated rats, the onset of respiratory failure was significantly delayed and the moment at which they resumed spontaneous respiration was significantly earlier than in those which received no EDTA. This means that the period during which artificial respiration was needed had been markedly shortened by administration of EDTA. Moreover, regular checks for spontaneous breathing during the period of respiratory failure revealed that the animals treated with EDTA maintained breathing for longer periods (see figure 13.3).

Plate 13.1. Bodies of rats injected with soman and ANCA (left) or killed in ether (right), five minutes after death

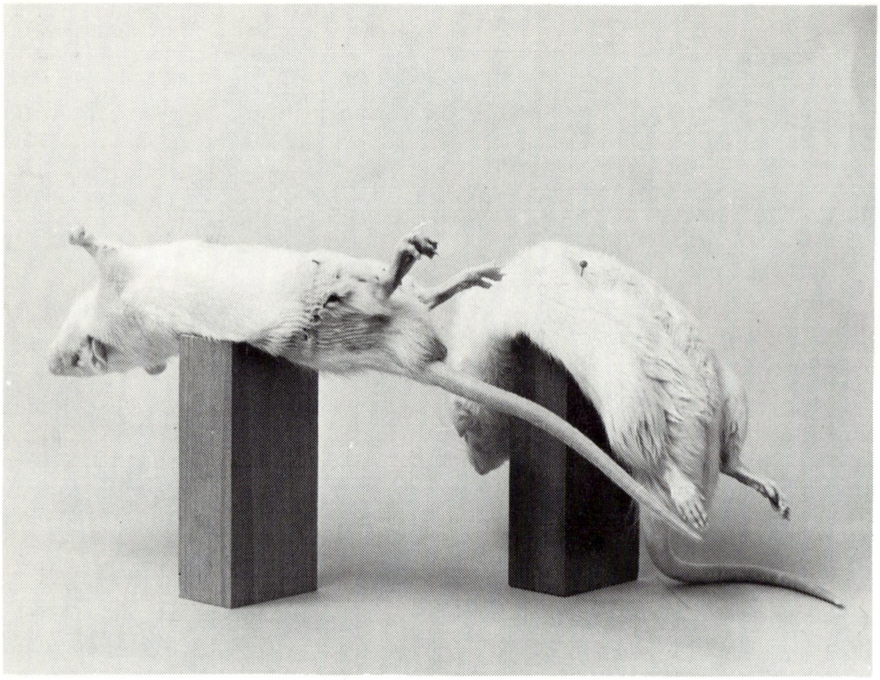

These results demonstrate that the (delayed) respiratory failure in soman-intoxicated, ANCA-treated rats is related to calcium accumulation in active muscles. It is interesting that the therapeutic efficacy of ANCA is not hampered if the accumulation of calcium is reduced. For future research, this means that if we succeed in controlling the calcium accumulation, respiratory failure might be prevented.

III. *Conclusions*

The present ANCA therapy only delays respiratory paralysis after poisoning with soman and possibly other organophosphates that cause a long-lasting respiratory failure. However, it was interesting to test whether treatment with ANCA in conjunction with atropine is able to save the lives of un-anaesthetized rats poisoned with sarin, an organophosphate which causes a respiratory paralysis of shorter duration. Recent unpublished results obtained by Dr L. A. Kepner in our laboratory showed that rats can be saved from at least 32 LD_{50}. These results, if confirmed, are encouraging, because a therapy with potentially useful oximes and atropine in our rats has never yielded a better protection than against 5 LD_{50} sarin.

Figure 13.3. Effects of ANCA and EDTA on the ability of anaesthetized, atropinized rats to breathe spontaneously after intoxication with soman

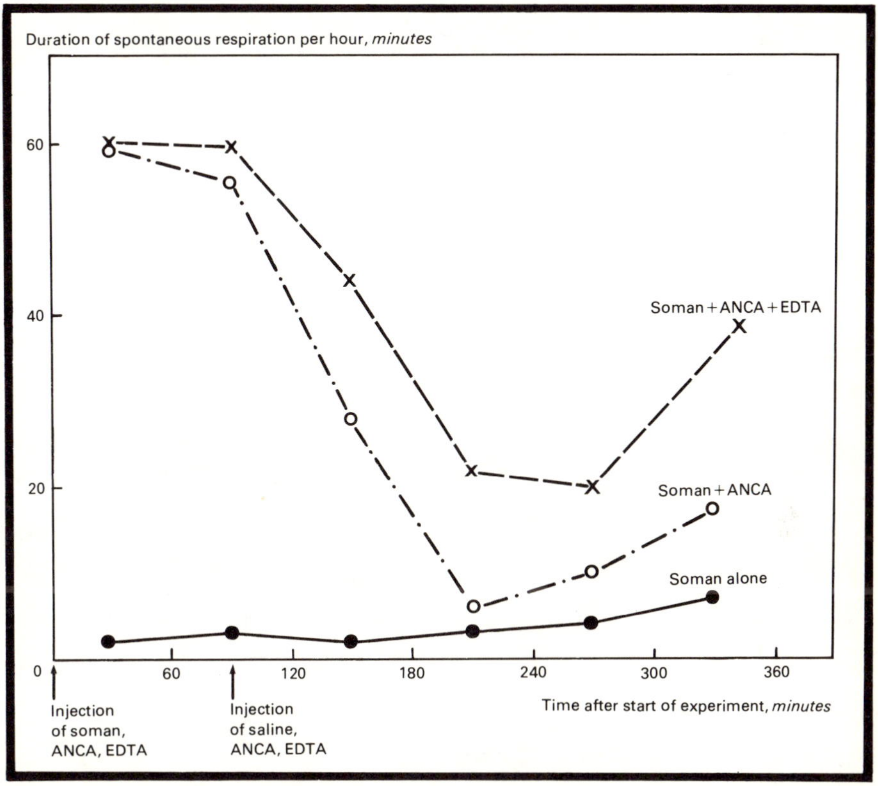

Note: Each point plotted represents the mean total time per hour that the animals could breathe spontaneously: 16 animals were treated with ANCA and EDTA, 17 animals were treated with ANCA alone, and 11 animals received no treatment.

Acknowledgements

The author wishes to thank Dr E. Meeter and Dr R. L. Polak for their critical discussions about the manuscript, and Dr C. A. van der Meer, Dr V. J. Nickolson and Dr L. A. Kepner for some of the data presented in this paper.

References

1. Wilson, I. B. and Meislich, E. K., "Reactivation of acetylcholinesterase inhibited by alkylphosphates", *J. Am. Chem. Soc.*, **75,** 4628–29 (1953).
2. Wilson, I. B. and Ginsburg, S., "A powerful reactivator of alkyl phosphate-inhibited acetylcholinesterase", *Biochim. Biophys. Acta*, **18,** 168–70 (1955).
3. Jandorf, B. J., "Chemical reactions of nerve gases (organophosphorus anti-

cholinesterases) in neutral solutions. I. Reactions with hydroxylamine", *J. Am. Chem. Soc.*, **78,** 3686–91 (1956).
4. Namba, T. and Hiraki, K., "PAM (pyridine-2-aldoxime methiodide) therapy for alkylphosphate poisoning", *J. Am. Med. Assoc.*, **166,** 1834–39 (1958).
5. Hobbiger, F., "Effect of nicotinhydroxamic acid methiodide on human plasma cholinesterase inhibited by organophosphates containing a dialkylphosphato group", *Brit. J. Pharmacol. Chemother.*, **10,** 356–62 (1955).
6. Wilson, I. B., "Promotion of acetylcholinesterase activity by the anionic site", *Discuss. Faraday Soc.*, **20,** 119–25 (1955).
7. Jandorf, B. J., Crowell, E. A. and Levin, A. P., "Role of hydroxamic acids in prevention and reversal of cholinesterase inactivation by DFP and sarin", *Federation Proc.*, **14,** 231 (1955).
8. Davies, D. R. and Green, A. L., "The kinetics of reactivation, by oximes, of cholinesterase inhibited by organophosphorus compounds", *Biochem., J.*, **63,** 529–35 (1956).
9. Berends, F., Posthumus, C. H., Sluys, I. van der and Deierkauf, F. A., "The chemical basis of the "ageing process" of DFP-inhibited pseudocholinesterase", *Biochim. Biophys. Acta,* **34,** 576–78 (1959).
10. Fleisher, J. H. and Harris, L. W., "Dealkylation as a mechanism for ageing of cholinesterase after poisoning with pinacolyl methylphosphonofluoridate", *Biochem. Pharmacol.*, **14,** 641–50 (1965).
11. Wilson, I. B. and Sondheimer, F., "A specific antidote against lethal alkyl phosphate intoxication. V. Antidotal properties", *Arch. Biochem. Biophys.*, **69,** 468–74 (1957).
12. Cohen, E. M. and Wiersinga, H., "Oximes in the treatment of nerve gas poisoning", *Acta Physiol. Pharmacol. Neerl.*, **8,** 40–51 (1959).
13. Fleisher, J. H., Michel, H. O., Yates, L. and Harrison, C. S., "1,1′-trimethylene bis(4-formylpyridinium bromide) dioxime (TMB-4) and 2-pyridine aldoxime methiodide (2-PAM) as adjuvants to atropine in the treatment of anticholinesterase poisoning", *J. Pharmacol. Exp. Ther.*, **129,** 31–35 (1960).
14. Loomis, T. P. and Salafski, B., "Antidotal action of pyridinium oximes in anticholinesterase poisoning; comparative effects of soman, sarin and neostigmine on neuromuscular function", *Toxicol. Appl. Pharmacol.*, **5,** 685–701 (1963).
15. Meer, C. van der and Wolthuis, O. L., "The effect of oximes on isolated organs intoxicated with organophosphorus anticholinesterases", *Biochem. Pharmacol.*, **14,** 1299–312 (1965).
16. Meer, C. van der, unpublished.
17. Heilbronn, E. and Tolagen, B., "Toxogonin in sarin, soman and tabun poisoning", *Biochem. Pharmacol.*, **14,** 73–77 (1965).
18. Wolthuis, O. L. and Cohen, E. M., "The effects of P_2S, TMB_4 and LüH6 on the rat phrenic nerve diaphragm preparation treated with soman or tabun", *Biochem. Pharmacol.*, **16**, 361–67 (1967).
19. Meeter, E. and Wolthuis, O. L., "The spontaneous recovery of respiration and neuromuscular transmission in the rat after anticholinesterase poisoning", *Eur. J. Pharmacol.*, **2,** 377–86 (1968).
20. Meeter, E. and Wolthuis, O. L., "The effects of cholinesterase inhibitors on the body temperature of the rat", *Eur. J. Pharmacol.*, **4,** 18–24 (1968).
21. Meeter, E., Wolthuis, O. L. and van Benthem, R. M. J., "The anticholinesterase hypothermia in the rat: its practical application in the study of the central effectiveness of oximes", *Bull. World Health Organ.*, **44,** 251–57 (1971).
22. Rump, S., Kaliszan, A. and Edelwein, Z., "Actions of curare-like agents on the

neuromuscular abnormalities caused by an organophosphate in the rat", *Arch. Int. Pharmacodyn. Ther.*, **173,** 173–81 (1968).
23. Ohnesorge, F. K., "Wirkungen und Wirkungsmechanismen von Alkan-bis-ammoniumderivaten bei der Organophosphatvergiftungen", *Naunyn-Schmiedebergs Arch. Pharmakol. Exp. Pathol.*, **263,** 72–88 (1969).
24. Cohen, E. M., unpublished.
25. Rump, S., Galecka, E., Grudzińska, E., Ilczuk, I. and Rabsztyn, T., "New trends in experimental therapy of organophosphate intoxications", in *Proceedings of the Third International Congress of Pesticide Chemistry, Helsinki, 3–9 July 1974,* abstract no. 302.
26. Lipp, J. A., "Effects of diazepam on soman-induced seizure activity and convulsions", *Electroencephalog. Clin. Neurophysiol.*, **32,** 557–69 (1972).
27. Lipp, J. A., "Effects of benzodiazepine derivatives on soman-induced seizure activity and convulsions in the monkey", *Arch. Int. Pharmacodyn. Ther.*, **202,** 244–51 (1973).
28. Barnes, J. M. and Duff, J. I., "The role of cholinesterase at the myoneural junction", *Brit. J. Pharmacol.*, **8,** 334–39 (1953).
29. Meer, C. van der and Meeter, E., "The mechanism of action of anti-cholinesterases II", *Acta Physiol. Pharmacol. Neerl.*, **4,** 472–81 (1956).
30. Wolthuis, O. L. and Meeter, E., unpublished.
31. Flacke, W., "Studies on veratrum alkaloids. XXXVI. The action of germine monoacetate and germine diacetate on mammalian skeletal muscle", *J. Pharmacol. Exp. Ther.*, **141,** 230–36 (1963).
32. Hofmann, W., "Newer drugs for myasthenia gravis; a microphysiologic study of effects", *J. Pharmacol. Exp. Ther.*, **160,** 349–59 (1967).
33. Standaert, F. G. and Detweiler, P. B., "The neuromuscular pharmacology of germine-3-acetate and germine-3,16-acetate", *J. Pharmacol. Exp. Ther.*, **171,** 223–41 (1969).
34. Moffet, R. B. and Tang, A. H., "Skeletal muscle stimulants. Substituted benzoic acids", *J. Med. Chem.*, **11,** 1020–22 (1968).
35. Tang, A. H., Schroeder, L. A. and Keasling, H. H., "U23223 (3-chloro-2,5,6-trimethylbenzoic acid), a veratrinic agent selective for the skeletal muscles", *Arch. Int. Pharmacodyn.*, **175,** 319–29 (1968).
36. De Candole, C. A., Douglas, W. W., Evans, C. L., Holmes, R., Spencer, K. E. V., Torrance, R. W. and Wilson, K. M., "The failure of respiration in death by anticholinesterase poisoning", *Brit. J. Pharmacol. Chemother.*, **8,** 466–75 (1953).
37. McNamara, B. P., Koelle, G. B. and Gilman, A., "The treatment of diisopropyl fluorophosphate (DFP) poisoning in rabbits", *J. Pharmacol. Exp. Ther.*, **88,** 27–33 (1946).
38. McNamara, B. P., Murtha, E. F., Bergener, A. D., Robinson, E. M., Bender, C. W. and Wills, J. H., "Studies on the mechanism of DFP and TEPP", *J. Pharmacol. Exp. Ther.*, **110,** 232–40 (1954).
39. Lundholm, L., "The effect of DFP on respiration and muscular function in the rabbit", *Acta Physiol. Scand.*, **16,** 345–66 (1949).
40. Karczmar, A. G. and Koppanyi, T., "Central effects of diisopropyl fluorophosphonate in urodele larvae", *Naunyn-Schmiedebergs Arch. Pharmakol. Exp. Pathol.*, **219,** 263–72 (1953).
41. Barnes, J. M., "The reactions of rabbits to poisoning by p-nitrophenyl-diethylphosphate (E600)", *Brit. J. Pharmacol. Chemother.*, **8,** 208–11 (1953).
42. Wright, P. G., "An analysis of the central and peripheral components of respiratory failure produced by anticholinesterase poisoning in the rabbit", *J. Physiol.*, (*London*), **126,** 52–70 (1954).

43. Meeter, E., ''Desensitization of the end-plate membrane following cholinesterase inhibition, an adjustment to a new working situation'', *Acta Physiol. Pharmacol. Neerl.,* **15,** 243–58 (1969).
44. Harris, L. W., Yamamura, H. I. and Fleisher, J. H., ''De novo synthesis of acetylcholinesterase in guinea pig retina after inhibition by pinacolyl methylphosphonofluoridate", *Biochem. Pharmacol.,* **20,** 2927–29 (1971).
45. Wolthuis, O. L. and Postel-Westra, K. B., ''Germine monoacetate and 3-chloro-2,5,6-trimethylbenzoic acid; therapeutic possibilities against inhibition of neuromuscular transmission by organophosphorus anticholinesterase compounds'', *Eur. J. Pharmacol.,* **14,** 93–97 (1971).
46. Masland, R. L. and Wigton, R. S., ''Nerve activity accompanying fasciculation produced by prostigmine'', *J. Neurophysiol.,* **3,** 269–75 (1940).
47. Wolthuis, O. L. and Cohen, E. M., "Veratrinic compounds in the therapy of organophosphorus anticholinesterase intoxication'', in Deichmann, W. B., ed., *Pesticides and the environment: a continuing controversy* (New York, Intercontinental Medical Book Corp., 1973) Volume II, pp. 469–77.
48. Nickolson, V. J., Clason-van der Wiel, H. J. and Wolthuis, O. L., ''Further studies on the therapy of organophosphorus anticholinesterase intoxication with veratrinic compounds; the role of calcium", *Eur. J. Pharmacol.,* **30,** 188–96 (1975).

14. Some toxicological consequences of the alkylating action of organophosphorus compounds

Kh. LOHS, W. GIBEL and G. W. FISCHER

Sqaure-bracketed numbers, thus [1], *refer to the list of references on page 149.*

I. *Introduction*

According to most standard textbooks of biochemistry and toxicology, the biochemical mode of action of organophosphorus compounds seems to be basically understood: by phosphorylating, and hence inhibiting, the enzyme acetylcholinesterase, these compounds block the transmission of impulses through the nervous system and may thus eventually cause paralysis and death. The problem of therapy against this type of poisoning has been studied in considerable depth, and although it is clear from the voluminous literature published during the past two decades that it has still not been completely solved and that a single universal antidote against these intoxications is yet to be discovered, the value of the cholinolytic properties of atropine and the enzyme-reactivating properties of the oximes (for example, PAM and its derivatives) in treating organophosphate intoxication is well appreciated.

The purpose of this chapter is to draw attention to the side-effects and delayed effects of exposure to organophosphorus compounds. This is a problem that has so far been largely ignored, because these effects are the result not of the well-understood phosphorylating action of organophosphorus compounds, but of their little-known alkylating reactions. The work described below is based on earlier studies carried out in 1966–67 on some phosphoric- and phosphonic-ester preparations used in veterinary medicine for ecto- and endo-parasite control (for example, "bubulin", a preparation containing the organophosphate trichlorphon, 0.5 per cent 2-PAM and 0.15 per cent atropine sulphate).

II. *Alkylating reactions of organophosphates*

It is well known from the studies of Hackley, Steinberg and Lamb [1–2] that sarin and other organophosphates react with pyridinium aldoximes to form highly toxic compounds. In our studies, we used 2-PAM to convert selected phosphoric- and phosphonic-acid derivatives (pesticides) to the corresponding N-methyl-pyridine-2-aldoxime salts, and we were able to obtain

Figure 14.1. Rate of alkylation of NBP by various organophosphates in 1.0 M methanol solution at 25°C

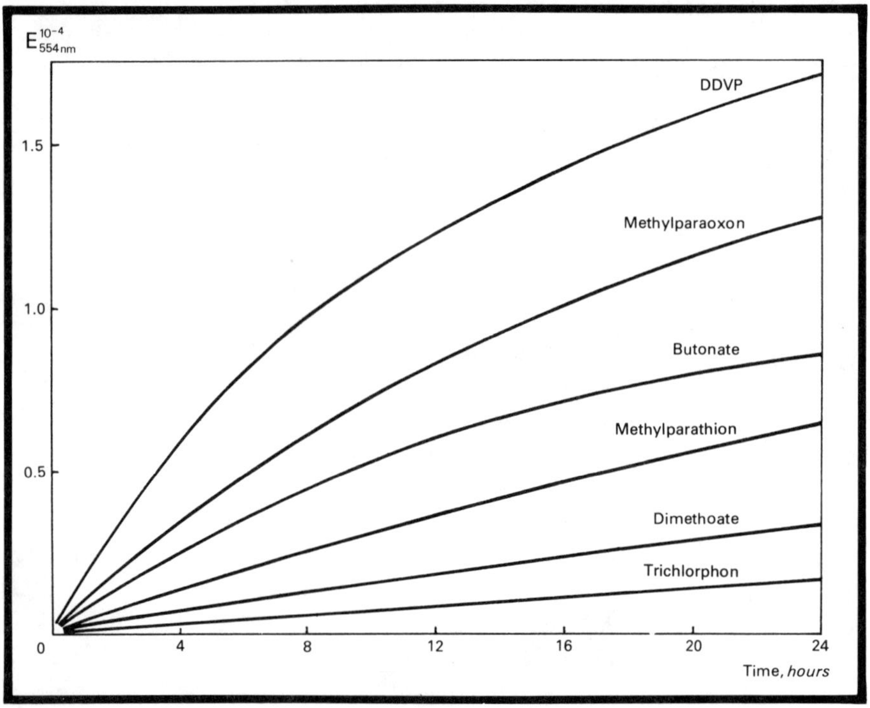

Note: $E^{10^{-4}}_{554\,nm}$=extinction at 554 nm, extrapolated to a 10^{-4} M solution.
Source: Fischer, G. W. and Lohs, Kh., "Zur Einschätzung des Alkylierungspotentials onkologisch bedeutsamer Phosphorsäureester mit Hilfe der NBP-Reaktion", *Arch. Geschwulstforsch.,* **42** (1), 34–40 (1973).

these salts in a crystalline form in order to study their toxicity in detail [3]. The most interesting aspect of this conversion is that phosphorylated oximes do not form, as might be expected: instead the oxime structure remains intact, and dealkylated organophosphorus esters, together with salts of the N-methyl-pyridine cations, are obtained:

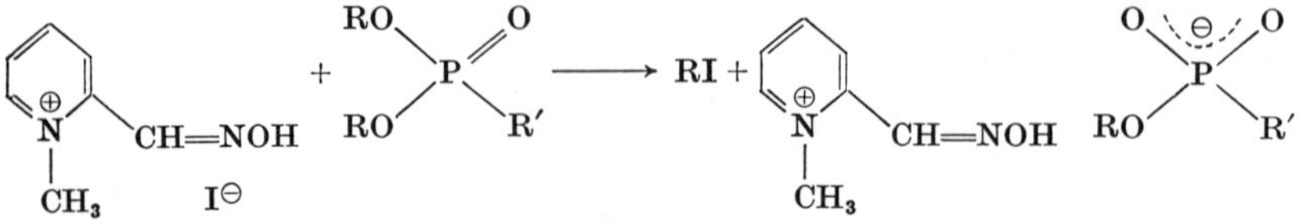

(This reaction is analogous to a conversion with potassium iodide, which also results in dealkylation.) From our preliminary investigations, we were not able to conclude whether such a dealkylation mechanism also operated *in vivo*. However, our findings prompted us to study in more detail the biochemical consequences of the alkylating effects of such organo-

Table 14.1. Incidence of tumours in rats after treatment with trichlorphon

Dose *mg/kg*	Route of application	Number of animals treated	Average time of survival *days*	Number of animals examined histologically	Number of tumours	
					Malign	Benign
Control[a]	Oral	40	743	36	–	3
Control[a]	Intramuscular	40	711	35	–	4
15	Oral	40	654	28	7	19
15	Intramuscular	40	565	27	4	7

[a] Saline (0.9 per cent NaCl).

phosphates. In 1963, the important work of Heilbron [4] and of Witter and Gaines [5–6] on the "ageing" of phosphorylated acetylcholinesterase, and the possibility that this reaction involves the hydrolytic splitting of an alkoxy group from the phosphorylated serine residue in the active site of the enzyme, were published. At that time, we were concerned basically with studies on the relationship between structure and function in organophosphorus compounds, with particular reference to alkylation. Thus, X-ray structure analysis of trichlorphon has revealed that, in the crystalline state, the binding gaps of the methoxy groups on the phosphorus atom are significantly different (1.53 Å and 1.58 Å) [7]. Parallel ESR spectroscopic studies on trichlorphon and other organophosphates have also suggested that phosphorylation may not be the only reaction in which these compounds may be involved [8–11].

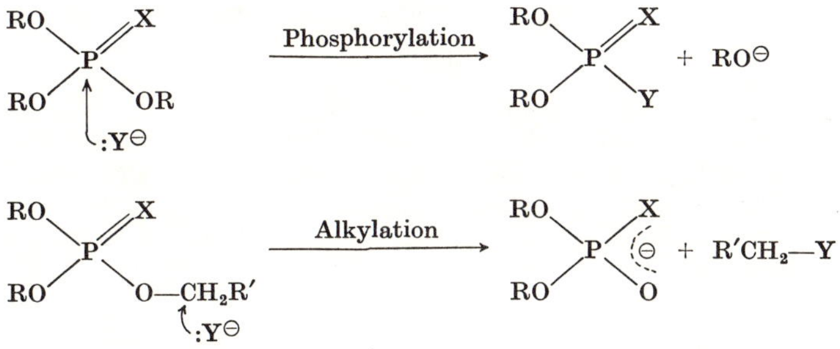

Table 14.2. Incidence of tumours in rats after treatment with dimethoate

Dose *mg/kg*	Route of application	Number of animals treated	Average time of survival *days*	Number of animals examined histologically	Number of tumours	
					Malign	Benign
Control[a]	Oral	40	743	36	–	3
Control[a]	Intramuscular	40	711	35	–	4
5	Oral	40	518	26	2	7
15	Oral	40	511	25	3	5
30	Oral	40	627	20	4	2
15	Intramuscular	40	570	30	6	5

[a] Saline (0.9 per cent NaCl).

Table 14.3. Location of tumours and histological diagnosis in rats after treatment with trichlorphon

Histological number	Single dose *mg/kg*	Total dose[a] *mg/animal*	Route of application	Time of survival *days*	Type and location of tumour	Histological diagnosis
24	15	186	Oral	440	Carcinoma: lung	Squamous-epithelial carcinoma
41	15	192	Oral	450	Malign reticulosis	–
85	15	252	Oral	562	Sarcoma: spleen	Reticulum cell sarcoma
94	15	243	Oral	569	Sarcoma: spleen	Reticulum cell sarcoma
142	15	303	Oral	710	Carcinoma: liver	Hepatocellular carcinoma
148	15	309	Oral	724	Sarcoma: upper jaw	Fibrosarcoma
177	15	348	Oral	813	Carcinoma: cardiac region of stomach	–
22	15	183	Intramuscular	433	Malign reticulosis	–
46	15	216	Intramuscular	510	Sarcoma: liver	Fibrosarcoma
88	15	249	Intramuscular	549	Sarcoma: spleen	Reticulum cell sarcoma
103	15	267	Intramuscular	629	Sarcoma: spleen	Reticulum cell sarcoma

[a] The total dose indicates the amount of trichlorphon administered to the animal (in "single-dose" aliquots) before it died.

In the meantime, we have carried out a number of studies on the alkylating potential of various organophosphorus compounds [12–14], and the results are shown in figure 14.1.

We also studied the question of the alkylating action of organophosphorus compounds *in vivo*. In animal experiments [15], we were able to show that, in addition to their haematotoxic and hepatotoxic effects, trichlorphon and dimethoate have a distinct carcinogenic activity (see tables 14.1–14.4). Together with the data on mutagenic and teratogenic effects of organophosphorus compounds presented by other authors, these findings suggest that the alkylation reactions operate on genetically relevant nucleic acids and on biochemically important protein structures that were not studied enough in earlier investigations into the effects of organophosphate cholinesterase inhibitors [16].

More attention should be paid to the psychopathological and neurological effects of organophosphorus compounds [17]. It may well be that biochemical alkylation processes involving, for example, biogenic amines such as serotonin, are responsible for the side-effects and delayed effects that have been observed [18].

In considering the mode of action of antidotes against organophosphate intoxications, the side-effects and delayed effects of organophosphorus pesticides and chemical-warfare agents have not so far received the atten-

Table 14.4. Location of tumours and histological diagnosis in rats after treatment with dimethoate

Histological number	Single dose *mg/kg*	Total dose[a] *mg/animal*	Route of application	Time of survival *days*	Type and location of tumour	Histological diagnosis
18	5	50	Oral	353	Malign reticulosis	–
44	5	77	Oral	538	Sarcoma: spleen (with different metastases)	Reticulum cell sarcoma
21	15	237	Oral	558	Sarcoma: colon	Polymorphocellular sarcoma
71	15	237	Oral	558	Sarcoma: spleen (with pancreas metastases)	Reticulum cell sarcoma
118	15	291	Oral	680	Carcinoma: liver	Hepatocellular carcinoma
27	30	256	Oral	451	Sarcoma: liver	Fibrosarcoma
49	30	522	Oral	609	Malign reticulosis	–
136	30	594	Oral	697	Sarcoma: spleen	Reticulum cell sarcoma
168	30	690	Oral	810	Sarcoma: spleen	Reticulum cell sarcoma
20	15	174	Intra muscular	410	Sarcoma: spleen	Fibrosarcoma
74	15	234	Intra-muscular	551	Sarcoma: abdomen	Spindle cell sarcoma
89	15	246	Intra muscular	572	Sarcoma: ovary	Alveolar sarcoma
177	15	279	Intra-muscular	655	Malign reticulosis	–
125	15	327	Intra-muscular	667	Sarcoma: spleen	Reticulum cell sarcoma
128	15	291	Intra-muscular	683	Carcinoma: liver	Hepatocellular carcinoma

[a] The total dose indicates the amount of dimethoate administered to the animal (in "single-dose" aliquots) before it died.

tion they deserve. The possibility of subacute damage and, consequently, the risk of carcinogenic and other delayed effects, must be accepted. The problem of the delayed effects of exposure to chemical-warfare agents is discussed in more detail in a SIPRI study [19].

References

1. Hackley, B. E., Steinberg, G. M. and Lamb, C. J., "Formation of potent inhibitors of acetylcholinesterases (AChE) by reaction of pyridine aldoximes with isopropylmethylphosphonofluoridate (GB)", *Arch. Biochem. Biophys.*, **80**, 211–14 (1959).
2. Lamb, C. J., Steinberg, G. M. and Hackley, B. E., "Isopropyl methylphosphonylated bisquaternary oximes: powerful inhibitors of cholinesterase" *Biochim. Biophys. Acta,* **89,** 171–74 (1964).
3. Kühn, G., Fischer, G. W. and Lohs, Kh., "Synthese, Toxizität und Cholinesterase. Hemmwirkung von N-Methylpyridinium-2-aldoxime-Salzen insektizider Phosphorsäureester", *Arch. Pharmazie,* **300**, 363–70 (1967).

4. Heilbronn, E., "*In vitro* reactivation and "ageing" of tabun inhibited blood cholinesterase. Studies with N-methylpyridinium-2-aldoxime methane sulphonate and N,N′-trimethylene bis (pyridinium-4-aldoxime) dibromide", *Biochem. Pharmacol.,* **12,** 25–28 (1963).
5. Witter, R. F. and Gaines, T. B., "Relationship between depression of brain or plasma cholinesterase and paralysis in chickens caused by certain organic phosphorus compounds", *Biochem. Pharmacol.,* **12**, 1377–86 (1963).
6. Witter, R. F. and Gaines, T. B., "Rate of formation *in vivo* of the unreactivatable form of brain cholinesterase in chickens given DDVP or malathion *Biochem. Pharmacol.,* **12,** 1421–27 (1963).
7. Höhne, E. and Lohs, Kh., "Die Kristallstruktur des Trichlorphons $C_4H_8O_4PCl_3$", *Z. Naturforsch.,* **24 b,** 1071–74 (1969).
8. Lassmann, G., Damerau, W. and Lohs, Kh., "Strahleninduzierte freie Radikale in phosphororganischen Verbindungen. I. Radikalausbeuten und Radikalkinetik bei Phosphonsäureestern vom Typ des Trichlorphon nach Röntgenbestrahlung", *Z. Naturforsch.,* **23 b,** 771 (1968).
9. Lassmann, G., Damerau, W. and Lohs, Kh., "Strahleninduzierte freie Radikale in phosphororganischen Verbindungen. II. Struktur freier Radikale in Trichlorphon nach Röntgenbestrahlung bei Zimmertemperatur", *Z. Naturforsch.,* **24 b**, 1375–80 (1969).
10. Lassmann, G., Damerau, W. and Lohs, Kh., "Strahleninduzierte freie Radikale in phosphororganischen Verbindungen. III. Bildung und Umwandlung primärer Radikale in Trichlorphon nach Bestrahlung bei 77°K", *Z. Naturforsch.,* **24 b**, 1381–84 (1969).
11. Damerau, W., Lassmann, G. and Lohs, Kh., "ESR of phosphorus-containing free radicals in aqueous solution. Evidence for angular dependence of β-phosphorus hyperfine couplings", *J. Magnetic Resonance,* **5**, 408–15 (1971).
12. Fischer, G. W. and Lohs, Kh., "Zur Einschätzung des Alkylierungspotentials onkologisch bedeutsamer Phosphorsäureester mit Hilfe der NBP-Reaktion", *Arch. Geschwulstforsch.,* **42** (1), 34–40 (1973).
13. Fischer, G. W., "Zur Reaktion von Phosphorsäurealkylestern mit 4-(4-Nitrobenzyl)-pyridine (NBP)", *J. Prakt. Chem.,* **315,** 901–908 (1973).
14. Jentzsch, R. and Fischer, G. W., "Kinetische Untersuchungen zum Alkylierungsvermögen insektizider Phosphorsäureester", *J. Prakt. Chem.,* **316**, 249–58 (1974).
15. Gibel, W., Lohs, Kh., Wildner, G. P., Ziehbart, D. and Stieglitz, R., "Über die kanzerogene, hämatotoxische und hepatotoxische Wirkung pestizider organischer Phosphorverbindungen", *Arch. Geschwulstforsch.,* **41**, 311–28 (1973).
16. Lohs, Kh., Gibel, W. and Dedek, W., "Experimente zur hepatotoxischen, hämatotoxischen und kanzerogenen Wirkung der Alkylphosphate", in Altmann, H., ed., *DNA-repair and late effects* (Eisenstadt (Austria), Rötzer Druck GmbH, 1974) pp. 207–11.
17. Spiegelberg, U., "Psychopathologisch-neurologische Spät- und Dauerschäden nach gewerblicher Intoxikation durch Phosphorsäureester (Alkylphosphate)", *Proceedings of the 14th International Congress of Occupational Health, Madrid, 1963, Excerpta Med. Found. Int. Congr. Ser. No. 62,* pp. 1778–80.
18. Lohs, Kh., "Zur Spätschadenproblematik der auf das Zentralnervensystem wirkenden synthetischen Phosphororganika", in *Festschrift zum 60. Geburtstag von R. Baumann* (Berlin, Berlin-Buch, 1971, Deutsche Akademie der Wissenschaften zu Berlin) pp. 103–107.
19. *Delayed toxic effects of chemical warfare agents,* A SIPRI Monograph (Stockholm, Almqvist & Wiksell, 1975, Stockholm International Peace Research Institute).

15. Blood and brain cholinesterase activity in human death cases, in normal human subjects and in some laboratory and domestic animals

A. R. ALHA, A. RUOHONEN and M. TELARANTA

Square-bracketed numbers, thus [1], *refer to the list of references on page 156.*

I. *Introduction*

During the past two years, the Department of Forensic Medicine at the University of Helsinki has been investigating cholinesterase activities in blood and brain. These studies form part of a research project, financed by the Finnish Ministry of Foreign Affairs, aimed at developing analytical techniques that could be used for verification of an international convention prohibiting the production, stockpiling and transfer of chemical weapons. In particular, the purpose of these studies is to discover whether the measurement of cholinesterase activity in the blood or brain of animals can provide an adequately sensitive indicator that the animals have, or have not, been exposed to cholinesterase compounds—chemicals which include the chemical-warfare nerve agents.

II. *Experimental methods*

Since 1959, we have been investigating (in the context of forensic medicine) the acetylcholinesterase activity in the blood of humans fatally poisoned by organophosphates (usually parathion, Bladan E 605). For these early studies, the electrometric method of Michel [1] was found to be quite successful, but it has been criticized. In addition, that method requires a relatively large volume of blood, which is a shortcoming when using small animals. Thus another method was sought, and after a literature survey, the modification by Zech *et al* [2] of the method of Ellman [3] was chosen. This method is based on the colorimetric determination of thiocholine with 5,5′-dithio-bis-2-nitrobenzoic acid (DTNB) after enzymatic hydrolysis of choline esters. Using acetylthiocholine iodide as the first substrate and butyrylthiocholine iodide, a competitive inhibitor of acetylcholinesterase, as the second, it is possible with this method to measure, in a single proce-

Table 15.1. Blood cholinesterase activities in humans and animals

Group	Number of subjects	Cholinesterase activities $\mu mol/min/ml$					
		Acetylcholinesterase			Butyrylcholinesterase		
		Min	Mean	Max	Min	Mean	Max
Humans							
Normal subjects:							
Male	73	6.1	8.2	12.7	2.3	3.6	6.4
Female	85	5.0	7.2	9.6	0.9	3.2	6.3
Death cases:							
Death not due to organophosphate poisoning	165	5.1	8.3	13.1	0.8	2.2	4.2
Death due to organophosphate poisoning (suicides)[a]	17	0.3	1.8	5.4	0.0	0.5	1.2
Animals							
Rat	7	1.1	1.8	2.3	0.5	0.9	1.3
Mouse	5	1.6	2.0	2.3	1.5	1.9	2.2
Cat	10	1.1	1.8	2.4	1.3	1.9	2.6
Dog	13	1.1	1.8	2.9	0.9	1.9	4.0
Horse	10	1.3	1.7	2.5	1.3	2.3	3.3
Sheep	10	1.3	1.7	2.2	0.4	0.5	0.6
Pig	10	1.7	2.0	2.5	0.4	0.6	0.7
Cow	10	2.5	3.0	3.5	0.2	0.3	0.5

[a] Details of these cases are listed in table 15.3.

dure, first the activity of acetylcholinesterase and then that of butyrylcholinesterase.

Both blood and brain were analysed: for analysis of the brain, either the total brain or one-half of it (whole brain) was used, or the cerebellum and the cerebrum were used separately, and in each case, the materials were homogenized and diluted to a suitable suspension. For the reaction, which was carried out at pH 8.0, an aliquot corresponding to 2.0 microlitres (of blood) or 2.0 mg (of brain) was used. Measurements were carried out at 25°C in a Beckman DU spectrophotometer at 405 nm using a one-centimetre cell. The cholinesterase activity of the sample, corrected for both spontaneous acid production and for non-enzymatic hydrolysis, was expressed as micromoles of substrate transformed per minute per millilitre of blood or gram of brain (μmol/min/ml(g)).

As is well known, it is not possible to isolate erythrocytes from the blood of dead subjects. The blood is often clotted, but the distribution of haemoglobin between the clots and the fluid phase does not correspond to that between the erythrocytes and plasma in live subjects. The measured acetylcholinesterase activity of blood from dead subjects was therefore corrected by dividing by the extinction coefficient at 412 nm, which was considered to represent the

Table 15.2. Blood and brain cholinesterase activities in humans and animals

	Number of subjects	Tissue analysed	Blood cholinesterase activities µmol/min/ml						Brain cholinesterase activites µmol/min/g					
			Acetyl-cholinesterase			Butyryl-cholinesterase			Acetyl-cholinesterase			Butyryl-cholinesterase		
			Min	Mean	Max	Min	Mean	Max	Min	Mean	Max	Min	Mean	Max
Humans (death cases)														
Death not due to organo-phosphate poisoning	38	Blood	5.3	7.3	10.2	0.9	1.9	3.1	–	–	–	–	–	–
		Cerebellum	–	–	–	–	–	–	6.3	9.6	11.9	0.9	1.6	2.8
		Cerebrum	–	–	–	–	–	–	1.2	1.7	2.2	0.7	0.9	1.1
Death due to organo-phosphate poisoning	3	Blood	1.4	2.1	3.1	0.1	0.4	0.6	–	–	–	–	–	–
		Cerebellum	–	–	–	–	–	–	0.3	1.5	2.8	0.2	0.5	0.7
Animals (normal)														
Rat	7	Blood	1.1	1.8	2.3	0.5	0.9	1.3	–	–	–	–	–	–
		Cerebellum	–	–	–	–	–	–	3.1	3.5	5.0	0.7	0.7	0.8
		Cerebrum	–	–	–	–	–	–	10.2	10.8	11.8	0.7	0.8	1.2
		Whole brain	–	–	–	–	–	–	10.0	10.4	11.1	0.7	0.8	1.0
Mouse	5	Blood	1.6	2.0	2.3	1.5	1.9	2.2	–	–	–	–	–	–
		Whole brain	–	–	–	–	–	–	12.5	13.3	14.4	1.0	1.1	1.3

Table 15.3. Blood and cerebellum cholinesterase activities in 17 fatal organophosphate-poisoning cases (suicides)

Case number[a]	Organophosphate	Extinction coefficient (E_{412})	Blood cholinesterase activities *μmol/min/ml*: Acetylcholinesterase, Measured	Acetylcholinesterase, Corrected	Butyrylcholinesterase	Cerebellum cholinesterase activities[b] *μmol/min/g*: Acetylcholinesterase	Butyrylcholinesterase
1070/73	Parathion	0.87	1.6	1.8	1.2	–	–
1134/73	Parathion	0.62	0.6	1.0	0.6	–	–
1158/73	Parathion	0.69	0.6	0.9	0	–	–
1177/73	Malathion	1.23	1.3	1.1	0	–	–
1210/73	Parathion	0.84	1.2	1.4	0.4	–	–
1214/73	Parathion	1.06	5.7	5.4[c]	0.8	–	–
1353/73	Dimethoate	1.45	0.4	0.3	0.5	–	–
1383/73	Parathion	0.74	1.4	1.9	0.9	–	–
1414/73	Parathion	1.33	6.6	5.0[d]	0.8	–	–
1532/73	Parathion	1.35	3.4	2.5	0.7	–	–
1564/73	Malathion	1.31	0.7	0.5	0.3	–	–
2398/73	Parathion	0.63	0.4	0.6	0.4	–	–
151/74	Parathion	0.80	1.1	1.4	0.3	1.5	0.7
181/74	Parathion	0.21	0.4	1.9	0.1	0.3	0.2
273/74	Parathion	0.95	2.9	3.1	0.6	2.8	0.5
564/74	Parathion	1.07	1.4	1.3	0.5	–	–
609/74	Dimethoate	0.54	0.4	0.7	0.4	–	–

[a] The serial number of the patient in the records of the University of Helsinki.
[b] Cerebellum cholinesterase activities were measured in only three cases, as also shown in table 15.2.
[c] Subject died because of inhalation of stomach contents.
[d] Subject was asthmatic.

haemoglobin content of the sample. Extinction at 412 nm varied widely (see table 15.3), and when the blood was badly deteriorated, it was not always possible to obtain a reasonable result.

III. *Results*

Blood cholinesterase activities are listed in table 15.1: in each case minimum, mean and maximum activities are shown. From some human death cases, and from rats and mice, both blood and brain were available and were analysed, and the results of these analyses are listed in table 15.2.

The blood acetylcholinesterase activity in normal human subjects is about 7–8 μmol/min/ml, while in subjects fatally poisoned by organophosphates it is only about 2 μmol/min/ml, that is, about 25 per cent of normal. In human cerebellum the difference is even greater: the normal activity (an average of 38 cases) is 9.6 μmol/min/g while the average activity of the three poisoning cases is only 1.5 μmol/min/g (see also table 15.3). All the 17 cases of fatal

Table 15.4. Blood and brain cholinesterase activities in rats and mice poisoned by parathion

		Blood cholinesterase activities μmol/min/ml		Brain cholinesterase activities μmol/min/g			
				Whole brain		Cerebrum	
Subject	Extinction coefficient (E_{412})	Acetyl-cholin-esterase	Butyryl-cholin-esterase	Acetyl-cholin-esterase	Butyryl-cholin-esterase	Acetyl-cholin-esterase	Butyryl-cholin-esterase
Rats							
Normal[a]		1.8	0.9	10.4	0.8	10.8	0.8
Poisoned	1.39	1.6	1.0	5.7	1.0	–	–
	1.38	1.5	1.0	5.1	0.9	–	–
	1.46	1.6	1.1	7.3	1.2	–	–
	1.34	1.7	1.1	6.9	1.0	–	–
	1.36	1.7	1.0	–	–	8.9	1.1
Mice							
Normal[b]		2.0	1.9	13.3	1.1	–	–
Poisoned	0.70	0.8	1.1	9.1	1.1	–	–
	0.93	1.2	1.5	9.0	1.2	–	–
	0.73	0.7	1.1	7.7	0.8	–	–
	0.72	1.1	1.3	13.2	1.4	–	–
	0.69	0.8	1.2	10.6	1.3	–	–

[a] Mean of 7 animals.
[b] Mean of 5 animals.

organophosphate poisoning (suicides) shown in table 15.1 are listed in detail in table 15.3. In only two cases did the blood acetylcholinesterase activity approach the lower end of the "normal" range and in both cases this was probably due to certain special features: in case 1214 the subject died because of "inhalation" of stomach contents and suffocation, while the subject of case 1414 was asthmatic and may have had less resistance to poisoning than normal subjects. But in these cases, blood butyrylcholinesterase activities were also reduced.

Blood enzyme activities in normal animals were considerably lower than in normal humans. While there were no large differences in acetylcholinesterase activities among the species investigated, butyrylcholinesterase activities differed considerably, those of mouse, cat, dog and horse being between three and eight times higher than those of cow, sheep and pig.

On the other hand, enzyme activities in the cerebrum or whole brain of rat and mouse were even higher than in human cerebellum. This result prompted us to perform a *preliminary experiment.* Five rats and five mice were fed crushed oats mixed with some parathion. The rats died in one day, while the mice lived for two days without external symptoms of poisoning, and were then killed. Blood was collected and brain prepared from both groups of animals and the enzyme activities were measured. The results, presented in table 15.4, show distinctly decreased acetylcholinesterase activities in whole brains of rats and mice and in the blood of mice, as well as decreased butyrylcholinesterase activity in the blood of mice.

References

1. Michel, H. O., "An electrometric method for the determination of red blood cell and plasma cholinesterase activity", *J. Lab. Clin. Med.,* **34,** 1564–68 (1949).
2. Zech, R., Franke, K. and Domagk, G. F., "Eine Mikromethode zur gleichzeitigen Bestimmung der Acetylcholinesterase und der Butyrylcholinesterase im Säugetierblut", *Z. Klin. Chem. Klin. Biochem.,* **7,** 547–50 (1969).
3. Ellman, G. E., Courtney, K. D., Andres, V., Jr. and Fetherstone, R. M., "A new and rapid colorimetric determination of acetylcholinesterase activity", *Biochem. Pharmacol.,* **7,** 88–95 (1961).

16. Medical protection against chemical-warfare agents

J. E. S. STARES

I. *Introduction*

The treatment of any case of organophosphorus poisoning is a medical emergency: ideally it requires constant care from a team of medical personnel, backed up by a well-equipped medical facility. Clinically, there are three main factors in the therapy, the order of priority depending on the condition of the patient.

1. *Blockade of excess acetylcholine.* By inhibiting acetylcholinesterase, organophosphorus poisoning results in an accumulation of acetylcholine, which leads to a variety of toxic symptoms. These symptoms can be partially alleviated by administering cholinolytic drugs that block the effects of excess acetylcholine. Atropine is the drug most commonly used for this purpose, and if the treatment is to be successful it must be administered as soon as possible after exposure to the poison, in adequate doses and by a means that promotes rapid absorption (intravenous injection is the best route of administration, although it is more convenient to give the drug intramuscularly).

2. *Oxygenation.* Inhibition of acetylcholinesterase may lead to paralysis including paralysis of the respiratory muscles and central nervous respiratory centres so that death is usually due to oxygen starvation. Hence artificial respiration is an essential component of therapy. The use of atropine is also beneficial in this context, since it promotes oxygenation by antagonizing the central respiratory depression, drying secretions and relieving the bronchoconstriction that might hinder artificial respiration.

3. *Reversal of acetylcholinesterase inhibition.* Since the effects of organophosphorus poisoning are caused by the binding of a foreign compound to the enzyme acetylcholinesterase, the logical means of reversing the toxic effects is to break the bond between the enzyme and the poison, that is, to "reactivate" the enzyme so that it is able once again to function normally. Drugs called oximes have just that biochemical effect, at least in the case of some organophosphorus intoxications, if they are administered quickly enough after exposure to the poison.

Provided adequate medical facilities are available, such treatment can be successful in saving the lives of individuals poisoned by organophosphorus compounds, even by some of the extremely toxic chemical-warfare agents, such as sarin. However, therapy may be considerably more difficult in practice: there is a vast difference between treating a poisoned individual in a well-equipped hospital and trying to treat poisoned individuals without the aid of advanced medical facilities or qualified medical personnel. And the difficulties would be even greater in the mass-casualty situations that would result from a chemical-warfare attack with organophosphorus nerve agents. In such cases, probably the only feasible form of treatment would be the administration of antidotes in the field. In fact, special autoinjectors filled with antidotes ready for intramuscular injection have been developed for this purpose, and are in standard issue in the armed forces of a number of countries. They can easily be used by laymen, even by the poisoned individuals themselves.

This chapter will examine whether the means and methods of treatment that are available now can provide adequate protection or treatment of troops or civilian populations in case of chemical-warfare attack. It will attempt to assess the effectiveness of currently available methods of treatment, when used under mass-casualty conditions, and will try to identify those areas where there are particular problems or limitations with the existing treatment methods. There will then be a review of the research work that is being carried out, a review based on the scientific papers that constitute chapters 1 to 15 of this book and on the discussions that took place at the international symposium in Herceg Novi in October 1974 (see page 7). Finally, there will be a brief discussion of how far the results from this international research effort can be expected to solve the outstanding problems of treatment and an assessment of the priorities for further research to try to solve the problems that still remain.

II. *Existing methods of treatment and their effectiveness*

Existing therapeutic measures against organophosphorus poisoning are limited in a number of respects. The standard drug therapy is based on the use of atropine, as mentioned above. However, the efficacy of atropine therapy is limited. Atropine treats only the symptoms of the intoxication, not the cause, and even then it is unable to reverse the paralysis of the respiratory muscles.

In addition to cholinolytic drugs such as atropine, another range of drugs is available for treating organophosphorus intoxications—the oximes. By reactivating the inhibited acetylcholinesterase so that its normal function of breaking down acetylcholine is restored, the oximes treat the cause of the intoxication, and are thus extremely valuable as adjuncts to the symptomatic atropine therapy. But as with atropine, there are several problems associated with the use of oximes.

While oximes can effectively reactivate inhibited acetylcholinesterase in the peripheral nervous system, they are ineffective against acetylcholinesterase inhibition in the central nervous system: none of the useable oxime reactivators has been found to have a significant effect *in vivo* on inhibited brain acetylcholinesterase. There are conflicting views on the reasons for this, but oximes are thought to be unable to cross the blood-brain barrier to enter the central nervous system because of their quaternary ammonium structure, and in fact studies have shown that while the blood-brain barrier is reasonably easily permeable to tertiary compounds, it is not permeable to quaternary compounds (see chapter 2).

Another limitation of oxime therapy is that the oximes are not effective against poisoning by all organophosphorus compounds. The most important example of this is their lack of effect against poisoning by the chemical-warfare agent soman, which is due to the extremely rapid "ageing" of the phosphonylated (inhibited) acetylcholinesterase—that is, dealkylation of the organophosphorus component of the enzyme/inhibitor complex which leaves the enzyme resistant to reactivation. The rate of ageing of inhibited acetylcholinesterase depends on the particular organophosphorus compound involved: for example, acetylcholinesterase inhibited by the chemical-warfare agent VX is not completely aged even after 48 hours, but in the case of soman intoxication, ageing is complete within minutes of exposure to the poison.

Apart from those cases where oxime therapy has no effect on the organophosphorus intoxication, there are reports of undesirable side-effects resulting from oxime treatment. For example, administration of an oxime is sometimes found to result in an additional toxic effect. In part, this may be due to the formation of toxic products in a chemical reaction between the oxime and the organophosphorus compound (see chapter 8): thus the use of some oximes against soman intoxication, apart from having no therapeutic effect, seems to be contra-indicated, according to some workers, because of the formation of more potent acetylcholinesterase inhibitors in a reaction between the oximes and the less toxic stereoisomers of soman. Among other side-effects, several workers have cited liver damage as a reason for not always using oxime therapy, although there is evidence that the liver damage seen in organophosphorus-poisoned patients treated with oximes is in fact caused by the organophosphorus compound itself rather than by the oxime (see chapter 3).

Many hundreds of different oximes have been synthesized and studied for their therapeutic efficacy against organophosphorus intoxications, but so far only three have been found suitable for widespread medical use. These are pralidoxime (of which there are two different pharmaceutical preparations commonly available—(2-hydroxyimino-methyl)-pyridine-1-methyl chloride or iodide (2-PAM) and (2-hydroxyimino-methyl)-pyridine-1-methyl methanesulphonate (P2S)), trimedoxime (1,3-bis-[(4-hydroxyiminomethyl)-pyridine-1-]-propane dichloride or dibromide) and obidoxime (bis-[(4-hydroxyimino-methyl)-pyridine-1-methyl]-ether dichloride). Pralidoxime (2-PAM) was first introduced in 1955, trimedoxime in 1958 and obidoxime in 1964, and since then no other oxime has been discovered that has therapeutic properties superior to those of these three.

It has been found from animal and human experiments and observations (see chapter 5) that obidoxime and trimedoxime are in many respects superior to pralidoxime: for example, they induce stronger and more rapid reactivation of inhibited acetylcholinesterase. Trimedoxime has the longest biological half-life of the three oximes, shows significantly lower excretion rates than the other two, and is, moreover, a more effective reactivator in some cases than is obidoxime. However, trimedoxime is more toxic than obidoxime, and both of these compounds are more toxic, on a weight basis, than pralidoxime. It is not surprising, therefore, that there is no general agreement about which of these three oximes is the "best". Indeed, there is no agreement that oximes should be used at all in treating organophosphorus poisoning: although a number of countries now issue their armed forces with special autoinjectors for use in case of a chemical-warfare attack, in some countries—the United States and the Netherlands, for example—the autoinjectors in standard issue contain only atropine, and no oxime. But this may be for bureaucratic rather than scientific reasons, that is, because of the difficulty of deciding which oxime to use, rather than because of a definite decision not to use oximes.

Other countries, for example Sweden and Yugoslavia, do issue their troops with autoinjectors containing an oxime as well as atropine, but the oxime used is different in different countries. In general, pralidoxime is the preferred oxime in Western countries, while either obidoxime or trimedoxime is chosen in East European countries. One of the reasons for these differing choices may be the different nature of the threat of chemical-warfare attack as perceived in different countries. The United States is known to stockpile only two organophosphorus nerve agents, sarin and VX, and so the Warsaw Treaty countries, in choosing drugs for protection against possible chemical attack from the West, can choose an oxime which is highly effective against these compounds. The nature of the chemical-warfare stockpile of the Soviet Union, however, is uncertain: the Soviet Union is thought to possess stocks of soman (which is not responsive to oxime therapy anyway) as well as another agent, code-named VR-55 in the West, the identity of which is unknown. NATO countries choose another oxime, pralidoxime, for use in their military autoinjectors: this oxime, although less effective as an antidote than either trimedoxime or obidoxime, has a rather wider spectrum of action against different organophosphorus compounds, and is thus more likely to be effective against an unknown chemical-warfare nerve agent.

The main problems that would be encountered in treating organophosphorus poisoning in the field, especially in mass-casualty situations, are that with existing methods of treatment: (*a*) There is a limit to the size of the exposure to organophosphorus compounds that can be treated successfully. (Under battlefield conditions the administration of atropine and oximes from an autoinjector would probably not be effective against a dose of more than about 5 LD_{50} of an organophosphorus nerve agent, even if the drugs were injected within 30 seconds of the exposure.) (*b*) There are no ways of giving artificial respiration in the field to large numbers of people. And (*c*) for some compounds, such as soman, there is no effective treatment at all. In practical terms, this means that, although atropine and the oximes are the best forms of treatment presently available, in the case of chemical-warfare attack with organophosphorus nerve agents, adequate medical protection of troops on the battlefield would, to say the least, be extremely difficult, and such protection of civilian populations would certainly be impossible. It is thus important to ask whether the research work that is currently under way on the problems of therapy of organophosphorus poisoning is likely to be able to offer solutions to these problems. Are there more effective antidotes that can counteract the effects of massive doses of organophosphorus poisons? Are there more effective ways of administering the available antidotes so that they might be able to counteract larger doses of the poisons? Are there other drugs that might be effective against soman intoxication and other cases of poisoning that are not responsive to the standard drug therapy? And are there ways to solve the problem of respiratory paralysis in the field or in mass-casualty situations? These questions will be explored in the next section.

III. *Current research on treatment of organophosphorus poisoning*

There are two basic approaches to developing improved methods of medical protection against organophosphorus poisoning: to try to improve existing treatment methods; or to try to find completely new means of dealing with the problem effectively. If a more effective treatment is found, it will probably be some combination of existing and novel methods.

The research aimed at improving existing treatment methods can be considered under two main headings. First, there are the attempts to find other cholinolytic drugs or oximes that are more effective than the currently used ones or that will be therapeutically effective against a wider range of organophosphorus compounds than are the present ones. A few cholinolytics other than atropine have been investigated, and in some cases have been found to be more effective than atropine, probably because they have a higher central-nervous-system activity (see chapters 1 and 10). But usually these other drugs have undesirable side-effects, and so on the basis of results to date, there seems to be little, if any, justification for substituting one of these other cholinolytics for atropine. Some workers have suggested that an enhanced therapeutic effect may be obtained by using two cholinolytic drugs together, but the results of experiments in animals seem to refute this claim, at least in the case of dimethoate poisoning (see chapter 11).

Among the oximes, a large number of new compounds have been synthesized and tested for therapeutic efficiency (see chapter 9). Some of the oximes that have been prepared and tested in animal experiments certainly seem to combine low toxicity with significant therapeutic effect, and thus seem to be worthy of further study. And further such pharmaceutical screening tests may perhaps result in the discovery of a highly effective drug. But, as was the case with the cholinolytics, the results that are available to date would hardly justify abandoning the three oximes currently in general use for one of these new ones. Moreover, the author of chapter 9 concludes from his studies that the protective effect of an oxime against an organophosphorus poisoning depends on the chemical structures of both the antidote and the particular organophosphorus compound involved. Therefore, he says, it is rather unlikely that a new oxime will be found that will be highly effective against a wide range of organophosphorus compounds without having undesirable side-effects or other properties that render it useless as a therapeutic agent.

It therefore appears that the chances of improving the prospects of therapy against organophosphorus poisoning by finding more effective cholinolytics or oximes, or by finding such drugs that are equally effective against all organophosphorus compounds, are rather slim. A number of researchers have therefore been investigating ways in which the therapeutic effectiveness of the existing drugs—atropine in conjunction with pralidoxime, trimedoxime or obidoxime—can be increased.

One possible way to increase the effectiveness of therapy is to add to the standard drug treatment other drugs that might in some way enable atropine and the oximes to act more effectively. For example, one of the limitations to the effectiveness of oximes is that they are excreted from the body rather quickly, and hence can only exert their biochemical effect for a limited period. Repeated administration of drugs is not always a suitable solution to this problem. However, it has been shown that some compounds—thiamine (vitamin B_1) was investigated in one study—can significantly increase the retention time of an oxime in the body (see chapter 1). It might be useful to investigate other chemicals in this context. But it is still not clear how high a concentration of an oxime must be present in the blood for how long in order to give effective therapeutic effect. Finding the answers to these questions is a task of some urgency.

Another line of research has been to investigate how the effectiveness of drugs varies with different routes of administration. One study has clearly shown that the administration of drugs with an autoinjector is preferable to injection with a conventional needle and syringe, and, moreover, that the drugs often exert their effects much more rapidly if they are administered in a small volume of highly concentrated solution. This would suggest that the development of a "mini-autoinjector" would be extremely profitable. Further study of the question of the most effective route of administration of drugs may well result in novel and highly effective means of drug administration. For example, administration in aerosol form, possibly from a special applicator that could be fitted inside a "gas mask" and that could spray the drugs into the nose, has been described. Results of investigations on this device indicate that while intranasal aerosol administration of atropine presents no problems, such administration of large doses of oximes gives rise to intense irritation, and is thus not possible at present. But there would certainly appear to be scope here for further detailed study (see chapter 1).

All of the work described so far has been concerned with the therapeutic treatment of organophosphorus intoxication, that is, with the administration of drugs *after* exposure to the poison. It has become clear that there are numerous problems associated with therapeutic treatment, problems that may or may not be solved in the future. Some workers have therefore been investigating the possibilities of prophylactic treatment against organophosphorus intoxication, that is, treatment that is administered *before* exposure to the poison (see chapter 12). A number of approaches to prophylaxis have been studied, for example, administering drugs that could inactivate organophosphorus poisons in the body before inhibition of acetylcholinesterase could take place, or using compounds that shield, and hence protect, the enzyme against organophosphorus compounds (see also chapter 4). Although such approaches have met with a certain degree of success, a rather more straightforward approach, described in detail in chapter 12, is the prophylactic use of therapeutically active oximes. The aim in these studies was to design oximes which would have a prolonged biological half-life and which therefore might be suitable as prophylactic agents. Although the results so far have unfortunately not been very promising, the studies are still in an early stage. Some compounds have been found which show some potential as prophylactic agents, and it is to be hoped that after more investigation, effective prophylaxis will become reality.

The discussion so far has been concerned with research that is being carried out with atropine and oximes. It is clear that while it may be possible to improve the effectiveness of the existing methods of therapy, and while it may even be possible to develop adequate prophylactic measures against organophosphorus poisoning, it will probably not be possible to solve all of the problems of treatment that exist at the moment. Other researchers have therefore been studying other means of medical treatment in an effort to find ways to overcome the limitations of the standard atropine and oxime therapy.

One of the outstanding problems is the lack of response of soman poisoning to oxime therapy. Some workers have been able to demonstrate, however, that drugs other than oximes may have therapeutic effects: for example, certain oxime-free bispyridinium compounds show an antidotal effect against soman. But it seems that this antidotal effect is not based on enzyme reactivation, and the exact biochemical mechanism of action has not yet been made clear (see chapter 9). There have even been reports of some oximes also having antidotal effects against soman, but once again it is thought that this is by a mechanism other than enzyme reactivation (see chapter 11).

Among the central effects and symptoms of organophosphorus poisoning, convulsions seem to play a major role in the mechanism of death. Oximes cannot be used to treat these symptoms, and many of the normal anti-convulsant drugs were also found to be ineffective. However, some benzodiazepines, for example diazepam, when used in conjunction with atropine and obidoxime, were found to be effective (see chapter 10): diazepam was found to be able to control convulsions in rats and rabbits poisoned with sarin or soman. As well as their anti-convulsant effects, diazepam and other benzodiazepines also have cholinolytic properties, but these are only of minor importance in organophosphorus therapy.

Probably one of the most promising research efforts described at the symposium concerns using drugs to reverse the respiratory paralysis that results from organophosphorus poisoning (see chapter 13): at present, respiratory paralysis can only be treated with artificial respiration. The work is based on a number of previous observations: (*a*) that even after a severe disturbance of the respiratory centres by organophosphorus poisoning, a few nerve impulses per respiratory cycle will still travel down the phrenic nerve; (*b*) that certain drugs are able to change the response of striated muscle fibres to a single stimulus—from a single twitch to a prolonged contracture; and (*c*) that if artificial respiration is applied over a sufficiently long period, a poisoned victim will resume spontaneous breathing. These observations suggest that if the period of respiratory failure can be bridged by a drug that converts single twitches in respiratory muscles into contractions of sufficient duration for adequate respiratory movements to occur, then eventually spontaneous breathing should be resumed without the need for artificial respiration.

The work so far reported shows that the use of the compounds 3-chloro-2,5,6-trimethylbenzoic acid (U23223) and 9-anthroic acid (ANCA), in combination with atropine, can prevent the respiratory paralysis caused by DFP and paraoxon in rats. More important, it has also been shown that when applied to soman intoxication, such treatment can postpone the onset of respiratory paralysis for about 2½ hours. While this delay is not a complete answer to the problem—the respiratory failure will still occur at the end of the delay period, and subsequent administration of more of the compounds only gives a very short additional delay—it could be extremely valuable in that it would provide the time needed to move a poisoned patient to a medical facility where artificial respiration could be given. There are also indications from preliminary experiments that ANCA treatment is able to prevent the respiratory paralysis resulting from intoxication by sarin, a chemical-warfare agent that causes a respiratory paralysis of shorter duration than that produced by soman.

There are still a number of problems with this treatment, but work is continuing and it is not impossible that a drug will be found that will completely prevent the respiratory-paralysis effects of organophosphorus poisoning. If such a treatment is developed to the point where it is effective and efficient in humans, one of the major problems of organophosphorus intoxication and its treatment, namely restoring breathing in a poisoned patient without using artificial respiration, may be in sight of being solved.

IV. *The need for further research*

The research that is being carried out on the problems of treating organophosphorus poisoning is certainly producing useful and valuable results, and the present methods of treatment may be considerably improved as a result of these studies. For example, there is a good chance that a drug, probably not an oxime, will be found that is effective against soman poisoning; there are drugs that seem to be able to counter some of the central effects of organophosphorus poisoning that are not responsive to oxime therapy; and there is promise that the problem of respiratory failure may be overcome with a new drug treatment. However, when one examines these advances in the context of mass casualties, for example, those that will almost certainly result from a chemical-warfare attack with organophosphorus nerve agents, the prospects are rather less promising. Even if some of the new drugs could be incorporated into military autoinjectors, all that can realistically be said of the new methods of treatment is that they will provide more time than is available with the existing treatment methods to move poisoned individuals to medical facilities. While this is certainly a valuable step forward, in times of war it is unlikely that medical facilities would be able to cope with the vast number of casualties.

There is therefore a need for much further work in this field to solve the problems that still remain. Many of the problems have already been pointed out above, but there may be others that have not yet even been identified. For example, some recent work has demonstrated that exposure to organophosphorus compounds may produce delayed effects and other side-effects, in addition to the well-documented acute effects. These additional effects appear in some cases to be a consequence of the alkylating properties of organophosphorus compounds, properties that, unlike the well-known phosphorylating and phosponylating properties of organophosphorus compounds, have until now been largely ignored (see chapter 14). Clearly, if an effective method of treating organophosphorus poisoning is to be developed, it should if possible take into account these other possible effects of the poisons.

The participants at the Herceg Novi symposium generally agreed that some form of international cooperation would be valuable in solving the problem of therapy of organophosphorus poisoning. Two broad areas in which cooperation might be beneficial were identified. First, there seems to be a need for standardization among scientists working on these issues. For example, toxicity determinations, cholinesterase-activity determinations and methods for evaluating therapeutic methods are all carried out in different ways in different laboratories and in different countries. The result is that it is often difficult to make valid comparisons of results from different sources. The important point here is not simply that the methods used in one laboratory are better, or worse, than those used elsewhere: that may or may not be the case. What is important is that scientists working on these problems should be able to communicate their results to each other, and for this communication to be optimally effective, an agreed set of standardized procedures for measuring, calculating and quoting results would be extremely useful. The means of deciding on which procedures to use were discussed briefly. For example, an international secretariat could be established with the task of investigating all possible experimental methods and recommending one. Alternatively, editors of scientific journals could perhaps be encouraged to request authors to quote results according to a standardized scheme. Clearly this is a question that deserves further detailed investigation.

The other area in which international cooperation would be useful is the dissemination of information. A need was expressed for a central data bank that could collect and distribute information relating to the problem of organophosphorus poisoning and therapy. There are obvious problems involved with establishing such a system, not the least being the cost, but it was generally agreed that any scheme that would speed up the circulation of research results and hence facilitate the solving of the outstanding problems of treating organophosphorus poisoning should be investigated fully.

In summary, it can be said that, with the techniques and drugs available at the moment, adequate medical protection against organophosphorus nerve agents used in war is not feasible. However, it is probably not unrealistic to conclude that if the research currently under way is continued, and especially if there is some form of international cooperation of research efforts, reasonably effective, even if not 100 per cent, protection may become feasible in the not too distant future.